Contemporary Cinema
of Latin America

Contemporary Cinema of Latin America

Ten Key Films

Deborah Shaw

continuum
NEW YORK • LONDON

2003

The Continuum International Publishing Group Inc
370 Lexington Avenue, New York, NY 10017

The Continuum International Publishing Group Ltd
The Tower Building, 11 York Road, London SE1 7NX

www.continuumbooks.com

Printed in the United States of America

Library of Congress Cataloging-in-Publication Data

Shaw Deborah.
   Contemporary cinema of Latin America : ten key films / Deborah Shaw.
      p. cm.
    ISBN 0-8264-1484-2 (hardcover : alk paper) – ISBN 0-8264-1485-0
   (pbk. : alk paper)
    1. Motion pictures – Latin America. Title.
   PN1993.5.L3S53 2003
   791.43′75′098 – dc21

                                           2002156028

Contents

List of Illustrations

Introduction

This is not a book about Latin American cinema; it is a book about some films made by selected Mexican, Brazilian, Cuban, Argentine, and Chilean directors.[1] There are many Latin American countries that are not represented and many excellent films that are not discussed. This is because the focus here is on a selection of films that international audiences have access to, whether at movie theaters, on television channels, or on video or DVD. Filmmakers from all over Latin America have produced interesting works that these audiences should have access to; however, because of the nature of the market and the difficulties in securing distribution deals with globally powerful companies, many high-quality films are never seen outside the countries in which they are made, and even then, many are shown in very few theaters for a limited time.[2] Although this is to be deplored, the aim of this work is to produce readings of films that can be seen without too much difficulty and to provide a social, economic, historical, and political context within which a better understanding of the films may be gained. Although some films have attracted some academic critical attention (*Memories of Underdevelopment, Strawberry and Chocolate, Like Water for Chocolate, Pixote*, and *I the Worst of All*), others have received very little notice, and it is hoped that the readings in this book will encourage debate, discussion, and dissent.

Aside from the issues of access, films have been chosen for a number of reasons. Some are interesting examples of movies by important directors who have produced a substantial body of work (Tomás Gutiérrez Alea, María Luisa Bemberg, Fernando Solanas, and Hector Babenco). Others, by directors who are just starting out on their careers, have been selected because they achieved the rare result of reaching an international film-going community and winning awards at national film festivals, with many breaking box office records (*Amores perros*, 2000; *Central Station*, 1998; *Like Water for Chocolate*, 1992; *The Frontier*, 1991; and *Amnesia*, 1994).[3]

So, how and why have the films selected been able to make an impact both domestically and internationally, in commercial and/or critical terms? The specific reasons for this are examined in each chapter; however, a more generalized explanation lies in the fact that each one seeks to represent themes related to national identity while addressing transnational concerns. Mette Hjort (2000) has applied literary critics Peter Lamarque and Steia Haugom Olsen's (1994) categories of perennial and topical themes to her analysis of Danish cinema, and these categories can be useful in assessing the success of the Latin American films selected in this book. As she explains:

> Perennial themes bring into focus subject matter that resonates across historical and cultural boundaries. They are universal or quasi-universal in their thrust.... Topical themes, on the other hand, involve only concepts that arise within, and remain relevant to, a highly specific historical or cultural formation. (106)

The Latin American films studied here all address specific national issues, yet they also transcend national borders through an appeal to wider concerns. To give some examples, Tomás Gutiérrez Alea's *Memories of Underdevelopment* (*Memorias del subdesarrollo*) (1968) and *Strawberry and Chocolate* (*Fresa y chocolate*) (1993) examine issues crucial to the Cuban social and political situation in the 1960s and 1990s, respectively, yet they also provide analyses of such perennial themes as the relationship between the individual and society, the role of the intellectual within a collective, and the nature of political and personal freedom. *The Voyage* (*El viaje*) (1991) by Fernando Solanas presents an analysis of exploitation, corruption, and the effects of neoliberalism and globalization in specific Latin American contexts; nevertheless, these themes are filtered through the protagonist, Martín, which allows the film to explore more general issues associated with adolescent self-discovery. Ricardo Larraín's *The Frontier* (*La frontera*) explores the highly topical issue of internal exile in Augusto Pinochet Ugarte's Chile, yet it also addresses a number of perennial themes, such as the role of religion in society, the nature of freedom and imprisonment, and the possibility of love following trauma.

Thus, the films studied in this book can be seen as important in both national and transnational terms, in that their subject matter is of interest to domestic and international audiences. This means that most were able to secure funding through coproductions and the interest of international distributors.[4] This use of the categories "perennial" and "topical" is not meant to produce a false dichotomy between domestic and foreign audiences. Foreign audiences are also attracted by the topical themes that the films address, and part of their appeal is the impression that entry is gained into another world. Likewise, domestic audiences want to see cinematic versions of their "realities" personalized through an exploration of "universal" concerns as they are represented back to them.

It is clear from the above that funding is a central concern in the case of every national cinema in Latin America. Néstor García Canclini (1997), writing in 1993, explains some of the difficulties facing filmmakers, including the decline in film going as a result of the privatization of culture, seen in the growth of home entertainment (248), the dominance of Hollywood distributors, and the fall in state funding (249). As John King (2000) points out, the decline in film going has been stemmed, and even reversed, thanks to the development of multiplexes in many of the urban centers throughout Latin America, although it must be recognized that Hollywood films dominate the programming (259–60). Nevertheless García Canclini's first two points are still relevant, and filmmaking throughout Latin America has only been able to survive by integrating within an international system of production and distribution.

This reality would clearly jar with the advocates of New Latin American Cinema in the late 1960s, who called for revolutionary filmmaking in opposition to commercial cinema. This political approach to producing films is known as Imperfect Cinema or Third Cinema. The term *Imperfect Cinema* was developed in the late 1950s by Julio García Espinosa to categorize Cuban revolutionary filmmaking, while in Argentina Fernando Solanas and Octavio Getino used the term *Third Cinema* to refer to oppositional filmmaking that was linked to the struggle for social justice.[5] However, as will be seen, even the directors who were originally part of the revolutionary cinema movements, Tomás Gutiérrez Alea and Fernando Solanas, came to accept the need for a change in attitudes to the film industry if they were to manage to secure funding for their work.

These two directors, along with María Luisa Bemberg, had international reputations that helped with raising the money needed to make their films in the ways that they wanted.[6] In the cases of new directors such as Alejandro González Iñárritu, Walter Salles, and Ricardo Larraín, production companies had to believe that their films would cross international borders to risk their support. It is no coincidence that these three directors, who broke into the international circuit in the 1990s and 2000s, came from a background in advertising, and as such are fully aware of the importance of commercial imperatives.

The role of the marketplace has inevitably led to a shift in the nature of filmmaking from the days of early New Latin American Cinema, with the emphasis on entertainment as much as on education.[7] B. Ruby Rich (1997) has argued that filmmaking has become less political, with a focus on the importance of individuals and private realities taking the place of revolutionary filmmaking, which advocates mass mobilization of the people to overthrow the government, or, in the case of Cuba, to support the revolutionary state. Rich writes: "In place of the explicitly and predictably political, at the level of labor or agrarian struggles or mass mobilization, we find an attention to the implicitly political, at the level of banality, fantasy, and desire and a corresponding shift in aesthetic strategies" (281). She adds that the changes in regimes, "from fascist to post-fascist," have led from "Revolutionary to revelatory" films (282).

Although Rich is writing about the 1980s, many of her observations are relevant to films made in the 1990s and 2000s. A number of the chapters in this book argue that in the films analyzed, made over three decades (the 1980s, 1990s, and 2000s), politics have been redefined. Only *Memories of Underdevelopment* was made in the 1960s, and it provides a useful point of comparison with the films made in the following decades. Each chapter presents an analysis of the ways in which national issues are represented and explores the ways that the films seek to explain social "realities" and suggest future directions while, in many cases, bypassing traditional political solutions. Only Solanas's *The Voyage* can be seen as an overtly political film in that it seeks to denounce the political system in much of Latin America and advocates popular resistance; however, even here, the film relies on satire, rather than the explicit rhetoric used in his and Octavio Getino's early film *The Hour of the Furnaces* (*La hora de los hornos*) (1968).

Politics, then, have not been abandoned in the films under analysis; rather, they have been redefined, and one of the questions the book addresses is how. What is striking is the way in which most of the films reject the path of revolution and look to groups of individuals for solutions to national problems.[8] It is as if faith in the political classes and political processes has been lost. Using some examples, chapter 5, which focuses on *Pixote* (1981) and *Central Station* (1998), examines the ways in which the implicit failures of the state are addressed and looks at how family units, both biological and symbolic, seek to provide a secure identity denied by the state. The study of *Amnesia* in chapter 3 explores the ways in which the problems of a nation have to be worked out on an individual level, in the absence of a political solution. The discussion in chapter 3 on *The Frontier,* among other issues, examines how and why the film prefers to focus on the personal trajectory of a man in internal exile, rather than denounce the murders and tortures carried out by the Chilean dictatorship. In the case of the most recent film studied, *Amores perros* (*Love's a Bitch*) the old revolutionary has become a disillusioned tramp and hired assassin, and in chapter 2 it will be seen how his abandonment of political ideologies and class warfare is linked to his personal redemption.

4

These points of focus — the commercial dimension of the films and the lack of faith in political solutions — do not mean that all of the films are, or should be, read in the same way; there is not, nor has there ever been, one type of Latin American film, nor is there a single approach filmmakers take that can be neatly theorized.[9] Each context in which the films are made is different. The films examined cover different historical periods (from 1968, *Memories of Underdevelopment*, to 2000, *Amores perros*); they are made in nations with their own specific social, political, and economic realities; and they are the result of the individual artistic visions of the directors, writers, cinematographers, set designers, and others.

For these reasons, the approach in the reading of each film is determined both by the subject matter of the film and by the context in which it was produced. As Julianne Burton (1997) has argued, "A film's contextual environment at the time of production is relevant to any historically sensitive subsequent interpretation of that text's content, form and function" (166). The chapters have been organized around national categories, and this provides the opportunity to ground the readings of the texts in the context not only of the social and political conditions but also of those of the national film industries. Thus, to give the example of the Mexican film industry, it will be seen how the shift from public to private sources of funding has affected national film production. The readings of two of the most commercially successful films of their time, *Like Water for Chocolate* (*Como agua para chocolate*) and *Amores perros,* aim to illustrate how these changes are reflected in the approaches to filmmaking in the 1990s and 2000s. This shift in funding is also explored in the analysis of *Central Station,* and it is asked whether economic imperatives account for the very different representations of children between this film and *Pixote.*

The readings, then, aim to respond to the subject matter of the films and provide a political and historical background in order to locate them in their context. In the case of Chile, for example, the dictatorship and transition to democracy are examined, along with discourses of human rights and those of the defenders of the dictatorship, as both *Amnesia* and *The Frontier* are better understood with some knowledge of the historical periods that the films address. This is also an approach taken in chapter 1 on two of Gutiérrez Alea's films, as the debates that they address represent a particular view of Cuban social and political life in the 1960s and 1990s. Likewise, Solanas's *The Voyage* cannot be understood without an explanation of what and whom the film is attacking; thus, an explanation of Argentine (and Latin American) economic and political policies of the 1980s and 1990s and a background to the government of Carlos Menem help to locate the film in its national context.

As well as rooting the films in their social, cultural, and political contexts, each chapter aims to provide readings that are sensitive to representations of gender and to examine their role in constructions of national identities. Feminist readings are applied to *The Voyage,* which, despite its call for equality in class terms, is criticized in its representation of women. It will be seen how Laura Mulvey's critical analysis of the dominance of the masculine gaze in Hollywood films can be applied to Solanas's representations of gender. Other films are criticized for their representations of gender roles. The discussion in chapter 2 of *Like Water for Chocolate* attempts to demonstrate that, although it has been conceived of as a "woman's film," it is an antifeminist text that seeks to promote a stereotypical feminine ideal and naturalize class divisions. Likewise, the reading of *Central Station* in chapter 5 aims to demonstrate that a variation of this feminine ideal lies at the center of the film's representation of a better, more compassionate Brazil.

The analysis in chapter 4 of the only explicitly feminist text to be included, *I the Worst of All (Yo la peor de todas),* explores the ways in which the creation of a female heroine has led to partial readings of history and asks whether the relationship between the two female protagonists can be seen as lesbian. *I the Worst of All* is the only film to be directed by a woman included in the book. This is because Bemberg is the only female Latin American director at the time of writing whose films are available in international circles. One hopes this will not be the case for long.

Representations of masculinity are also examined in these chapters, particularly in the case of the films that present a critique of patriarchy and machismo. The study of *Pixote* in chapter 5 explores the constructions of gender identity and seeks to demonstrate the ways that a cult of violent machismo is seen to be at the root of many of Brazil's social problems. Variations on patriarchal constructs of masculinity are also the focus of attack in a number of other films analyzed. Thus, *Strawberry and Chocolate* addresses homophobia in Cuban society, *I the Worst of All* denounces institutionalized misogyny, both *Amnesia* and *The Frontier* link the abuses of the Pinochet dictatorship to a brand of masculine militarism and its fixation on power, and *Amores perros* exposes a similar kind of violent machismo that is seen in *Pixote.* The readings aim to explain the various ways in which the films critique the types of patriarchal constructs that are represented and to examine the alternative forms of masculinity that each proposes.

The combined aims of this book are thus to highlight important Latin American films made over four decades, with a focus on films produced in

6

the 1990s; to provide a social, political, and economic context that grounds the films in their national contexts; to assess their place within their national film histories; and to provide "original" interpretations. I make no claims that the book will produce definitive readings of the texts; rather, I hope that it succeeds in contributing to the growing field of Latin American film studies and generates debate in its views on the films analyzed.

Notes

1. For a comprehensive book about Latin American cinema that includes a study of the film industries of Argentina, Uruguay, Paraguay, Brazil, Mexico, Cuba, Chile, Bolivia, Ecuador, Peru, Colombia, Venezuela, Central America, and the Caribbean, see King (2000); see also Chanan (1983). For a theoretical approach to Latin American cinema, see Stock (1997).

2. For a discussion of this situation in Mexico, one of Latin America's strongest film industries, see Rashkin (2001).

3. See individual chapters for details.

4. See each chapter and *www.imdb.com* for details. The only film included here that received full state funding was *Memories of Underdevelopment*, which was fully funded by the Cuban Film Institute; see chapter 1. *Pixote* by Hector Babenco also received most of its funding from the Brazilian state company Embrafilme, along with Babenco's own company, HB Filmes; see chapter 5. For more theories on transnational and national cinema, see Higson (2000); for an analysis of the debates in a Latin American context, see Stock (1997).

5. For discussions on Imperfect Cinema, see the section on *Memories of Underdevelopment* in chapter 1. For an explanation of Third Cinema, see the section on Solanas in chapter 4. For more on New Latin American Cinema, see Martin (1997), Burton (1983), and King (2000).

6. Sadly, both Tomás Gutiérrez Alea and María Luisa Bemberg died of cancer (see chapters 1 and 4).

7. All the national cinema movements of the late 1960s emphasized educating "the masses." In one example, Octavio Getino, looking back on the aims of Third Cinema, writes, "This cinema, revolutionary in both its formulation and its consciousness, would invent a new cinematographic language, in order to create a new consciousness and a new social reality" (Getino, 1997, 99).

8. Once again, *The Voyage*, a film that is closer in spirit to the revolutionary films of the late 1960s than any others, proves the exception. *Memories of Underdevelopment* does not fit into this category, as it was made in the late 1960s.

9. Writing on New Latin American Cinema, B. Ruby Rich (1997) has argued that a false sense of thematic and aesthetic unity was created by critics. Films that did not conform to such an image were simply written out of the history of film (279–81).

Tomás Gutiérrez Alea's
Changing Images of the Revolution
From *Memories of Underdevelopment* to *Strawberry and Chocolate*

This chapter focuses on *Memories of Underdevelopment* (*Memorias del subdesarrollo*) (1968) and *Strawberry and Chocolate* (*Fresa y chocolate*) (1993), by both Cuba's most celebrated director, Tomás Gutiérrez Alea (1928–1996).[1] It examines how these two films reveal the ways in which the position of a major cultural figure of the Cuban revolution shifted. This is particularly apparent in the change of direction Alea took in his representation of the masculine individual in his relationship with revolutionary society, as well as in the films' attitudes toward "popular" and "high" art, or revolutionary and bourgeois culture. There are many links between *Memories* and *Strawberry*, with the latter reformulating some of the key issues introduced in the earlier film. Alea himself said of *Strawberry*, "[T]here were times in the initial conversations regarding the script in which the presence of this film [*Memories*] was very strong" (Evora, 1996, 52; my translation). The aim of this chapter is to explore the relationship between the two and to examine each film in the social and cultural context in which it was made.

These two works, one made at the beginning of Alea's career and one toward the end, are the films for which the director is best known. *Memories of Underdevelopment* is considered a classic of Latin American cinema and established Alea's reputation internationally. Of the film's achievement, Julianne Burton wrote that *Memories of Underdevelopment* is "not only, among the greatest Latin American films ever produced, but among the most significant films of [its] decade worldwide" (Burton, 1984, 67). The film won a number of prizes in the 1970s, including the National Society of Film Critics award (United States, 1973), and has been praised for its innovative techniques, principally the combination of fictional forms with newsreel and documentary footage and the use of nonchronological (narrative) time, as well as its editing (Myerson, 1973).[2] For its part, *Strawberry* is considered groundbreaking, as the first Cuban film to examine the theme of homosexuality in any depth. It was an extremely popular film in Cuba and broke box office records. The film was also successful outside Cuba in commercial and critical terms, winning a number of awards and being featured at several top international film festivals.[3] In addition, *Strawberry* was the first Cuban film to be nominated for an Oscar for best foreign language film (1995).[4]

As a director, Alea held an interesting position in the Cuban cultural system. He was a self-declared revolutionary, yet he used many of his films to criticize flaws in the Cuban political system. This is particularly true of his later films, as will be seen. Alea was, in fact, one of the cofounders of the Cuban Institute of Art and Industry (ICAIC),[5] although he believed that the triumph of Fidel Castro's forces in 1959 was just the beginning of the revolutionary process. Film would contribute to that process by acting as society's critical conscience and by helping to educate and stimulate Cuban citizens. In his words:

> [Spectators] should not return complacent, tranquil, empty, worn out and inert; rather, they should be stimulated *and* armed for practical action. This means that show must constitute a factor in the development, through enjoyment, of the spectators' consciousness. In doing that, it moves them from remaining simple, passive (contemplative) spectators in the face of reality. (Martin, 1997a, 125).

Alea was thus an evangelical director in that he aimed to change the attitudes and ways of thinking of his audience through his films.[6] Although he was broadly supportive of the Castro regime, throughout his career, in both his films and public statements, he sought to challenge aspects of Cuban society. Alea always asserted the director's right to be critical of revolutionary society, if that criticism could be put to constructive use. In his words: "For the development of the revolution, criticism of the revolution is fundamental. Our silence is the greatest weapon of the enemies of the revolution" (Evora, 1996, 126, my translation). He also spoke out against the servile relationship between artists and politicians (Gutiérrez Alea, 1975, 106), and claimed that the revolutionary filmmaker should have a "permanent critical spirit" (Gutiérrez Alea, 1975, 105).

Alea's perspective on the Cuban revolution changed significantly from the early 1960s to the mid-1990s. A comparative analysis of his two most successful films, along with the contrasting messages Alea sought to deliver in each film, provides a number of insights into the changes in ideology for this artist working within the Cuban state institution.

The movement initially associated with Cuban revolutionary film, known as Imperfect Cinema, was first defined in 1969 by Julio García Espinosa in his essay "For an Imperfect Cinema" (Martin, 1997a, 71–82).[7] One of Espinosa's theses is that art should eventually be made by the people, for the people. However, until conditions become possible for that to happen, filmmakers should create a partisan, socially committed art form, which will become "the heritage of all" (76). According to Espinosa, notions of quality have been contaminated by elitist, Europeanized values, and thus, within Imperfect Cinema, questions of taste and quality need to be reexamined. For Espinosa, "The only thing it [Imperfect Cinema] is interested in is how an artist responds to the following question: What are you doing in order to overcome the barrier of the 'cultured' elite audience which up to now has conditioned the form of your work?" (82).

This question of the relationship between the bourgeois revolutionary artist and the culture that has formed him or her is crucial when tracing the trajectory of the filmmaking of Tomás Gutiérrez Alea. *Memories of Underdevelopment* directly takes up Espinosa's challenge by providing a lengthy critique of bourgeois culture. The film's protagonist (played by Sergio Corrieri), adheres to an elite, foreign (European) lifestyle, which casts him as an antimodel. His understanding of the terms *development* and *underdevelopment* has been tainted by a value system that is alien to the majority of the Cuban people. In *Strawberry and Chocolate,* in contrast, Alea critiques this conceptualization of culture. Here, the debasement of bourgeois art forms, which has seen the work of national artists rejected and brought about isolation in terms of international culture, is viewed as having caused a form of underdevelopment that the film challenges. Diego (played by Jorge Perugúrria), an elite, intellectual outsider, is not to be shunned; rather, he is to use his knowledge of neglected (and censored) cultural figures to educate the young revolutionary and to create a better leader for the future.[8] Clearly, this issue is further complicated by the fact that Diego is a homosexual in a homophobic state, something that will be examined later in this chapter.

An awareness of the historical period in which each film was made can explain these shifts in attitude. *Memories of Underdevelopment* is set in postrevolutionary Cuba; it covers the years 1961–1962, which saw two of the most important events in recent Cuban history, the Bay of Pigs invasion and the missile crisis with the United States. This was a period in which revolutionaries were seeking to establish a new collective identity while protecting themselves from a hostile neighbor, the United States, amid cold war tensions. *Strawberry and Chocolate* is set in 1979 at another time of crisis for the revolution, just before the mass exodus of dissatisfied Cubans in the so-called Mariel boat lift. An estimated 125,000 Cubans left for the United States from the port of Mariel, a number that included many gays (Skidmore & Smith, 1992, 281). The regime attacked those who left, focusing on "delinquent" homosexuals (Lumsden, 1996, 78); as a result, there were mass antihomosexual demonstrations in the streets of Havana. Both films were made some years after the periods in which they were set, *Memories* in 1968 and *Strawberry* in 1993, and thus offer reflections both on key historical periods in Cuban history, and on the periods in which they were made.

In 1968, both revolutionary society and the ICAIC, just nine years old, were seeking to establish and consolidate their identities. The Cuban film industry was, in fact, created as part of the revolution; Alfredo Guevara, a filmmaker and former schoolmate of Fidel Castro, was asked to establish a Cuban film institute, and in March 1959 the ICAIC was founded. Before the revolution, there was very little in terms of a national film industry. Cuba provided cheap locations for Hollywood films, and local production was limited to poor-quality pornography, newsreels, and copies of Mexican commercial melodramas (Myerson, 1973, 18–19). With the creation of the ICAIC, the culture of Cuban filmmaking was transformed. Between 1959 and 1987, the production of feature films doubled, compared to the period 1930–1958, while, particularly in the early years of the revolutionary government, many documentaries and newsreels were produced to promote the state's policies (King, 2000, 146).[9] One of the aims of the ICAIC was to create a new national film culture to reflect Cuban reality and thus move away from foreign cultural models. As Alea himself said in an essay written in 1968, "[T]he Revolution is a radical break with everything that until that moment had denied and deformed our needs and possibilities as a free and sovereign nation" (Gutiérrez Alea, 1975, 99).

Memories of Underdevelopment critiques outdated value systems, anchored in generations of imperialism, and attacks nonproductive intellectuals, who nurture notions of individualism at a time of collective endeavor. The film takes as its subject a bourgeois intellectual who has been brought up to believe that foreign models are superior and that Cuba is doomed by its own cultural underdevelopment. These ideas are challenged as viewers are shown Sergio's decline in a new world, where his way of thinking has become redundant. The film demonstrates that political structures may have changed, but bourgeois values permeate the national culture. Of the intended outcome of this process, Alea wrote, "[T]he spectators feel caught in a trap since they have identified with a character who proceeds to destroy himself and is reduced to... nothing" (Burton, 1977, 9).

By the 1990s the Cuban film industry had proven that it could make high-quality, internationally recognized films, but it was facing financial difficulties.[10] Also, by 1990, Fidel Castro had declared a "Special period of peace," in response to the economic crisis left by the disintegration of the former Soviet bloc, and the subsequent loss of aid to Cuba. The government took new measures against corruption and the black market, and within three months, beginning in November 1990, 500 people had been arrested (Chanan, 1997, 2). The economic climate affected the industry with fewer films made and an increasing dependence on coproductions to ensure financing.[11] These hardships were reflected within Cuban films made during this period, and tensions were becoming more visible between the ICAIC and the Cuban government, with one film banned, *Alicia en el pueblo de las maravillas* (*Alice in Wonder Town*) (1991).[12] Mirta Ibarra (Alea's wife and the actress who played Nancy in *Strawberry and Chocolate*) argued that the reason *Strawberry* was not censored was because of the controversy generated by *Alicia,* with the subsequent outcry by intellectuals and filmmakers (Ibarra, 1995, 79). One of the reasons that *Strawberry and Chocolate* was made at all was that it was very cheap to film. Of this, Senel Paz noted, "[T]he producer [Miguel Mendoza] said it was the best of all scripts he had read, because it didn't need petrol. There's no movement, very few exteriors, everything's filmed in one house.... It's a film written to be very cheap to make" (Paz, 1995, 29).

Thus, with the economic crisis and cultural censorship, film directors in the 1990s could no longer look to the Cuban government for financial backing. As Ana López explained: "The fissures of Revolutionary Cuban identity are only too apparent today, as the economic and social crises of the 'special period' have permanently invalidated the Revolutionary Utopian promise and have unmoored the fictions of insular national identity that once sustained the Revolution ideologically" (López, 1995, 6).

Alea, who had always claimed the right to be critical within the framework of the revolution, reflected the climate of his times by directing his criticisms toward the government in his later films. In them he expressed his frustrations with the insistence on cultural orthodoxy, and represented the resourceful and illegal ways citizens dealt with censorship and economic hardships. *Strawberry and Chocolate* makes a case for the need for alternative voices, even if these voices run counter to party orthodoxy and, through the character of Nancy (Mirta Ibarra), represents black market dealings as an essential part of everyday life.[13] In his last film, *Guantanamera* (1995)

Alea would go on to show the resourceful ways people dealt with the chronic shortages of goods (in this case, gasoline), and attacked the inefficiency of bureaucrats.[14]

Although it is well known that Cuba in the 1990s was suffering from the effects of the long-established U.S. blockade and its recent abandonment by the former Soviet Union, Alea used *Strawberry* to highlight another form of impoverishment of the Cuban state's own making, that is, cultural isolation. The director made his feelings clear in an interview, when he said, "[W]e live on an island in all senses, we have isolated ourselves too much. Culturally we have become impoverished; we aren't being stimulated by so many things that the world produces everyday" (Evora, 1996, 133; my translation). This call for a cultural and political perestroika is one of the principal messages of *Strawberry*.

Strawberry and *Memories*, then, are films with very different ideological messages due to changes in social, political, economic, and cultural circumstances. The key shift in approach in the films is demonstrated in the representation of bourgeois culture in these different contexts, seen through the lives of Sergio and Diego. A comparative character analysis of the protagonists of each film can shed light on the ways in which Alea used his characters to generate changing images of the revolution. This chapter looks at each character's relationship with his culture, society, class, and sexuality. It goes on to contrast Sergio with David (played by Vladimir Cruz), two characters who act as antimodel and model, respectively, and serve to highlight the directions Alea proposed for his country, at two important historical moments. Each section also draws attention to the cinematic forms used and the ways in which they give shape to the vision in each film.

In both films, the focus is on the relation of intellectuals to revolutionary society. In *Memories*, the individual is seen to be going in the wrong direction. Society is moving forward; the people are preparing to forge their own identity and resist invasion by U.S.-backed counterrevolutionaries. Sergio, in contrast, cannot take part in any form of collective action, because of the bourgeois mind-set in which he is trapped. Alea, in describing a scene in which Sergio walks in the opposite direction of people on their way to a political gathering, said, "[T]he scene is very significant, because Sergio is always heading in the other direction from everyone else. As an image it functions very well" (Gutiérrez Alea, 1977, 8). *Strawberry*, in contrast, argues that it is society that is going in the wrong direction (isolation, censorship, and unrealistic economic policies) and, in a reversal of position, that it is the role of the bourgeois intellectual to guide the young revolutionary future leader back on track.

14

Memories of Underdevelopment:
Sergio, the Useless Intellectual

One of the most interesting aspects of the film is its exploration of the nature of the individual, and the possibilities of maintaining this identity in a society that focuses on the collective. Through carefully chosen cinematic techniques, Alea revealed that Sergio's self-perception is flawed and that the accusations of underdevelopment which Sergio levels at the Cuban people are more appropriately directed toward himself. Alea's understanding of the bourgeois intellectual relied on a Gramscian conceptualization, which is in direct conflict with that of Sergio. For political activist and theorist Antonio Gramsci, intellectuals are not "independent [and] autonomous, endowed with a character of their own," but are part of "a system of relations" in which intellectual groups have their place within a structure of social rela-tions (quoted in Hoare & Nowell Smith, 1971, 8). Sergio is unable to see his place in the new social system, believing that his self-appointed status of intellectual situates him above any social structure. He prefers to see himself as a superior being in an underdeveloped culture, an alienated individual in the mold of a protagonist of a European existentialist novel. He believes he has gained this status of true individual in his refusal to leave for Miami with his friends and family and in his separation from the revolutionary society forming around him.

When Pablo (played by Omar Valdés), Sergio's only remaining friend, leaves Cuba for the United States, Sergio walks away from him at the airport, relieved in the belief that he is shedding the last remainder of his identity. He says to himself: "I realize that Pablo isn't Pablo; it's my own life. Everything I don't want to be. It's good to see [him] leave. . . . I keep my mind clear. It's a disagreeable clarity, empty."

The two have moved away from their prerevolutionary friendship and are symbolically separated by the glass divide in the airport lounge. Pablo mouths words that Sergio cannot hear, as communication with his old world has come to an end. Nevertheless, despite Sergio's relief, his overwhelming emotion is one of emptiness, as he has no new identity to replace the old. He claims that the revolution is his revenge against the bourgeoisie, yet he has no involvement in the new society. He does not work, has no friends, and spends his time in critical thought about the old and new Cuba, with little sense of his place in either. He does not realize that he cannot shed his identity by simply isolating himself. This is highlighted in the film by the sequence of the editing. As soon as Sergio says good-bye to Pablo, he is invaded by memories of his school days, and the audience is shown images of

15

his childhood world: the school run by priests, his school friend's mansion, and the brothel where he had his first sexual relations. This is the world that has formed him, a world characterized by unequal class and gender relations. The film suggests that Sergio cannot begin to change until he uses his education and privilege to understand the power relations of which he is a part, then employs this knowledge to take on a role in his changing society.

These unequal power relations are at the root of ordinary people's lack of opportunity and, in Alea's view, are responsible for Cuba's underdevelopment. However, Sergio does not make the connections, just as he cannot understand how he fits into Cuban society. He blames the (proletarian) people themselves and appears to believe that contact with them will contaminate him. One of his contacts with the "other" Cuba is Elena (played by Daisy Granados), a young working-class woman whose ambition it is to be an actress. When assessing his relationship with Elena, he says, "I always try to live like a European. And Elena forces me to feel underdeveloped at every step." The film counters the self-image Sergio has by showing the audience his place in a bourgeois system of relations in both economic and social terms. He may have abandoned the lifestyle of marriage and dinner parties, but this is a passive acceptance of changes in circumstances, and although his thought processes remain anchored in prejudices and scorn toward his countrymen and women, he cannot be integrated into Cuban society.

Sergio's greatest mistake is to believe that his thoughts and actions are somehow above the society in which he lives. As Julianne Burton (1977) writes:

Sergio fails to make any connection with his own life. He fails to realize that he too is an accomplice of reactionary forces precisely because he won't desert his position of critical superiority to participate, to act, to engage himself in the world around him. (20)

This is seen most clearly in a scene in which Sergio reads an extract from a revolutionary book, *Bourgeois Morality and Revolution,* written on the capture of the Cuban CIA-backed mercenaries during the failed invasion of Playa Girón (known as the Bay of Pigs to English speakers). Sergio reads out the thesis of the author, Leon Rozitchner, while newsreel footage illustrates his ideas.[15] This thesis is that all the components of a capitalist dictatorship, including landowners, priests, intellectuals, and political leaders, refuse to see how the murderer-torturers act on their behalf to maintain their place of privilege in society. The scene's screen title in capitals, THE TRUTH OF THE

GROUP IS IN THE MURDERER, highlights this message. Sergio is heard reading about those put on trial after the Bay of Pigs invasion:

> In none of the cases considered was there a recovery of the true dialectic relationship between individuals and the group. Those who came with [Ramón] Calviño (the torturer-murderer) didn't recognize themselves as part of the system which entangles them in their own acts. (Myerson, 1973, 65)

Following this, several members of the invading party are shown denying any individual responsibility. Alea shows the interdependence of this relationship by editing together disparate documentary images of former Cuban president Fulgencio Batista examining weapons, the trial of Calviño, the victims of state murders, and the members of the bourgeoisie at grand dances.[16]

The great paradox in this scene is that Sergio, who provides the voice-over to the documentary images, shows no awareness of his own place in Cuban society. At one point, he reads about the group dynamic, which even includes a passage about the strategy that he has adopted: "Everybody refers to his own personality when he wants to get away from another person's contaminating misery.... Or he sinks into the group when he has to hide his own responsibility"(Myerson, 1973, 64).[17] Sergio has clearly taken the former path; however, he shows no recognition of this. His identity and lifestyle have been made possible by the former regime, yet he takes no responsibility for this, and is simply pleased that he is able to live off the money given to him by the state for his expropriated apartment block.

Sergio reserves his critical judgment for others; he appears to be satisfied with the idea of himself as an intellectual. However, the very notion of intellectual has changed with the revolution, something that Sergio is unaware of. The supporters of the revolution, including the filmmakers of the ICAIC, shared Gramsci's notion that intellectuals will eventually be formed within the process of revolutionary society. For Gramsci, intellectuals would evolve organically from within a worker's party; members would be turned into "qualified political intellectuals, leaders and organisers of all the activities and functions inherent in the organic development of an integral society, both civil and politically" (quoted in Hoare & Nowell Smith, 1971, 16–17). In line with this, Espinosa declared in his manifesto for Imperfect Cinema that the ultimate aim of art is to belong to and come from the people. In his words: "[A] complete aesthetic activity will only be possible when it is the people who make art" (Martin, 1997a, 79). The aim of the privileged intellectual, then, is to help to create the conditions for this to happen and to produce a genuinely popular culture. For Alea, the term *popular* can only be used when cinema responds to people's authentic interests. He claimed that "a people's cinema can be fully developed only in a society where the people's interests coincide with the state's interests; that is, in a socialist society" (Martin, 1997a, 115).

Through Sergio, an antihero is created to promote the above position. In contrast to the Gramscian model, he relies on an elitist concept of culture, in order to see himself on a higher plane than the rest of society. The interests of the majority of the Cuban people do not interest him. After he has left a round table conference on the subject of "Literature and Underdevelopment" (an actual conference that Alea incorporated into the film), he muses: "How does one get rid of underdevelopment? It marks everything. Everything. What are you doing down there, Sergio? What does all this mean? You have nothing to do with them. You're alone." As he goes on to say that without family, work, a wife, he is nothing, already dead, the initial close-up of the camera intensifies and becomes so close that Sergio's face dissolves into grainy material. He literally disappears, with the image reflecting his words. Despite these insights, Sergio has missed the point of the conference. He has not seen that, as one of the speakers, Giani Toti, says, the term *underdevelopment* is in itself "sickly," a linguistic trap that is an "accomplice of an already wasted culture."[18] What Toti perhaps means here is that the term has been used historically to blame "third world" cultures for the centuries of exploitation and oppression imposed by "developed" countries. Sergio sees other Cubans as being "down there," while he is forced to share their position, before ultimately preferring to disappear.

Alea cleverly has the audience question Sergio's sense of superiority by deconstructing and reversing this key concept of underdevelopment. It is Sergio who is, in fact, underdeveloped in both an emotional and an intellectual sense. His only contact with others is seen through his attempts to seduce women, and, even when successful, he is unable to choose appropriate partners or to sustain relationships. His relationship with Elena serves to illustrate this. He is attracted by her looks and sexuality, but when she fails to allow herself to be educated according to his Western standards, he loses interest in her and dumps her with no regard for her feelings. She later falsely accuses him of rape, and although he is acquitted at the trial, he recognizes that he is not entirely innocent, as he used the trappings of his privileged lifestyle to seduce her. In addition, Sergio is unable to adapt to the changes in social circumstances; his attempts to live like a bourgeois European in a socialist country with no community around him make no sense and serve no purpose. As Edmundo Desnoes explains, "The key of the character is that he does not assume his historical involvement" (Myerson, 1973, 45).

Alea takes the opposite position to Sergio, as the intellectual who can use his privilege to challenge hegemonic bourgeois values through his filmmaking. The appearance of the director in *Memories* highlights this distinction. In a meta-filmic scene, Alea meets with Sergio and shows him clips of a film he is making that "will be a collage, that'll have a bit of everything." This clearly is *Memories of Underdevelopment*, a film that makes use of a range of narrative registers, including sections of documentaries made by ICAIC filmmakers, television footage, and documentary-style street scenes filmed with a hidden camera. The interaction between the social world, as seen in the documentary footage, and the private world of Sergio is the cause of the audience's shift from a position of identification with Sergio to alienation from him. There has been much excellent analysis of this, so I will not repeat ideas already expressed.[19] The point being made here is that Alea and Sergio represent two poles of the position that can be taken by the artist within a revolutionary society.

Sergio is thus an anachronism in the Cuba of the early 1960s. The desired role of the intellectual had shifted from passive critic to central participant working with the state to create a new society. Gramsci's model of the intellectual within a revolutionary society seems particularly apt for the Cuban model. For Gramsci,

> The mode of being of the new intellectual can no longer consist of eloquence, which is an exterior and momentary mover of feelings and passion, but in active participation in practical life, as constructor, organizer, permanent persuader, and not just simple orator. (quoted in Hoare & Nowell Smith, 1971, 10)

Sergio, out of step with his society, is the antithesis of the Gramscian model; he is a voyeur whose sign is the telescope. He is seen on a number of occasions from his balcony, surveying the city below, demonstrating the distance he creates between himself and the people below. Sergio is a consumer, not a producer, of culture. He feeds his fantasies through literature and art, and is seen buying Nabokov's *Lolita* and running his finger over a print of Botticelli's *Venus*. He may buy respectable classical culture, yet this does not lead to spiritual enlightenment, but rather acts as soft porn. His association with *Lolita* also highlights the film's critical view of his relationship with Elena, who is only sixteen years old. Likewise, his only interest in filmmaking (i.e. the new revolutionary art form) is as a vehicle to seduce Elena, who wants to become an actress. He claims he wants to be a writer,

Sergio (Sergio Corrieri), the voyeur, in *Memories of Underdevelopment*.

yet the audience only ever sees him produce a line of his memoirs.[20] He is, in short, a nonproductive intellectual, with theories on the nature of Cuba, Cuban women, and underdevelopment expressed only in private thoughts. The film gives the audience access to these thoughts; however, Sergio does not enter into a productive debate or discussion with his fellow countrymen or women. In addition, he has no job and, as has been seen, lives comfortably on state money, taking from society without giving anything back.

Strawberry and Chocolate:
Diego, the Redeemed Bourgeois Intellectual

In *Memories of Underdevelopment*, the protagonist, Sergio, is engaged in a process of self-destruction, as he is unwilling or unable to change his bourgeois identity in line with the new historical realities surrounding him. On this, Desnoes said, "the character's world is closed; the Revolution, however, is open to everybody" (Myerson, 1973, 46). By the time *Strawberry and Chocolate* was made, in 1993, it had become clear that the revolution was not open to everybody, certainly not to its protagonist, Diego, a non-conformist, bourgeois Catholic homosexual. This focus on a discriminated minority shifts the object of criticism from the individual to the collective (the state), which has been unable to integrate him into the body politic. Castro's regime has had a poor record on human rights for gay men in particular. Homosexuality was associated with a decadent, bourgeois lifestyle and with crime, delinquency, and disease (Lumsden, 1996, 65), and gays were prevented from having influence over young people and children, particularly in the field of education (Lockwood, 1990, 107). Leading gay cultural figures in Cuba were dismissed from posts or detained (Lumsden, 1996, 59–60), and from 1965 until 1968 many homosexuals were sent to work camps, or Military Units to Aid Production (UMAP).[21] This discrimination led to the exile of key members of the Cuban cultural arena. The most prominent of these were the cinematographer Néstor Almendros, and the writer Reinaldo Arenas.[22] This has been one of the main areas of concern for many socialists outside Cuba, who might otherwise be supportive of the Castro regime.

It should be noted that, although the film mentions that Diego has had problems with the system and is laughed at because of his effeminacy, state and individual homophobia is underplayed, with only the dogmatic young communist student Miguel (played by Francisco Cattorno) seen to be genuinely homophobic.[23] There is only one brief reference to UMAP, with no explanation, which would go unnoticed by a foreign audience, and there is no mention of the mass homophobia that led to the street demonstrations of 1980. In addition, although José Lezama Lima's memory is rescued, there is no mention of either Arenas or Almendros. It is interesting that Almendros made a film with Orlando Jiménez, *Improper Conduct* (1983), which features testimonies from former UMAP prisoners, including Reinaldo Arenas. Alea was highly critical at the time of its release, claiming the film damaged the reputation of Cuba an open socialist society. He later claimed that *Strawberry* was, in a sense, an attempt to reopen the debate, while calling for an end to discrimination against gays (Santí, 1998, 413–414; Smith, 1996, 82).

Despite the downplaying of historical state homophobia in *Strawberry*, it is clear that revolutionary Cuba has rejected Diego, if not principally as a result of his sexuality, then because of his questioning of cultural policies and his defense of Catholicism and forbidden art and literature.[24] There is, then, a radically different representation of the bourgeois intellectual than that seen in *Memories*. In *Strawberry*, Diego, a gay intellectual with a love of high culture (art, classical music, opera, and canonical literature), is presented as a neglected positive force that needs to be valued and allowed to contribute to the education of culturally deprived Cubans. Because of the change in circumstances, the Gramscian model of the bourgeois intellectual was no longer relevant in the 1990s to Alea, codirector Juan Carlos Tabío, and Senel Paz. Diego, unlike Sergio, is no longer seen as part of a hegemonic system, but part of a counterculture. He is one of the voices of opposition speaking against censorship and in favor of cultural inclusiveness.[25] In addition, he actively promotes culture, mentoring David (played by Vladimir Cruz) in his quest to become a writer, and initially taking charge of the planning an art exhibition by Germán (played by Joel Angelino). As such, Diego is actively engaged in the development of society, unlike the aloof, passive Sergio. Another Gramscian notion is questioned in *Strawberry* as David, the organic intellectual produced by a revolutionary society, is represented as lacking because of the cultural isolationism and censorship of Cuban society in the late 1970s.

In *Memories of Underdevelopment,* Alea gradually encourages the audience to shift from a position of identification with Sergio to alienation from him. In contrast, in *Strawberry,* the initial prejudice that David (and the implied audience) has toward Diego shifts toward a steady approximation to the character. The most obvious difference between Diego and Sergio is their sexuality, both in terms of orientation and in how they practice it. This is used in each film to generate antipathy and sympathy, respectively. Audiences are encouraged to like Diego, partly because he has been discriminated against, and partly because he is a safe (nonsexual) gay man, who helps David to find love with a woman. In contrast to Sergio, who is a sexual predator and sees women as objects, Diego's sexuality is subsumed in culture and is thus made more palatable for David and straight audiences.[26] Diego is never seen to be sexually active in the film, and the only hint of his pleasure is seen in briefly glimpsed naked photos of young men in nonsexual poses, discovered early on by David, suggesting little more than a voyeuristic interest. In addition, despite his attraction and love for David, Diego never makes a pass at him, and even fixes him up with Nancy (played by Mirta Ibarra), his unstable neighbor and friend. In this way, through a conservative representation of Diego's gayness, the filmmakers are able to appeal to mainstream audiences for tolerance toward a discriminated minority.[27]

Strawberry and Chocolate makes no claims to be a gay film (i.e., a film made by gays, for gay audiences). Paz, Alea, and Tabío are all straight, the perspective is that of David, while audiences are presumed to be heterosexual and are encouraged to challenge their assumed prejudices and accept Diego. Those involved in the making of the film have stressed that tolerance, not homosexuality, is the main theme of the film and that homosexuality should

Diego (Jorge Perugorría) and David (Vladimir Cruz) in *Strawberry and Chocolate*.

be seen as a metaphor. In an interview, Tabío stated, "our film represents a hymn to tolerance, to the possibility of mutual comprehension and to the mutual enrichment of two persons who are profoundly different" (West, 1995, 20). Likewise, Paz rather defensively asserted that "intolerance in respect of sexual attitude is a metaphor. So the film also addresses religious and racial intolerance and intolerance on the level of ideas, which is the most important of all.... The film was never intended, nor did it ever occur to us, to campaign on behalf of homosexuality" (Paz, 1994, 33).

If the perspective of the film is heterosexual and there is no intention to campaign for homosexuality, then why are audiences encouraged to accept the gay character? Who is Diego, this creation of straight writer and directors, and what purpose does he serve? Once again, Alea chose a project that he believed would change the way that Cubans think about a subject.[28] One of the functions of the representation of homosexuality is the promotion of high culture. As Diego is seen to have suffered discrimination, he is in the paradoxical position of being a marginalized elitist; this allows the filmmakers to call for high art to be rescued from neglect, without embracing dominant bourgeois culture, as represented by Sergio. Thus,

Strawberry uses the theme of tolerance toward homosexuality to challenge other social taboos. The film calls for a pluralistic society without censorship or state interference in cultural affairs; it attacks cultural isolationism and calls for a recognition of the need to liberalize the economic system. All these issues are personalized through the characters of Nancy, David, and, in particular, Diego. It can also be said that, as the first homosexual to be represented sympathetically in a Cuban film, the focus on Diego ensures that the controversial political criticisms are less apparent.

As homosexuality in the film is a metaphor for tolerance, an acceptance of Diego by David and the audience stands for the creation of a more open-minded, democratic society, able to accommodate difference. Diego is a rather stereotypical, effeminate gay man with aristocratic tastes, who comes to embody forbidden or neglected bourgeois culture. His early references to André Gide, Oscar Wilde, Federico García Lorca, Lezama Lima, and Ernest Hemingway help to immediately place his sexuality in a cultural context, and take the emphasis away from sex. His aim is to teach the proletarian David (and, by extension the viewer) about high art (literature, opera, and music) and the joys of luxury food and drink.[29]

On first meeting, Diego appears to conform to stereotypical images of the predatory queer and reactionary bourgeois. He brings David back to his apartment on false pretenses, then lectures him on well-known cultural figures who were gay. He is also seen to be racist, associating blacks with the chaos of the streets and thieves who would steal your best china. He adds that he well knows the value of black men, but they are not made to drink tea, implying that they are only of value to Diego as sexual objects. As the friendship develops and David (with the audience) gets to know him, he reveals himself as an improbably selfless character who sacrifices his own needs for David's. Diego is there for his friend whenever he needs him without appearing to ask for anything in return. He feeds David, providing him with expensive luxury food and wines at the dinner based on a chapter of Lezama Lima's *Paradiso* (1966).[30] He provides David with shelter, understanding, and whiskey, when he is suffering the pain of a failed relationship, he acts as a cultural mentor in David's education as an aspiring writer, and he plays matchmaker for David and Nancy despite the fact that he is clearly in love with David. He is also extremely handsome, charming, and witty.[31] Diego's opinions on Cuban blacks are never referred to again, which allows the audience to forget that he is racist. This is a problematic aspect of the film, as he is redeemed without having to confront these views.[32]

This positive representation is clearly part of the strategy to ensure that mainstream audiences warm to Diego and, by implication, challenge their homophobia. However, it begs the question of how "real," flawed, sexually active homosexuals would be received. Perhaps this form of representation only becomes possible when there is a range of gay characters in Cuban film, and one character does not have to bear the burden of embodying a heterogeneous group.[33] Despite Diego's goodness, identification is maintained for David, as implied straight (male) audiences share in his journey of cultural awakening and (hetero)sexual initiation.

Diego sees his principal role in Cuba as a spokesman for artistic freedom and a preserver of forgotten culture. He plays music by neglected Cuban composers and pianists Ernesto Lecuona and Ignacio Cervantes. The music is a significant part of the soundtrack; Cervantes's "Farewell to Cuba" ("Adiós a Cuba") and "Lost Hopes" ("Ilusiones perdidas") anticipate Diego's exile from Cuba and his disillusionment with the regime.[34] His hero is José Lezama Lima, an author whose difficult masterpiece, *Paradiso*, was initially banned in Cuba, partly because of its references to homosexuality. The emphasis on *Paradiso* in the film is significant. Cuba has lost its utopian projection as great figures like Lezama Lima have been marginalized in the national cultural arena. The film calls for an inclusive cultural world where Lezama's homosexual paradise can sit alongside Che Guevara's utopia visions of Cuban society.

Diego is a symbol, an embodiment of a position. Audiences never gain access to his inner world or his private thoughts, and, in contrast to David and Nancy, he is rarely seen alone. He is always seen in relation to an "other," usually David. This is because the film functions through the use of dialectics. The position the film takes is reached through dialogue between the young, revolutionary aspiring writer and the older, nonconformist promoter of culture. Each character states his position, with both learning from each other, until a new, better position is reached. In one key scene, David tries to explain to Diego why the whole process of the revolution cannot be rejected and abandoned because of the way it has treated Diego and other gays. He, in line with official policy, claims that "the mistakes aren't the revolution. They're part of the revolution but they are not the revolution."[35] Alea himself clearly shared this view; his comments in an interview in 1979 could have been made by David: "we have to do our best so that fewer errors and injustices are committed. What we cannot do is to take those errors and injustices as a justification to abandon the struggle" (Stone, 1997, 125–26).

In the exchange between the two, there is a brief mention of the UMAP work camps, with no explanation, and David reassures Diego (and the audience) by stating that that era has passed. Diego pushes David, asking him to look at who pays the price for the mistakes, and David responds by looking forward to a more enlightened time. He says, "I'm sure that one day there will be more understanding for everyone; if not, this wouldn't be a revolution." This new, better world is shown through symbols, illustrated at the beginning of this scene, when David seals his friendship with Diego by adding the iconography of the revolution to Diego's baroque altar dedicated to Cuban culture. To ballet shoes, photographs of writers and leading Cuban cultural figures, and angelic statues, David adds photographs of Che and Fidel when they were young, along with a July 26 armband.[36]

Dialogue forms the basis of *Strawberry*, unlike *Memories*, which acquires its overall meaning through a series of disparate yet connected images and Sergio's voice-over. *Strawberry* largely takes the format of a play in terms of structure and setting; aside from a few outdoor shots, the emphasis is on interiors, principally Diego's home, and there is a general lack of movement.[37] In *Memories*, the audience has to work out the politics of the film by contrasting the "objective" documentary images with Sergio's subjective images. This, in fact, led to the film being misinterpreted outside Cuba, with a number of critics in the United States and Britain believing that audiences are meant to identify with Sergio. For them, Sergio is a character who is used to critique revolutionary Cuba (Alea, 1977, 8). There are no doubts as to the message of *Strawberry*: the revolutionary project can be saved if there is a more democratic, inclusive brand of communism and cultural perestroika.

Part of the reason for the change of format in the two films is that each film has a different intended effect on the audience. *Memories* aims to make viewers deconstruct their own bourgeois ideology, and so takes a more subtle approach. *Strawberry* is a defense of the prohibited and hidden identities of others, and this is why much of the dialogue takes the form of justification. In one example, David attributes Diego's sexuality to illness and bad upbringing; hence Diego's defensive explanation that his sexuality is not the fault of his parents and is not a glandular problem. He adds, "I like men and I'm perfectly normal," and insists that this does not stop him from being as decent and patriotic as David.

Despite the emphasis on dialogue to state the filmmakers' position, symbolism in *Strawberry* is also used to compound the message of the film. This is seen principally in Germán's papier-mâché sculptures, housed in Diego's den, as he is seeking to exhibit them, both in Cuba and in Mexico. The sculptures take the form of martyred religious figures and feature both Jesus and Karl Marx as members of the Holy Family.[38] The first glimpse the audience has of the statues is during David's first visit to Diego's home. As Diego is talking about the pleasures of tea, his home as a refuge from the streets, and important gay cultural figures, the image of the martyred Christ figure with pierced hands and a crown of thorns can be partially seen, covered by a plastic sheet. The Christ figure appears to provide a cross for Diego as the statue's outstretched arm is seen behind the seated Diego, all to a soundtrack of Maria Callas, the suffering opera diva. The symbolism is clear: Diego as a Catholic, a homosexual, and a promoter of high, marginalized culture, has been sacrificed in the quest for a cultural and sexual orthodoxy. Just as Jesus is partially hidden from view, Diego can only be himself in his *guarida,* his den, a refuge from the outside world with all its prejudices.

While Germán is prepared to agree to censorship of his exhibition if it means he can present it in Mexico, Diego refuses to accept any form of state interference. The authorities have said that the work can be shown if some of the sculptures are dropped, presumably referring to the image of a Christianized Marx, clearly blasphemous in communist (and Catholic) terms. However, for Diego, the exhibition represents a statement of artistic freedom and cultural inclusiveness. In a highly significant scene, the two men fight over their respective positions, with Diego holding the martyred Jesus and Germán, the martyred Marx. Diego and Jesus and Germán and Marx are caught in a symbolic battle, as the scene plays out the struggle for religious freedom in a Marxist society. Marx is wearing a crown of thorns, as the bourgeois artists, represented by Diego and Germán, have rejected his beliefs. Likewise, Jesus has been sacrificed, killed again by atheist revolutionaries.

The exhibition has to be complete with both Jesus and Marx accepted as part of the pluralist culture for which the film is calling. Yet the authorities are not ready to accept this pluralism, insisting on a censored version, and the gay artist cannot work within the communist state. Germán, in a state of frenzy, destroys his statue of Marx, while repeating over and over that the pieces are his. Germán takes the role of the egocentric artist and refuses to acknowledge the larger issues that are represented in this battle. Germán's destruction of Marx while claiming exclusive ownership over him suggests that he is unable to work for a collective project. Diego, through his promotion of Germán's work, comes to represent a call for an acceptance of homosexuals and Catholics in Cuban cultural life. For this, he is prepared to sacrifice himself, creating an artistic parallel with the sculptures. He is sacked and forbidden from working in any cultural arena as a result of a letter he has written complaining about the refusal of the cultural authorities to allow Germán to exhibit all of his statues and at the lack of freedom in Cuban artistic life.

The fundamental paradox at the heart of *Strawberry* is that the world of the cultural elite is that of a member of a discriminated minority. Diego's love of high culture is elitist, but not exclusive to the bourgeoisie. In *Memories,* bourgeois culture is associated with the hegemonic structure of the Cuban society of the Batista regime, and Sergio represents a world of class privilege. Diego's aim is to bring a broader culture to Cubans, as seen in his circulation of prohibited literature among the young (admittedly, just men) and in his insistence that the exhibition be shown in its entirety.[39] Unlike Sergio, he is not a passive intellectual, but aims to have an active role within society. It is this active involvement that causes Diego to leave Cuba to go into exile in the United States. His cultural world, then, is seen to offer no threat to Cuban society; on the contrary, the film argues that he can educate a young revolutionary and help produce a new version of the "new man" called for by Fidel and Ché in the 1960s. It is worth mentioning that although Diego is helping to forge the new, new man, it is never suggested that he, as a homosexual, could be that new revolutionary man.[40]

David: A Future Revolutionary Leader

Diego, then, has an important role: to help in the creation of a future revolutionary leader. He does this by acting as David's cultural mentor, introducing him to Cuba's forgotten and rejected cultural past, and by teaching David to accept him as a homosexual. David ends the film as a man who is capable of accepting difference and of understanding the wealth of cultural diversity. A key point is that he needs to change if the revolution is to progress. In the preceding analysis of *Memories,* it was noted that in 1968 the hope for the future lay in the Gramscian model of the organic intellectual, an idea echoed in the concept of the "new man" called for by Fidel Castro and Che Guevara. At the time, there was a general optimism in Cuban society that a new society was being formed and that the new revolutionary worker-intellectual would replace bourgeois intellectuals. *Strawberry* argues that this hoped for organic intellectual is in many ways incomplete. David has been able to study thanks to the revolution, and he is the first member of his family to go to a university.[41] However, his education has been limited by a restricted access to Cuban and international culture as a result of censorship and isolationism. David is ignorant of anything that is not officially sanctioned, while his own creativity has been quashed by a sense of duty. He has, for example, chosen to study political science, despite his interest in literature, as he feels this is more useful, and his own writings are flawed by a reliance on political propaganda. Diego, as a cultural mentor, picks up where the university has failed and helps to turn David into a more complete writer/cultural leader.

David is a student in 1979 when the film is set, and thus represents an identity in formation. When he is living within the confines of the university, David is "protected" from the realities of the outside world. Only when he meets Diego does he grow aware of the "other" Cuba. Not only does he become friends with a gay, Catholic man who has had problems with the state, he also falls in love with Nancy, who is emotionally unstable, deals on the black market, and practices Santería (an Afro-Cuban religious practice that combines Catholic and Yoruban beliefs).[42] The "other" Cubans, represented by Diego and Nancy, have little to do with Miguel's image of law-abiding, exclusively heterosexual, rationalist Marxists. This ideal of the model citizen can only be maintained in the film within the walls of the university residence in the Student Communist League. Paradoxically, much of David's life education begins when he leaves this world behind.

In both Senel Paz's novella upon which *Strawberry* is based, *The Wolf, the Woods and the New Man* (Paz, 1995), and the film, David, the young Revolutionary, has to enter the woods of a heterodox Cuba and learn to understand the "wolf," the homosexual hiding in the woods, in order to emerge as a new man. The idea of a new man originates in Cuban revolutionary language. Fidel Castro and Che Guevara called for the creation of a new socialist man after the overthrow of Batista's dictatorship. This man was an idealized figure who would lead the country to economic and spiritual independence and renewal. The ideal Cuban communist was to be guided by heroism, a spirit of sacrifice, and a love for his country (Bonachea & Valdés, 1969, 155–69). Castro saw this figure in utopian terms, as "a self-sacrificing idealist who willingly and gladly works not for his private gain, but for the welfare of society" (Dolgoff, 1976, 153). Virility and heterosexuality were prerequisites for this revolutionary, and there was no place for the homosexual, or an acceptance of homosexuality, within this conceptualization. In a much-quoted interview, Castro explained that a homosexual could never be a revolutionary. In his words:

> Nothing prevents a homosexual from professing Revolutionary ideology, and consequently, exhibiting a correct political position.... And yet we could never come to believe that a homosexual could embody the conditions and requirements of conduct that would enable us to consider him a true Revolutionary, a true Communist militant. A deviation of that nature clashes with the concept we have of what a militant Communist must be. (Lockwood, 1990, 107)

Alea appears to have shared many of Castro's ideas of "new man" in *Memories* (although there is no mention of homosexuality), as seen in his creation of an antihero, Sergio, who is the antithesis of this idealized revolutionary figure. Sergio has no love for his country, only a concern for the individual self; he does not contribute in any way to the development of society and is cowardly, paralyzed by fear at the thought of U.S. attacks on Cuba during the missile crisis, as the rest of the country is seen to be preparing to defend itself.[43] However, by the 1990s, Alea and his collaborators felt the need to make substantial alterations to Che and Castro's original prototype. Neither revolutionary leader made mention of the rights of the individual, something that Alea believed had been neglected. In an article published in 1992, just before *Strawberry* was released, he wrote:

> The fundamental objective of the Revolution is man, the improvement of man, the perfecting of the human condition...the creation of a new, more humane, man.... Due to an enthusiasm for social justice, for ideological purity, the Revolution began to ignore man's personal interests, his individual needs. (cited in Evora, 1996, 135; my translation)[44]

Through the character of David, *Strawberry* represents a new, new man who, while remaining true to earlier revolutionary principles of social justice, learns an awareness of individual rights and needs. Both versions of the new man are imaginary utopian creations, but the earlier type, represented in the film by Miguel, has been discredited because of his dogmatism, intolerance of difference, and willingness to punish others for their nonconformity. Miguel has David expelled from the university for his suspected homosexuality and his expression of new ideas, and is happy at the thought of Diego's being imprisoned for his "counterrevolutionary" behavior. Yet David is still working for the revolutionary project, and it is significant that, like Castro and Che's original model, he is still a card-carrying communist. Diego never tries to encourage his friend to leave the party; on the contrary, he welcomes the idea of a democratic communism and tells David, "the revolution needs more activists like you."

Conclusion

At the root of *Memories of Underdevelopment* and *Strawberry and Chocolate* lie two very different conceptualizations of underdevelopment. In the earlier film, historical oppression of the masses and the unequal power relations between the classes are seen as the causes of underdevelopment. High culture is seen to be the preserve of the middle and upper classes, and has only served to lend them a false sense of superiority, and to alienate and subjugate the poor. In *Strawberry*, underdevelopment is seen in terms of cultural impoverishment and isolation due to state policy. The suggestion throughout the film is that high art, whether "correct" or not in the eyes of the state, can bring both intellectual and spiritual enlightenment to the Cuban people. The whole notion of popular culture radically changes from one film to another, and one historical period to another. The key to this lies in Alea's definition of popular culture, seen earlier. In *Memories*, it is felt that the people's interests coincide with those of the state; this is why Sergio is represented as out of step with society. However, by the 1990s, this is no longer seen to be the case, which is why culture disapproved of by the state has a newfound appeal, as does the recognition of the practice of Catholicism and Santería, and the acknowledgment of the illegal, but much used, black market.

Both *Memories of Underdevelopment* and *Strawberry and Chocolate* are films directed by a man who was actively involved with creating images that reflected, and even shaped, the cultural period in which they were made. In the two films, Alea provided guides for the interaction between individuals and their society, with a focus on masculine identities. Sergio is Alea's anti-model, the man who cannot adapt to the requirements of a changing society; David is Alea's model, as he can and does change from a dogmatic defender of the status quo to a potential future leader, who is both a revolutionary and a democrat. Diego is a reworked version of Sergio in that he comes to represent culture that has been associated with the bourgeoisie. However, whereas Sergio is condemned as he fails to embrace a common revolutionary identity, Diego represents the rights of the individual that have been wrongly sacrificed in collective nation building.

Whether consciously or not, Alea established a dialectic between these films. They not only reflect the sociohistorical periods in which they were made but also mirror each other, with *Strawberry* reversing images and ideas first seen and proposed in *Memories*. Sergio, the bourgeois elitist, martyrs himself unnecessarily in an attempt to hold on to a sense of individuality that means little and offers nothing to the revolutionary society. European culture (art, literature, music, film, and fashion) is used to cultivate an image and a lifestyle which makes him feel superior to others and helps him seduce impressionable women. Diego, the cultured gay man is, in contrast, an unwilling martyr to the macho revolutionary culture. Diego opposes Sergio's use of high culture and argues with his predecessor that it is not exclusively for those of his class, and that it is not to be used superficially as a weapon of seduction; rather, it should be made popular, that is, available to the people. True art, for Diego, has a classical definition: it is seen as a means of self-improvement and spiritual elevation and transcendence, and should be used to educate, enlighten, and encourage debate among Cubans. There is, then, a silent dialogue between these two films and, in particular, between the two main characters, as the individual who can point his society in the right direction challenges the individualist who does not believe in society.

Notes

1. *Memories of Underdevelopment* is based on the short story "Inconsolable Memories" (1963) by Edmundo Desnoes, which was rewritten and retitled after the release of the film. The screenplay was written by Desnoes and Alea. The film is sometimes translated from the Spanish *Memorias del subdesarrollo* as *Memoirs of Underdevelopment*. *Strawberry and Chocolate* is based on the novella *The Wolf, the Woods and the New Man* (*El lobo, el bosque y el hombre nuevo*) by Senel Paz. The film was codirected by Juan Carlos Tabío, because Alea was suffering from cancer during the shooting, although he was in charge of the project. Alea died in 1996.

2. The film also won prizes at the London Film Festival (1970), as well as three special prizes at Hyères, France (1970). See *http//us.imbd.com/Tawards?0063291* for details of other awards. Significantly, Alea was refused a visa by the U.S. government to accept the National Society of Film Critics award because of his association with the Cuban government.

3. Of the enormous success of *Strawberry and Chocolate*, Alea said that it, "may hold the record for the greatest number of Cuban viewers . . . [I]t is the film which has attracted the greatest number of viewers in the shortest period of time" (West, 1995, 20).

4. Among the prizes the film won are the Silver Bear at the Berlin Film Festival (1994), a Goya for best Spanish-language foreign film (Spain), and most of the top prizes at the International Festival of New Latin American Cinema in Havana (1993). See *http://us.imbd.com/Tawards?0106966* for more details.

5. ICAIC stands for Instituto Cubano del Arte e Industria Cinematográficos.

6. Alea said that "films serve to change the attitude of the people with regard to a particular subject" (Evora, 1996, 99; my translation).

7. With Alea, Espinosa was one of the founding members of the ICAIC. He became the head of the institute in the early 1980s and remained in this position until 1991.

8. Of this reevaluation of bourgeois culture, Paul Julian Smith has written: "[I]n proletarian and puritan Cuba the abjection (expulsion, denigration) of the bourgeoisie renders their remainder curiously seductive" (Smith, 1996, 95).

9. Between 1959 and 1987, 164 feature-length films were produced in Cuba; of these, 49 were documentaries, and 3 were animations. In addition, 1026 short films were made (King, 2000, 146). For more on the Cuban film industry and the ICAIC, see King (2000, 145–67) and Chanan (1985).

10. For an overview of the position of the Cuban film industry in the 1990s, see Chanan (1997).

11. Both *Strawberry and Chocolate* and *Guantanamera* (1994), Alea's last film, were coproductions. The production companies involved were from Cuba, Mexico, and Span in the case of *Strawberry,* Cuba, Germany, and Spain in the case of *Guantanamera.*

12. *Alicia en el pueblo de las maravillas* (1991) directed by Daniel Díaz Torres, provoked a crisis in the ICAIC. The film was seen as satirizing the Castro regime and was pulled from

theaters in Cuba. The government threatened to curb the ICAIC's independence by merging it with the Institute of Radio and Television (IRT) under the control of the Armed Forces film section; however, this move was successfully resisted by the directors in the ICAIC (Chanan, 1997, 6–7; King, 2000, 275).

13. In an interview, Alea spoke of how everyone in Cuba had, at some point in his or her life, been forced to break the law by turning to the black market, because of the impossibility of buying basic materials in official shops and the lack of technicians and craftspeople such as plumbers and mechanics (Evora, 1996, 138).

14. *Guantanamera* is a black comedy that tells the story of the attempt to transport the body of a well-known Cuban singer from Guantánamo to Havana (the same route the revolutionaries took in their march to Havana in 1958). The funeral director of the province is the nephew of the dead singer, and he takes charge of the proceedings, attempting to overcome the problem of the lack of gasoline. The narrative combines the comic nature of the journey with a love story between a truck driver (Jorge Perugorría) and the funeral director's wife (Mirta Ibarra). Despite of the humor of the story, there is a serious and critical message in Alea's final film: revolutionary society is seen to be dying from a lack of resources and official incompetence. For further analysis of the film, see Chanan (1997).

15. For details of the footage used and the coverage of the news on Cuban television, see Chanan (1985, 241).

16. Ramón Calviño, an assassin in the service of President Batista, is known to have murdered two men and raped and tortured a woman (Johnson, 1965, 206).

17. Of this scene, Michael Chanan has written that Sergio's voice-over with the newsreel commentary "allows the film to elaborate the sense of social anatomy through which Sergio himself is refracted" (Chanan, 1985, 241).

18. The round table discussion actually took place in 1964 (Burton, 1977, 19), another example of Alea's interplay between fiction and reality. On the panel is author Edmundo Desnoes; as with the meeting between Sergio and Alea, this is used to create a meta-filmic moment. Giani Toti is an Italian novelist (Myerson, 1973, editor's note 87).

19. See Alea in an interview with Julianne Burton (1977), Burton's own analysis (1977), and Chanan, (1985).

20. Desnoes's original novel includes a collection of Sergio's short stories. It is significant that the Sergio of the film version is nonproductive; for an analysis of the relationship between the original text and the film, see Fernández, Grossvogel, and Monegal (1974).

21. UMAP comprised forced labor camps where prisoners endured hard labor in sugar-cane fields, working 11-hour days (Lumsden, 1996, 69). Others who were sent to the work camps included Jehovah's Witnesses and Seventh-Day Adventists. In 1979, homosexuality was decriminalized, yet until 1987 it was a criminal offense to publicly demonstrate ostentatious homosexuality.

22. Arenas documents his sexual encounters, counterrevolutionary writings, and imprisonment in his autobiographical novel *Before Night Falls* (1990). This is the basis of the recent film of the same title directed by Julian Schnabel (2000), for which Javier Bardem, playing Arenas, was nominated for an Oscar for best actor. See Smith (1996, 59–80) for a discussion of Almendros and Arenas.

23. Of this, Paul Julian Smith (1996) has written, "[The film] fails to address the structural reasons for Revolutionary homophobia, reinscribing a properly political question in terms of the conflict between individuals...and sublimating that conflict into metaphysical terms: an abstract and wholly disembodied request for universal tolerance" (93).

24. Steve Wilkinson (1999) argues that Diego faces problems with the regime as a result of his dissident cultural politics, not because of his homosexuality.

25. Diego identifies this need early on in the film when he laments the fact that Cuba has not produced a voice like that of Maria Callas and insists that Cubans need to listen to another voice, in a clear reference to the single-party line, and Fidel Castro.

26. José Quiroga (1997) has argued that *Strawberry and Chocolate* presents a partial view of homosexuality, with Diego essentialized to represent culture. It would be interesting to compare this representation with that of Reinaldo Arenas. In his autobiography, there are tales of Arenas's frequent sexual adventures, which are interspersed with stories of his love of literature and his attempts to write while under surveillance and in hiding; in other words, there is no conflict between Arenas as a sexual being and as a cultural figure (Arenas, 1992).

27. It is worth noting that *Strawberry and Chocolate* has been criticized for its conservatism in terms of sexual politics and aesthetics (West, 1995), as well as for its "pallid and patronising images of gay men" and Diego's excessive effeminacy (Smith, 1994, 31). The film has also been criticized for its heterosexist focus with the camera almost always adopting David's gaze (Santi, 1998, 418). In defense of the film, Senel Paz (1995) says, "It is a film which is aimed at heterosexuals. It is heterosexuals who have to be educated. Heterosexuals have to understand how inhumane, how barbaric it is to deny the possibility of other forms of expression, of relationships" (35).

28. *Strawberry and Chocolate* was made primarily for a national audience. Paz (1995) said, "We always made this film with Cuba in mind and never thought it would make an impact elsewhere" (31).

29. Of this, Paul Julian Smith (1996) writes, "Gutiérrez Alea delights with his alter ego-witness [David] in the elite pleasures of high culture" (95).

30. The meal costs Diego $100, an enormous amount of money in the Cuba of 1979. This is an additional sacrifice, as Diego has just been fired from his job and is trying to save some money for his exile in the United States.

31. Paz commented on the reaction of others to the casting choice of Jorge Perugorría to play Diego: "A girlfriend of mine said, 'So they've chosen Perugorría? Well, if David doesn't fall for him, he's as hard as nails.' ... And others said, 'If he's going to play the homosexual, I'm turning homosexual' " (Paz, 1995, 22).

32. In fact, David's "anti-racist" opinions are just as problematic. He counters Diego's views with the unthinking official line that all blacks are from Africa, a notion that is clearly false, as Diego points out. I am grateful to Conrad James (personal communication, 2002) for this observation.

33. There has been no sign of lesbian representation in a successful Cuban film or, to my knowledge, any Latin American film that has appeared on the international market.

34. Alea incorporated Lecuona and Cervantes because of a personal desire to have these two musicians recognized. In an interview with Dennis West, he explained, "The music of Ignacio Cervantes and of other Cuban musicians from the last century is virtually unknown. Nevertheless, that music possesses excellent quality and great richness" (West, 1995, 19).

35. Emilio Bejel (1997) has noted that "the dialogue between [David's] Socialist and [Diego's] homosexual discourse can be interpreted as two oppressed discourses aspiring to a utopian alliance in the face of the hegemonic power of capitalism" (68–69).

36. On July 26, 1953, Fidel Castro led his forces in an attack on the Cuban army barracks in Santiago de Cuba. This is considered the beginning of the revolution.

37. There were, in fact, four stage versions of Paz's novella *The Wolf, the Woods and the New Man*, which played to packed audiences in Havana simultaneously, before the film was made (Paz, 1995, 20).

38. It is interesting to note that, despite the intended sympathetic account of homosexuality, *Strawberry* won the OCIC (International Catholic Film Organization) award for exemplary film (Bejel, 1997). This is most likely because of the promotion of religious freedom in the film and the fact that the character of Diego is never seen as sexually active.

39. This is another example of culture replacing sex, as Diego reverses the prejudice of the gay man corrupting young men, by providing an alternative education for them.

40. Catherine Davies (1996) has argued that, "as in all successful therapies, once recognised and understood, once brought under the control of language, he [Diego] is no longer of use" (179).

41. There are autobiographical links between David and Senel Paz here. Paz himself was also able to study thanks to the revolution and stated, "I was the first person in my family to study at university and the first to bring books home" (Paz, 1995, 6).

42. For a fascinating study on the character of Nancy and her symbolic role in the film, see Davies (1996).

43. In a speech shown in newsreel form in *Memories*, Fidel Castro addresses the Cuban nation, assuring them that they will stand together to resist any invasion. He ends his speech with the assertion that they are all one, which only serves to highlight Sergio's isolation.

44. It is worth noting that Alea was concerned mainly with male identity. In an interview (Evora, 1996a, 165), talked of a possible future project with his wife, Mirta Ibarra (Nancy in *Strawberry*), based on an idea of hers. This film would have a female perspective and would tell the story of a Cuban woman's return to Cuba after years of voluntary exile in the United States. Unfortunately, his death prevented the completion of the project.

2

Seducing the Public
Images of Mexico in
Like Water for Chocolate
and *Amores Perros*

There has been a mini boom in Mexican cinema in recent years. Three films in particular — *Like Water for Chocolate* (*Como agua para chocolate*) (1991), *Amores perros* (*Love's a Bitch*) (2000), and *Y tu mamá también* (2001) — have been extremely popular both in Mexico and internationally. This chapter presents analyses of two of these films, *Like Water for Chocolate* and *Amores perros*, which offer audiences contrasting images of Mexico. Both discussions examine the national images that the films promote and look at the ways that they succeed in seducing the public using very different approaches. The works are analyzed within the context of the Mexican film industry. Commercial factors arising from the shift away from state-produced cinema to independent productions are also discussed.

The first discussion in this chapter focuses on the ways in which *Like Water for Chocolate* promotes a tourist-friendly view of the country; it is examined as an ideal national product of the Salinas regime in the way that it masks social inequalities and political discontent. The film also relies on romantic ideals and conservative social values for its success. The discussion examines the ways that the film creates a heroine with traditional feminine "virtues" and looks at the way she is used to attack values associated with contemporary feminism. The second discussion of the chapter provides a reading of *Amores perros* and examines the very different images of Mexico that the film presents. In contrast to *Like Water for Chocolate*, the setting of *Amores perros* is Mexico City at the end of the 1990s, and it is therefore interesting to look at the ways in which the film represents modern life in the metropolis. The characters are from a cross section of the city, and the film attempts to create links between individuals from these sectors of society. The section discusses whether this works and argues that the realities of the distinctions between social classes are minimized in order to promote a vision of the universality of the human condition. Gender relations are also analyzed, and the ways in which the film represents the marginalization of women and critiques dominant forms of masculinity are examined.

Like Water for Chocolate
and the Mexican Film Industry

The film project for *Like Water for Chocolate* was never likely to be risky. Laura Esquivel's novel by the same name, published in 1989, was a long-running best-seller in Mexico, and it spent over a year on the best-seller list of the *New York Times* (Esquivel, 1995). By 1994, 780,000 copies had been sold in the United States in English and 75,000 copies in Spanish (De La Rosa, 1994, 200), showing that there is a vibrant potential market for Spanish-language texts (and therefore Spanish-language films) in the United States. It was translated into twenty-nine languages, laying the ground-work for the subsequent profits made by the film in international markets. The film was directed by Alfonso Arau (b. 1932), Esquivel's husband at the time, with the screenplay written by the novelist. It is not surprising, then, that it has also enjoyed enormous success, with the novel and film clearly boosting each other's sales.

Like Water for Chocolate was, in fact, the most commercially successful Mexican film of the 1990s. The film was a box office hit in Mexico and was shown in six theaters in Mexico City for six months (Castrillón 1993, 54). In addition, it was the highest grossing foreign language release in the United States in 1993. Miramax released the film through over one hundred screens in the United States (Galvin, 1993/1994, 25), something that is extremely unusual for a foreign-language film. As a result, a film costing $2 million grossed $21.66 million in the United States alone ("Business data," n.d.). It was also popular in many other national markets, in particular in the Spanish-speaking world; for example, the film was shown in one Madrid theater for eight months (Pérez Turrent, 1994, 9). *Like Water for Chocolate* also won a degree of critical acclaim, despite a number of poor reviews. It won eighteen international awards in 1992, including Arieles (the prestigious Mexican film awards) for best film, best director (Arau), and best screenplay (Esquivel); a prize for best foreign film at the Tokyo International Film Festival; and Audience Awards at the Gramado Film Festival in Brazil and the Guadalajara Mexican Film Festival.[1]

The film has come to symbolize the development of Mexican film in the 1990s. David Maciel has talked about the "major cinematic renaissance" that took place during the *sexenio* (six-year presidential rule, 1988–1994) of Carlos Salinas de Gortari (Maciel, 1999, 214).[2] During this period, thirty-two Mexican directors completed and exhibited their first work. This has been attributed to Ignacio Durán's successful presidency of the Mexican Film Institute, or Instituto Mexicano de Cinematografía (IMCINE). Despite a number of shortcomings, Durán achieved his objective, which was to promote quality filmmaking while accommodating the government's policies of privatization and reduced funding. This was done principally by developing coproductions and supporting new talent (Maciel, 1994, 214; Rashkin, 2001, 14).[3]

Nevertheless, the success of *Like Water for Chocolate* could give a false impression of the state of the Mexican film industry. Although more films were financed by IMCINE, most films made in the 1990s with artistic pretensions were given limited release in the domestic market and were unlikely to be shown to international audiences beyond film festivals (Rashkin, 2001, 14–15). The national market was dominated by low-quality genre films that relied on sex and violence to pull in the crowds. Despite the talk of promoting national cinema, the Mexican government did not increase its investment in filmmaking. The Cinema Law of 1992 meant that IMCINE reduced its funding from 100 percent to 60 percent of the production costs (Segre, 1997, 43). In addition, screening quotas for national films were greatly reduced, with a view to abandoning the quotes altogether (Rashkin, 2001, 16). The fragility of the situation was highlighted when in 1995 virtually all state-sponsored filmmaking ceased following the financial crisis of 1994.

The Salinas regime is now notorious for its failed modernization program, its corruption, and the increasing gap between the extremely wealthy and the extremely poor. In 1991, some 17.3 million Mexicans lived in extreme poverty, and another 24 million lived in poverty (Tarrés, 1992, 27). Such figures are notoriously difficult to gauge accurately, but this gives some indication of the scale of the problem at the time. On the other extreme, Erica Segre (1997) commented that "out of the 24 listed Mexican billionaires, all but one owed their meteoric wealth to the Salinas presidency" (37).[4] During his term in office, however, Salinas attempted to win legitimacy for himself and for his neoliberal reforms. One method of achieving this, at limited financial cost, was through the development of the cultural sector. In light of this aim, *Like Water for Chocolate* was a model product for the regime. As Nuala Finnegan (1999) pointed out, "it [*Like Water for Chocolate*] is one of the most successful cultural products of Salinas's infamous rule" (312).[5] The film followed the government's model of public and private investment, as it was made with a combination of funding arrangements: producers of the film included IMCINE, Aviasco (a Mexican airline), the Mexican Ministry for Tourism, and the state government of Coahuila, where a large part of the action was set and filmed.[6] It promotes a conservative, romantic image of rural Mexico that would please the Ministry for Tourism and that belied the reality of mass poverty and ever increasing urbanization, seen in Mexico City's vast shantytowns.[7]

Alfonso Arau has indirectly acknowledged that *Like Water for Chocolate* is very much an establishment film. He commented that the Ministry for Tourism "[is] very grateful because *Like Water . . .* did a great job in promoting tourism and the image of Mexico" (Espinosa, 1995, 26, cited in Segre, 1997, 45; my translation).[8] The film, in its content, style, and reception, can be read as a reaction to a range of social changes, including modernization, the increase of social inequality, and the growth of feminism. This can be seen in the way that it ignores all of these issues and reinvents the past in such a way as to negate social history. The images of Mexico sold to national and international audiences through the film are filled with nostalgia for a mythical past. In this reinterpretation of the past, gender roles are clearly delineated, class and ethnic tensions are ignored, and nobody goes hungry. Also, despite the focus on Tita (played by Lumi Cavazos), a Cinderella-like heroine, the film does not comment on the oppression of women; rather, in the tradition of melodrama, the problems are located within the private space of the home and are the fault of one bad woman, Mamá Elena (played by Regina Torné).[9] Without this problem, Tita would live an idealized life with the man of her dreams and would be fulfilled, cooking and attending to the needs of her husband and children, with the help of her indigenous servants, who are happy to work for her as a kind, considerate mistress of the house.

Gender and Class Conservatism in Like Water for Chocolate

Laura Esquivel, the author of the novel and the screenplay, has repeatedly stated that her intentions are to challenge the kind of feminist thinking that advocates changes in women's traditional roles. She claims that in the 1960s and 1970s

> [we] [women] thought the things worth fighting for were outside the home, not inside. . . . Now we understand that the system and the progress that we established [are], in fact, destroying us. Right now we're seeing women in the work force and we're seeing that the subsequent changes are altering and destroying our values. (Loewenstein, 1994, 602)

Esquivel's remarks depend on static, unitary notions of natural womankind, which is being destroyed by a new breed of women, corrupted by progress. The reference to "our values" assumes that there is only one set of true values, possessed by women who have not been denaturalized or masculinized in the work force. It would, in fact, appear that her attack on materialism and modernity is a cover for what is really an attack on women's place within it, for at no point is men's place in modernity challenged. In the film, Arau attempts to translate Esquivel's vision, clearly helped by her screenplay. Arau said, "I deliberately put aside my ego to make my wife's film" (Billen, 1993, 35), and that one of the main challenges in making the film was "to express on the screen such delicate and feminine feelings" (Feay, 1993, 72).[10] As will be seen, the essentialist image of women shared by Arau and Esquivel sustains the representation of the female characters in the film, who are divided into categories of "natural" women, who are nurturing home-builders (Tita, Nacha, Esperanza, and Tita's great-niece), and "unnatural" women, who are failed mothers and homemakers (Mamá Elena, Rosaura, and Gertrudis).[11]

At a time when women were beginning to make their mark in Mexican cinema as directors and both male and female directors were developing more complex female characters, Esquivel and Arau created a female heroine whose strength lies in her cooking and her potential wifely and maternal attributes. Charles Ramírez Berg argued that "since the late 1960s, we have seen the existing female images multiplied...amplified...made more realistic...and more sympathetic" (Ramírez Berg, 1989, 179). In contrast to Esquivel's vision of the 1960s as a period in which "women's values" were lost, a current generation of women directors in Mexico, including Marisa Sistach, Busi Cortés, Guita Schyfter, María Novaro, and Dana Rotberg, have represented the 1960s in their films as a period in which women's liberation became possible (Rashkin, 2001).

Like Water for Chocolate bypasses the 1960s altogether to return to more stereotypical representations of femininity. The central action of the film takes place during the Mexican Revolution (1910–1917). The time of the film passes from Tita's birth in 1885 to 1910 and beyond. The film jumps to 1934 toward the end, with the wedding of Alex (played by Andrés García Jr.) and Esperanza and the deaths of Tita and Pedro and ends with the narrative present, as the audience comes back to the narrator, Tita's great-niece, speaking from her modern kitchen. This creates a link between a pre-1960s past and the 1990s. The link is emphasized by the fact that the unnamed great-niece is seen at the end of the film framed by the figures of Tita and Esperanza, her mother. She vows to continue to keep Tita's memory alive by following the recipes left to her in her great-aunt's recipe book, which also contains the story of her romance with Pedro (played by Marco Leonardi). Changes in gender roles in the 1960s through the 1980s are not represented in any way. Thus, it is suggested that models for a current generation of women should be found in what is represented as a prefeminist era.

The historical setting of the film could have provided a radical back-drop to the story. However, the political and social causes and effects of the conflict are ignored. The revolutionaries themselves are reduced to folkloric caricatures and are seen drinking, dancing, and singing, rarely fighting. In addition, only one side is ever seen, that of the Villistas, so it is not clear whom they are fighting. There is one violent attack in the film, resulting in the rape of the family's servant Chencha (played by Pilar Aranda) and the murder of Mamá Elena. However, the audience is not told who is responsible for this, as the ranch hand asks the attackers in English, "What do you want?" While audiences might assume they are revolutionaries, the ranch hand would not speak to them in English if this were the case.[12] The novel clears up the confusion, referring to the attackers as bandits, which contributes to the soft representation of the revolutionaries (Esquivel, 1989, 122). Nuala Finnegan has argued that the film follows the Hollywood tradition of representing the Mexican Revolution, particularly in the emphasis on Pancho Villa as the principal revolutionary and in the evasion of political and social issues (Finnegan, 1999, 314–15).

Like Water for Chocolate re-creates a preindustrialized, rural Mexico through its costumes, lighting, and theatrical setting. Tita is a paradigm of femininity in her long, flowing skirts and loose-fitting blouses, which contrast with Mamá Elena and Rosaura's tightly buttoned restrictive dresses, and Pedro and John (played by Mario Iván Martínez), the family doctor who is in love with Tita, are rarely seen out of their formal suits and bow ties. Sepia tones, used for the interior scenes, create an old-fashioned stage for this old-fashioned love story. Most of the action takes place on the ranch, providing the unity of place of classical tragedy. This creates the opportunity for several highly staged social events, such as Rosaura's wedding celebration, the baptism of Roberto, Tita's nephew, and Esperanza's and Alex's wedding, which serve as showcases to exhibit the colorful and "exotic" dishes that Tita makes.

A historical period is re-created, then, to provide local color, to offer an escape from the polluted, overcrowded realities of Mexico City, and to promote a particular image of feminine identity. The obstacles that sustain the romance between Tita and Pedro are located within family history, not national history. The De la Garza family tradition stipulates that the youngest daughter cannot marry or have children, as she must look after her mother until her mother dies. This, along with Mamá Elena's cruel treatment of Tita, is where the injustice lies and is the sole reason for Tita's unhappiness. There are no other obstacles to Tita and Pedro's relationship: they share class, ethnic origins, and age,[13] and as the narrative makes clear at every possible moment, they are meant to be together. In this filmic version of history, it is presented as natural, right, and good that a woman should be nothing other than wife, mother, and cook. All the class issues raised by the revolution are ignored, and the model for femininity is the middle-class woman as embodied by Tita.

This failure to consider class and ethnic divisions results in essentialist representations of womankind. Tita and Nacha are seen as united in the film through the model of the universal Earth Mother. The film relies on a form of ethnic romanticism, which praises the magical abilities and healing properties of indigenous women, while suggesting that these skills can be passed on to sympathetic nonindigenous women.[14] The fact that they are exploited as servants and that Nacha's dedication to the De la Garza family has meant that she is unable to have a family of her own is not problematized. Nacha and Chencha's devotion to Tita masks the injustice of their servitude, which is a result of their social condition. Once again, the problem is seen to be caused by one woman, Mamá Elena, who is an example of a bad mistress, not by the class system that generates inequalities between women. As John Kraniauskas (1993) has noted, this is part of the reason for the popularity of the film with middle-class audiences. In his words: "Despite all the changes brought about in Mexican society by the Revolution and its aftermath, they [audiences] can still feel comfortable with those things that have remained the same: the servants in their kitchens" (42–43).

The film thus reassures the middle and upper classes that there is no ethical problem with having servants, provided they treat those servants well. The contradictions arising from the fact that Tita belongs to the landowning class with its roots in the Spanish conquest are never examined.

The Creation of a Feminine Heroine

The film's tendency to focus on private emotions, and to concentrate the action within the home and the family, while excluding an analysis of larger scale historical forces, places *Like Water for Chocolate* in the category of "woman's film" operating within a melodramatic mode.[15] This point is made by Kraniauskas (1993), who argues that the film "retreats from the masculinized terrain of high politics and the battlefield and concentrates our attention on the so-called private sphere of a household run by women" (9).

The idea of *Like Water for Chocolate* as a woman's film needs some explanation, as an understanding of what this means in this specific case can shed light on the type of femininity the film advocates. The concept itself, when applied to film reception, can be seen as essentialist, as it suggests a shared approach to a certain type of film on the part of an implied homogeneous female audience.[16] Nevertheless, it is less problematic when applied to character construction, particularly in the way that the film "centres both our narrative identification and its structures of looking on a female protagonist" (Thornham, 1997, 52).

Like Water for Chocolate promotes and naturalizes a specific feminine subject position, through the centralizing and idealization of Tita, its protagonist. There is a single feminine point of view throughout. The third-person narrative voice of Tita's great-niece always provides a first-person perspective. She recounts each scene from her great-aunt's point of view, telling the audience how each event in the film affects Tita emotionally. A repeated technique is for the voice-over to tell the audience how she is feeling, while the camera provides a close-up of her, and her emotional state is revealed through her body language. An illustration of this can be found in the scene with Tita miraculously breastfeeding her nephew, Roberto. The audience is shown her desire to comfort and feed the crying baby and her successful attempt to do so. The voice-over details what is happening and describes Tita's emotions, as the audience is being shown the events. Lumi Cavazos's body language, facial gestures, smiles, and sighs illustrate the narrator's words, in what could be seen as redundant narration. Thus, the voice-over tells the audience how Tita's virginal breasts produce milk as we see Roberto suckling.

This single perspective and process of idealization ensure that audiences are given no freedom of interpretation. Tita is good, her cooking is wonderful and is a magical art form, she is the victim of a cruel family tradition and her wicked mother, and she should be married to Pedro. The film throughout constructs the viewer as Tita's accomplice through her characterization and that of the other characters. They are all seen in the way that they affect her. Thus, Mamá Elena is her tormentor and prevents her from being fulfilled as a woman, Rosaura is her enemy and rival in love, Gertrudis is her ally, John is her savior, Nacha is her surrogate mother and guide, Chencha is her supportive servant, Pedro is her love interest, and Roberto and Esperanza are her surrogate children.

Tita's status as romantic heroine is based on her gifts as a cook. The representation of the preparation of food is central to the construction of a feminine identity. The creation of delicious, traditional, and exotic dishes is seen as a magical skill that is shared by only special women (Nacha and Tita), with a link to a mythical pre-Columbian past. Tita rules in the one part of the house where she is not under the control of her domineering mother, and she is able to influence events by altering the other characters' constitutions through her cooking. Through her dish of quail in rose petal sauce, inspired by a vision of Nacha, she arouses the sexual passions of the eaters (except for Rosaura) and literally sets Gertrudis on fire with passion. Likewise, she is indirectly responsible for Rosaura's flatulence and halitosis (and premature death from digestive problems). This is set off by the dark thoughts she has for her sister, when Rosaura reveals that she intends to raise Esperanza to look after her in accordance with the family tradition. She transmits her anger to the dish of frijoles that she prepares for her sister.[17] In this way, Tita is presented as having a power that transcends the kitchen but not the domestic sphere, as her cooking is used principally to attempt to seduce Pedro and is ultimately born of her frustrated desire to be a housewife and mother.

Because of these episodes, the film has been tagged with the label *magical realism,* which has clearly helped to promote the film in international markets, as this is the "style" that has for many, erroneously, come to define most Latin American culture.[18] Magical realism has been defined as the "proposal of a method for giving to magic the status of reality" (Rowe, 1997, 506), which *Like Water for Chocolate* does through Tita's cooking and through the appearance of the ghosts of Nacha, and Mamá Elena. Nevertheless, when applied, for example, to the works of such writers as Gabriel García Márquez, Juan Rulfo, Miguel Angel Asturias, and Isabel Allende, the term is linked to a realism that highlights central social concerns, such as poverty, corruption, and abuses of power and human rights. In *Like Water for Chocolate,* much of the realism is dropped in favor of the magical: there is none of the social commitment found in the above-mentioned writers. The term *magical femininity* would be more appropriate to describe the way in which magical realism is adapted in the film, as each instance of Tita's powers serves to contribute to a characterization of a perfect, feminine woman.

Tita has been created, then, to promote a particular notion of womanhood: woman as romantic heroine, cook, and homemaker. Esquivel has argued that women's natural place is in the home, and she suggests that it is time for them to return to that rightful place. She claimed in one interview that women through their entry into the workplace have abandoned the home, a "marvellous and sacred centre" (De La Rosa, 1994, 204). These views are illustrated in both the novel and the film by making the kitchen the primary source of all the action and an exclusively female space. It is the warm heart of an otherwise cold house, the site from which humanity emanates. In another interview, Esquivel claimed that there are two reactions to the film or the novel that she particularly relishes. One is when people confess that they cried in the movie theater. The other is when they tell her that after reading the book or seeing the movie, "they have returned to the kitchen and started cooking" (Donahue, 1993, 9A).

Feminist or Feminine?

Laura Esquivel has argued that *Like Water for Chocolate* furthers the women's movement by raising the status of women's creativity in the kitchen, which has been devalued (De La Rosa, 1994, 197). A number of critics, particularly of the novel, have shared this view and have chosen to see a feminist message in the text. It is worth briefly examining these critics, as their readings are also relevant to the film, which, as has been seen, adopts Esquivel's vision of ideal femininity. Their argument, that it is a feminist enterprise to elevate cooking to an art form and value the work that women do in the kitchen, follows a particular tradition of what has been called domestic feminism, feminism of difference, or, for critics, "essentialist" feminism.[19] That position holds that women come to identify with the spaces that have been assigned to them in patriarchal structures, reclaiming these spaces and filling them with positive meanings (Riquer Fernández, 1992, 54).[20]

Beatriz González Stephan (1991) is one critic who sees an affirmation of feminine popular culture in recipe writing and cookery, and praises the way that the novel promotes a respected and neglected art form. In her essay, she celebrates the fact that women's work, traditionally denigrated in (masculine) high culture, is finally given the recognition it deserves rather than questioning the legitimacy of separate male and female spheres. For her part, Kristine Ibsen (1995) interprets the novel's affirmation of feminine qualities as an attack on patriarchal structures. In her words: "The appropriation of popular discourse, with its emphasis on such 'feminine' values as nurturing and selflessness, is a means of undermining the patriarchal system" (137).[21]

These views can be challenged by those advocating a feminism of equality, which has traditionally argued that women's oppression is in large part due to the gendered division of labor, and the association of femininity with domesticity. The above critics do not appear to acknowledge that the institution of the housewife has relied on such values as nurturing and selflessness for its survival, whereas patriarchal systems have always relied on women as domestic cooks for their survival. This celebration of what is presented in both the novel and the film as exclusively female territory serves principally to endorse through culture the notion that women belong in the kitchen.[22] In this respect, *Like Water for Chocolate* shares many of the belief systems commonly upheld by both traditional romantic fiction and women's films made in the United States in the 1920s and 1930s.[23] Janice Radway (1984) pointed out the problematic nature of the glorification of femininity in romance narratives:

> Despite [the] proclamation of female superiority, in continuing to relegate women to the area of the domestic, purely personal relations, the romance fails to pose other more radical questions. In short, it refuses to ask whether feminine values might be used to "feminize" the public realm or if control over that realm could be shared by women and by men. (217)

Despite raising the status of a traditional female art form and placing a female character center stage, *Like Water for Chocolate* is a film that challenges many of the agreed principles of contemporary feminism, such as advocating women's equality in the work force, the view that a woman cannot be entirely fulfilled by a man, a family, and the home, and the notion that many aspects of gender difference rest on cultural constructs, not biological factors. Tita as heroine challenges these principles: she is endowed with a simplistic, childlike view of the world where Manichean notions of right and wrong, good and evil are not questioned, with this value system underpinned by an appeal to the emotions of the audience. The film thus naturalizes domesticity and places romantic love within a domestic tradition. As Roger Bromley (1989) pointed out in his study of popular fiction, the naturalization of such cultural constructs as individualism, marriage, masculinity, femininity, and property is a common, insidious feature of much popular culture. He wrote:

> These are all presented as universal, they are superstructural forms re-presented in the deep, hidden, structures of the discourse: the permanent foundations of life, which are unsigned in the text because in society they are unsigned — not seen as structures but are personalized as natural presences. (153)

The naturalization processes are more likely when these foundations of society are seen as being under threat from, in this case, feminism and modernization.

Like Water for Chocolate is then a film that constructs feminine subject positions for the protagonist and the viewers, but it also accepts patriarchal discourses about gender. This is seen in the way that Tita's cooking and sexuality depend on Pedro, the romantic "leading man," for their meaning and in the representation of an essentialist form of femininity. Pedro himself is a weakly drawn character. All the characters, including him, have adopted a passive position in response to the masculinized Mamá Elena, and for most of the film he accepts the family tradition that keeps him from Tita. He only initiates a sexual relationship after many years of longing looks and after the death of his mother-in-law. In addition, Marco Leonardi, the Italian actor who plays Pedro, gives a rather stilted performance, not helped by his sparse but formal lines, or the fact that he had to learn to produce these lines in Spanish, which were then dubbed over.[24] Nuala Finnegan (1999) sees Pedro as an archetypal Latin lover (321); he is defined purely by his desire for Tita and his good looks. These, in contrast to John's plainness, qualify him to be the center of Tita's world, making a weak man the focus of an extraordinary woman. The fact that the camera frequently sees him through Tita's eyes frames him for the audience as an object of desire.

In one key scene this is reversed, as Pedro's gaze is seen to turn Tita into a sexual being. She is shown sensually grinding ingredients, when she is interrupted by Pedro. She is kneeling on the floor, and he looks down on her, dominating her with his look. The narrator describes how his gaze "transforms her breasts from chaste to voluptuous" in a few seconds without touching them, and explains that "a breast that has not passed through the fire of love is a passive breast." Here, female voices articulate a patriarchal discourse, as the female narrator relates Tita's thoughts, in lines written for her by Laura Esquivel, expressing how a man gives meaning to a female body. In the following scene, Tita is shown breastfeeding Roberto, Rosaura and Pedro's baby. She miraculously produces milk for him. The sequence of events is important: Pedro brings her breasts to life through his gaze, and immediately they are put to use to feed his baby. She is shown in close-up feeding Roberto, with her face apparently illuminated by candlelight; the next shot shows Pedro kissing her on the forehead and, in a husbandly gesture, wrapping her shawl around her. This is a scene full of echoes of Marianist mythology, as for a brief moment they form a tableau of the Holy Family, until they are interrupted by Mamá Elena, with Tita as the virginal mother in the center of the frame.

These scenes highlight the fact that there are two categories of women in the film: "natural" and "unnatural," with the maternal instinct used as the organizing principle for these categories. Interestingly, biological mothers are failed mothers (Mamá Elena and Rosaura), whereas successful maternal figures, Tita and Nacha, are surrogate mothers. Tita embodies the "natural" woman; she is maternal and sensual, and is motivated principally by

Tita (Lumi Cavazos) and Pedro (Marco Leonardi) in *Like Water for Chocolate.*

romantic love and by a desire to nurture (feed) others. "Unnatural" women (Mamá Elena and Rosaura) are unable to provide love, dominate others, and, most importantly, are unable to cook or to provide milk for their children. Tita, as a baby, has to be fed by Nacha's teas, as Mamá Elena is unable to breastfeed her, and Rosaura cannot produce milk for her two children; in fact, Roberto dies when he is moved away from Tita, as his mother cannot make him eat without his aunt.[25] Tita is thus represented as a form of Earth Mother, who nurtures others through her cooking and breast milk.

Gertrudis does not appear to belong to either category; she is also unable to cook and is not interested in the domestic space, yet as Tita's ally, she is sympathetic character and is the only one in whom her sister can confide. She is the sole character who takes advantage of the social circumstances to seek power in the public domain when she leaves the matriarchal home to eventually become a general in the Mexican Revolution, after (unrealistically) sating her repressed sexual desires in a brothel. Despite the lack of feminist sexual politics, she might have been held up as a feminist heroine in another narrative. However, this was not the intention of the film or novel. Esquivel explains that Gertrudis represents the path taken by feminists, that of "total sexual liberation [which] is in fact a masculinization" (Loewenstein, 1994, 594). Despite the intentions of the author and the outdated and offensive racial stereotyping, Gertrudis does provide an antidote to Tita's idealized femininity and is an enjoyable character.[26] Nevertheless, Gertrudis is used as a foil for Tita and is not intended to serve as any kind of model. Her revolution is contrasted unfavorably with Tita's, who "makes her own revolution in the family environment" (Esquivel quoted in Loewenstein, 1994, 594). This is paradoxically a conservative revolution, as the family codes she eventually transgresses, by temporarily rebelling against her mother, run counter to the most basic societal codes of Mexican femininity, which stipulate that women should be wives and mothers above all other roles.

The film's conception of ideal womanhood is essentialist, as it relies on the notion of a feminine core that motivates all of Tita's actions. The providing of food and the nurturing of others lie at the very center of her being. This can be seen when Roberto is taken from her as Mamá Elena forces Pedro, Rosaura, and their baby to leave the family ranch. As they leave, Tita's breasts leak milk as her body calls for the child to feed. Her being is so bound up with feeding that she suffers a temporary breakdown of identity and descends into madness and silence as a result of the baby's death due to hunger. Before the birth of the baby, all her energies are spent cooking. Her role as provider of food takes on particular significance when Pedro moves to the family ranch. If she is to be denied other wifely roles, she will make the most of the one area where she is given almost unrestricted freedom, and her cooking becomes her principal weapon of seduction.

This is illustrated in the scene in which Tita prepares the quails in rose petal sauce. Pedro has given her the roses to congratulate her on her excellent culinary skills on the anniversary of her first year as the house cook, and she uses them in defiance of her mother in this dish. The cooking process is represented as an expression of her love for Pedro. She is seen in close- up, and her smiling face is illuminated. This scene is accompanied by lush piano music that highlights the connection between romance and the culinary process.[27] The rose thorns pierce Tita's skin, and some of her blood escapes into the sauce, which produces an aphrodisiac effect. The narrator tells of how "in a strange act of alchemy not just Tita's blood but her whole being had dissolved in the rose sauce." In this way, "she penetrated Pedro's body, fragrant, voluptuous and completely sensual." Her cooking and her relationship with Pedro define her to such an extent that she becomes embodied in the sauce and, through this, united with her love.

Her inability to exist independently of Pedro is best illustrated in their romantic final union. They are finally free to be together as Rosaura and Mamá Elena have died and Esperanza has left home with her new husband, Alex. The ghost of Nacha has made a room for them in the barn, filled it with lit candles, and prepared their lovers' bed. The lovemaking experience is so intense that Pedro dies on top of Tita at the moment of orgasm, thus embodying John's grandmother's theory of death due to excess happiness. According to this theory, narrated again by John as Pedro dies, a powerful emotion lights all the matches inside a person and reveals a brilliant tunnel of light that takes the person back to his or her divine origins. Tita, unable to bear Pedro's death, eats a box of matches one by one, making this metaphor literal, and achieves her desired effect. We are shown outline images of two naked bodies in this tunnel of love. As in the Hindu custom of suttee, Tita chooses self-immolation, rather than a life without her lover, an ending that should trouble feminists.

Conclusion

Like Water for Chocolate is in the paradoxical position of marking the high point for Mexican cinema in commercial terms, at the time of its release, and being unrepresentative of trends in the Mexican film industry. The representation of gender and sexuality, in particular, hark back to a pre-1960s era, when women were represented as being more innocent and submissive, and gender divisions were more clearly delineated. The film is also exceptional in its commercial success, with no other Mexican films of the 1990s achieving such profits. As Guillermo del Toro, the director of *Cronos* and *Mimic,* commented, "I jokingly say that the first foreign territory for a Mexican movie is Mexico itself, because Mexican people hardly ever go to see Mexican movies" (Patterson, 2001).

It is unfortunate, then, that the most widely seen image of Mexico in the 1990s was one that deliberately avoided social reality, relied on clichéd images of revolutionaries, provided an antifeminist representation of Mexican women, and showed a world where indigenous women are happy to work as servants. *Amores perros* (2000) and *Y tu mamá también* (2001) subsequently showed that domestic and international commercial success does not depend on the traditional representations of class, gender, or ethnicity that sustain *Like Water for Chocolate*. This film provided an image of a country that fit the notion of the ideal tourist location for the wealthy Western filmgoer. Mexico is represented as a country unlike the metropolises in which the film was so successful (including Mexico City). It is represented as a rural land, which has maintained its culinary and social traditions. By naturalizing and idealizing the ideology of femininity through Tita and by demonizing the masculine Mamá Elena, *Like Water for Chocolate* suggests that women can reach fulfillment only within patriarchal codes. This seemingly harmless romance thus conceals an antifeminist subtext. Not only does Tita seduce Pedro through her cooking, beauty, and submissiveness, as well as her brand of magical femininity, she is also used to seduce the public. She is constructed to act as a role model for implied female audiences and an ideal fantasy wife/mother for implied male audiences.

Amores perros and Commercial Mexican Cinema

No film had matched the national and international commercial success of *Like Water for Chocolate* before *Amores perros*. The film was hugely popular in Mexico, taking in over $8 million in box office and DVD-video sales (Franco Reyes, 2001). It won the Taquilla de Oro (Golden Box Office award) at the Expocine at Guanajuato in 2001 for the highest selling Mexican video and DVD. This is not to say that no other Mexican films were seen outside the country; a few films, such as del Toro's *Cronos* (1992), Jamie Humberto Hermosillo's *La tarea* (*Homework,* 1992), Arturo Ripstein's *Profundo carmesí* (*Deep Crimson,* 1996), were either given brief art house release or brought out on video; however, none of these had the impact of *Like Water for Chocolate* or *Amores perros*. The latter film grossed $5.4 million in the United States alone (Koelher, 2002); it was the fifth most successful independent film at U.S. box office's from January to July 2001, and the most successful foreign language film of that period ("Limited Release B.O.," 2001). That success was repeated elsewhere, and the film was eventually shown in thirty countries (*http://us.imdb.com/ReleaseDates?0245712*). As with *Like Water for Chocolate,* the profits are particularly impressive when considering that the film was made on a budget of $2 million (Hernández Cerda, 2001). In addition, *Amores perros* won a number of prestigious awards at film festivals in 2000–2001, including prizes for best film at Cannes, Flanders, Chicago, Bogotá, Valdivia, São Paulo, and Tokyo. It was also the Mexican entry in the best foreign film category at the Oscars in 2001, with the award won by *Crouching Tiger, Hidden Dragon,* directed by Ang Lee.

The success of *Amores perros* seems to have opened the way for a new style of Mexican film with international appeal, as seen in the success of the sexually explicit *Y tu mamá también* (2001) by Alfonso Cuarón. This film has been even more successful in Mexico than *Amores perros* and was the second highest grossing in terms of box office receipts behind the sex comedy *Sexo, pudor y lágrimas* (*Sex, Shame and Tears*) (1999), directed by Antonio Serrano (Hernández Cerda, 2001). In its first year of release, *Y tu mamá también* took in $13.65 million in the United States alone.[28]

The emergence of *Amores perros* and *Y tu mamá también* marks the resurgence of the independent Mexican film industry in response to the failure of state-run IMCINE to adequately manage and fund filmmaking.[29] After a brief period of success for the Mexican film industry in the early 1990s, by the mid-1990s national film production had fallen to a low point. Only twelve or so films were produced in 1995, 1996, and 1997 (King, 2000, 263); this figure worsened in 1998, with just seven films made (Patterson, 2001). Directors saw that they were unable to bring projects to fruition if they relied on IMCINE and consequently turned to private sources for funding. In effect, by the end of the 1990s, there was no full state funding, with IMCINE requiring filmmakers to have raised 80 percent of the expected production costs before a project was accepted (Hershfield & Maciel, 1999, 289).

This changing state of affairs has had an impact on the types of films being in Mexico. Commercial concerns clearly have to match artistic ones if private financing is to be raised. As Marta Sosa, executive producer of *Amores perros,* said, "The difference between today's filmmakers and those of 10 years ago is that now they are thinking about the audience the whole time" (Tegel, 2001a). This ethos is clearly shared by the film's director, Alejandro González Iñárritu (b. 1963), and writer Arriaga Jordán, who have also spoken of a desire to reconnect emotionally with audiences and to avoid artistic, elitist, "difficult" films. In Iñárritu's words: "We loathe government-financed moviemaking, which seems to operate by the maxim 'If nobody understands and nobody goes to see a movie, that must mean it's a masterpiece' " (Pérez Soler, 2001a, 19).

This desire to please the audience has borne fruit in terms of profit, with three films, including *Amores perros*, financed by Altavista, earning the company $10 million.[30] Altavista is a production company financed by Sinca Inbursa, the financial conglomerate owned by Carlos Slim Helu, believed to be the wealthiest man in Latin America. Although there are ethical and political concerns about the marriage between filmmaking and big business in Mexico, it cannot be disputed that more movies are now being produced, with thirty films made in 2000 and 2001 (Patterson, 2001). In addition, theaters have improved, with the introduction of a number of new multiplexes. This increased choice of nationally produced films is reflected in the viewing figures, with domestic films taking 13 percent and 14 percent of the national box office in 2000 and 2001, respectively, compared to an estimated 3 percent in 1998 (Tegel, 2001b). The Mexican film industry has also been helped by an amendment to the 1992 Cinema Law, passed in March 2001, which guarantees 10 percent of screen time to domestic products (Tegel, 2001c). It appears as if the government of Vicente Fox (2000), the first president not of the Partido Revolucionario Institucional (PRI, Institutional Revolutionary Party) to be elected in seventy-one years, is happy to further reduce the state's role in financing and policing culture, in line with his neoliberal policies.[31]

Although *Amores perros* and *Y tu mamá también* are the first films to repeat the commercial success of *Like Water for Chocolate* in international markets, both present an image of Mexico that is very different from Arau's film. The latter, as has been seen, was marketed as a "woman's film." *Amores perros,* in contrast, was marketed to appeal to a more universal audience, and *Y tu mamá también,* with its story of adolescent self-discovery, is aimed at a younger audience.[32] These differences, in the case of Arau and Iñárritu's films, are reflected in the structures of the films and in the soundtracks. *Like Water for Chocolate* has a linear, chronological narrative structure, whereas *Amores perros* makes complex use of time, and each narrative sequence includes cuts to the lives of the others characters.[33] Tita's story is accompanied by classical, harmonious piano music to highlight the romance of the film. Iñárritu uses a modern soundtrack, made up principally of Mexican rock and rap, and electronic ambient music, which generates a cool, modern image.[34]

Like Water for Chocolate and *Amores perros* demonstrate two formulas for success. The former represents a Mexico that stands for difference. It is a film that offers an escape for city dwellers to a more "authentic," traditional world symbolized by the natural products used in the time-consuming recipes. *Amores perros* presents another model, one that shows images of modern Mexicans that are not "other" to European and U.S. audiences, but images of people who are apparently like us or, at least, are like images with which we are familiar.

Class: Connections and Divisions

Inárritu has spoken of his intentions to challenge stereotypes of Mexicans, seen in such Hollywood films as *The Mexican* (2001) and *Traffic* (2000):

> I am not a Mexican with a moustache and a sombrero and a bottle of tequila....Nor am I a corrupt cop or a drug trafficker. There are millions like me. And this is the world I live in and the one I want to show. (Patterson, 2001)[35]

The world he and Arriaga Jordán create shows characters divided by class and socioeconomic circumstances, but linked to each other (and to audiences) through such universal concerns as love, desire, hate, power, and loneliness. Octavio (played by Gael García Bernal), Susana (played by Vanessa Bauche), and their family unit are working class, and their only means of making significant sums of money are through either robberies or dog fighting. Daniel (played by Alvaro Guerrero) and Valeria (played by Goya Toledo) are upper middle class; he is the editor of a fashion magazine, and she, until her accident, is a top model. El Chivo, meaning "The Goat" (played by Emilio Echevarría), is in a curious position in terms of class. He was a middle-class college lecturer who left his job and family to become a revolutionary; after years in prison he is living as a tramp while working as a hired assassin for a corrupt policeman. He initially appears to be the character to whom audiences would least relate. However, once we are shown his story and gain an insight into his loneliness and the love he has for his daughter, we begin to be moved by his plight. We ultimately witness his redemption, seen visually when he showers, shaves, and cuts his hair, so that by the end of the film, he is no longer characterized as different by his appearance, or indeed by his value system.

It is worth mentioning that, despite the appearance that the film is showing a range of classes, there is a glaring omission. There are no images of the extremely poor, indigenous shantytown dwellers who make up the majority of Mexico City's population, while the three male actors, playing the protagonists, are all of European origin. This is a common omission in Mexican cinema, with overrepresentation of the middle classes (Rashkin, 2001, 194). The notable exception to this is Dana Rotberg's *Angel de Fuego* (1991), which focuses on marginalized characters, circus and street performers, and prostitutes working in the slums of Mexico City.[36]

The plot and structure of *Amores perros* emphasize the theme of "the interconnectedness of human beings" (Chumo, 2000, 10), despite the separate spaces that social groups inhabit. The structure and editing of the film aim to demonstrate the connections between the characters and their worlds.[37] *Amores perros* is a film that tells three stories, or as Iñárritu put it, "It's not so much a movie split into three separate stories as one single story split into three chapters" (Pérez Soler, 2001b, 29). If the car crash is taken as the central organizing scene, the first chapter, "Octavio and Susana," can be said to be set in the past, the second chapter, "Valeria and Daniel," in the present, and the third, "El Chivo and Maru," in the future. The connections and separations of the characters and the three sections of the film are well illustrated in the car crash, which is shot four times, once to introduce the film, and three other times to show the event from the perspectives of Octavio, Valeria, and El Chivo. Each shooting of the crash has its own style and pace and marks a key moment in all the characters' lives. The collision itself occurs at a crossroads, signifying the life-changing aspect of the event. Iñárritu explains that nine cameras were used, set at different angles to capture the multiple perspectives of the crash (DVD, "Behind the Scenes").

This pivotal scene is shot the second time from the perspective of Octavio and his friend, Jorge (played by Humberto Busto). There is a frenetic car chase with members of Jarocho's gang, while the dog Cofi lies bleeding in the back seat. This replays as a summary of the dramatic events already seen at the start of the film, shown then as a hook for the audience. In this return to the scene, the audience now has a context for the events. We witness the buildup to the accident, as the director, after a brief blackout in place of the collision, cuts to a sequence of Valeria in the television studio (chronologically in the past). The excitement and tension of the car chase are represented using blurry tracking shots to capture the speed of the movement. Close-ups of the brothers, short bursts of animated dialogue, and rapid cuts to the car chasing them, accompanied by loud rock music, add to the excitement. The crash is later seen from Valeria's perspective, and the tone here contrasts directly with the earlier scene. It occurs as she is calmly driving out to buy a bottle of wine to celebrate living with Daniel. The heightened sound of the

Octavio (Gael García Bernal) in *Amores perros*.

collision, the shattered glass and smoke from the engines, and the interruption of her gentle rhythm ensure that the impact of the crash is dramatic. The fourth representation of the crash is seen from El Chivo's perspective. The crash is glimpsed in the background as he is interrupted watching Luis Miranda Solares (Jorge Salinas), the businessman he has been hired to kill. However, it soon transfers to the foreground of his life, as the implications of saving Cofi's life ultimately lead to his redemption, and potentially save the life of the businessman.[38]

The collision comes to represent the ways in which lives are interconnected, with the actions of characters dramatically affecting those of the others and changing the course of their lives. Octavio's feud with Jarocho (played by Gustavo Sánchez Parra) leads to the accident that badly injures him and kills his friend. The crash, in turn, causes Valeria's injuries, which ensure that she and Daniel significantly rethink their lives and their relationship, while it leads to El Chivo's moral redemption. The accident thus brings apparently disparate people together, then attempts to identify universal emotions that connect them. In this desire to seek out the universal, the film underplays the specifics of class, and is more interested in personal motivations of the characters than in the political implications of their actions.

Despite the apparent divisions in *Amores perros,* the connections are emphasized between the three principal male characters, Octavio, Daniel, and El Chivo. Arriaga Jordán explained that they were conceived of as a single man at different periods of his life. It is, he has said, "a story of a man divided in three characters — there's a boy of less than twenty, a man of forty and a man of sixty" (Chumo, 2000, 11). This is reflected in the chronology of the film, with the stories of the characters following each other. There is something both effective and troubling about taking characters of different ages and backgrounds and, despite their different environments, highlighting their commonalities. "Universal" human emotions are seen to unite the characters, and make national and international audiences able to identify with them, despite their individual circumstances. In Iñárritu's words, "It's a story that deals with human pain, love and death — which make no distinction of social class" (Pérez Soler, 2001b).

Despite the proclamations of the writer and the director, the film can be read against the grain of universalism. Pain, love, and death are not all universal and are clearly influenced by social class. Susana, for example, would not be forced to stay with a violent husband and an infatuated brother-in-law, were it not for the fact that she has no economic independence. Ramiro (Marco Pérez) would not be shot dead while robbing a bank, if crime were not the only way to get rich for a man of his class. Daniel would not have been able to buy an apartment for Valeria and him to start their new life together were he not comfortably off. Indeed, the very plot depends on class; the dogfights, the violent feud between Octavio and Jarocho, the resulting car chase and crash, which dramatically change the lives of Valeria and Daniel and El Chivo, all stem from a working-class brand of machismo.

Each "chapter" has its own style, yet is not a self-contained unit, as the film provides a number of crosscuts to the characters that feature in the other sections. In addition, there are recurring themes, such as infidelity, the absence of a father figure, and the rivalry between brothers, which aim to connect the sections. The dogs that feature in each "chapter" also link the characters while signaling their distinct characters. Octavio and Ramiro's mastiff, Cofi, demonstrates the violence of the streets that condition the brothers' behavior; Richie, Valeria's pretty pet, symbolizes the spoiled life she has lived before her accident, then shares a similar fate to her in its fall; while El Chivo's love of his strays reflects his initial rejection of people.[39]

Octavio, Cofi, and El Chivo

The first section of the film is the most exciting in terms of pace and action. As Iñárritu said, "It has more music, more young people, more drive and edge" (Oppenheimer, 2001, 24). The car chase is the culmination of a series of action-packed sequences, which feature the affair between Octavio and Susana, Ramiro's violent behavior toward his wife and his drug store robberies, Cofi's victories over Jarocho's dogs, Jarocho's shooting of Cofi, and Octavio's revenge stabbing of Jarocho. The story, while focusing on Octavio, also cuts to scenes of his brother's life. There are also six cuts to El Chivo and two cuts to scenes of Daniel with his wife and young daughters. Valeria is seen once before the crash from Octavio and Jorge's perspective, on Jorge's television.

The editing in this section is rapid; fast cuts from one scene to another intentionally disrupt the narrative process and generate interest and intrigue. There are a number of unanswered questions regarding El Chivo, whose name the audience does not know at this point.[40] Who is he? Why does he kill the businessman? What is his connection with the story of Octavio, Susana, and Ramiro? Why does he have no relationship with his daughter, even after her mother has died? None of these questions are answered until the final chapter, and all the audience is given are snapshots of his life. As well as ensuring the audience's interest, the crosscutting serves to create a thematic connection. The editing deliberately creates links between El Chivo, the brothers, and Cofi. In one scene, the brothers are arguing over the profits made on their dog's victories. Ramiro aims a gun at Cofi's head, threatening to shoot him if Octavio does not share his winnings with him. This is juxtaposed with a short shot of El Chivo watching his daughter. In another sequence, a scene in which the brothers are again arguing over money at the dinner table is followed by a cut to El Chivo coolly assassinating a businessman eating his lunch at a restaurant. Cofi's first fight is again followed by a cut to El Chivo at a distance watching his wife being buried. These juxtaposed scenes aim to make evident the links between the brothers, their dog, and El Chivo, and to highlight the violence, materialism and machismo in society, where men fight, risk the lives of their dogs, and kill each other, all for money and a sense of power. The characters are symbolically united after the car crash when El Chivo rescues Cofi, and nurses him back to health. Cofi, the dog who kills dogs, finds his natural owner in the man who kills men. It is Cofi who teaches El Chivo the implications of his own actions; El Chivo's horror when Cofi kills all of his dogs leads to his redemption. Feuding brothers are also used in the final story to illustrate this change. Here, El Chivo is not linked to the brothers; on the contrary, he distances himself from them in his refusal to kill one brother on behalf of another.

The ex-guerrilla who is now a hired assassin is initially compared through the use of editing with Octavio and Ramiro. Characters are clearly intended to act as a reflection of Mexican society in *Amores perros* and serve to critique violence and the loss of humanity (Niogret, 2000, 26). Arriaga Jordán argued that *Amores perros* is an exposé of "a world where we are losing our social values, our sense of fraternity, and focus only on individual values" (Chumo, 2000, 11). The editing aims to create a sense of commonality: the characters are trapped in the violent world of Mexico City, and the crosscutting gives the impression of parallels in the characters' behavior. However, the circumstances of the violence of the characters are very different. Octavio and Ramiro belong to a world where violence denotes masculinity, as do the material gains that come through the robberies and the dogfights. El Chivo's violence has very different motives; his job as a hired assassin has deep psychological and political roots. It is a manifestation of his anger against a society that has incarcerated him. The anger and loneliness caused by the lack of family and his failed political goals have led him to distorted acts of class warfare, seen in his assassination of members of the business elite on behalf of other wealthy businessmen.[41]

Through El Chivo, the film suggests the demise of the revolutionary left, yet fails to explore this idea in any depth or to make meaningful links with the current revolutionary Zapatista movement. Gustavo Garfias (played by Rodrigo Murray), the man who hires El Chivo to kill his brother, does make a brief connection between El Chivo and the Zapatistas, but this is not developed. More is learned about the ex-revolutionary in the third "chapter" of the film, "El Chivo and Maru." However, the film is more interested in the human dimension of the story than in the specific political circumstances that led El Chivo to become a guerrilla. The film never explains what he was fighting for beyond the vague explanation to his daughter in a telephone message that he wanted to put the world right and then share it with her. It is made clear that he was wrong to leave his family and middle-class life for his political cause, and that he has failed in his struggle, as he also tells his daughter. The audience is given only minimum information regarding his past. Leonardo (played by José Sefami), the corrupt policeman, tells Garfias that El Chivo was a guerrilla who planted bombs in shopping malls, kidnapped businessmen, and killed policemen. He was imprisoned for many years and went mad on his "release," until Leonardo "rescues" him. In this way, the film blames El Chivo for both abandoning his family and murdering civilians, and does not examine his cause or question the role of the state in its repression of oppositional political activity. In fact, the PRI brutally repressed any guerrilla organizations that emerged in the 1960s and 1970s, with others imprisoned and leaders assassinated by a Mexican military trained by the U.S. Army in counterinsurgency (Hellman, 1978, 127).

The film is interested in the personal as separate from the political, and locates the problems of the characters within dysfunctional family units. The thematic link with the first story is maintained as it becomes clear that the idea of the absent father is central. Octavio and Ramiro are two young men without a father who are vying for supremacy in the household. They have no positive masculine role model, which, in turn, causes Ramiro to be a failed father to his son. In one scene, he is shown with no idea of how to behave in his baby son's presence; he wakes him up and explodes in a fit of violence when Susana berates him. His reckless robbery of the bank leads to his death and ensures that his son will not have a father. The story of El Chivo is of a man who has learned from his mistakes. However, he, as a young man, is compared to Ramiro, as he too has failed a young child. The cause of his pain lies in the fact that he abandoned his daughter when she was only two years old. As he tells her, not a day has passed that he has not thought of her, and he ultimately reenters society in the hope that he can renew a relationship with her. These themes are developed in the second "chapter" through the characters of Daniel and Valeria, as will be seen.

It is argued in the analysis of *Central Station* and *Pixote* (see chapter 5) that the reference to failed paternal models can be used as a metaphor for a failed state. Despite the focus on the personal over the political, *Amores perros* also makes a connection between absent fathers and an ineffective state. Iñárritu has said that "it is not a political film, but it has a lot to do with the consequences of a political system that existed in my country for 71 years" (Franco Reyes, 2001; my translation). Although there are no references to the PRI, in its last years in power when *Amores perros* was made, this is a film that reflects a society without any effective government. There is corruption, sleaze, and dishonesty at all levels, seen in the unregulated dogfights, in the arrangement Daniel and Andrés (played by Ricardo Dalmacci) come to in which Andrés appears on the front cover of the magazine that Daniel edits in exchange for posing as Valeria's boyfriend, in the fact that a businessman pays to have his partner murdered, and in the fact that it is a policeman who organizes this. Nevertheless, each class experiences the failures of the state in very different ways, yet the extreme poor, who suffer the most, are absent from this tableau of life in Mexico City.

Valeria and Daniel

The middle chapter, "Valeria and Daniel," is a story of an initially privileged couple who have their lives shattered by a car crash. This section is a good example of how the film shows separate social spaces while establishing thematic links with the other "chapters." Although this narrative is more coherent, the editing in the first section has already highlighted the inter-linking structure of the film. Their story is introduced in the first part with two short scenes of a frustrated Daniel with his family. The phone, which has a symbolic function, rings twice, alerting the audience to the fact that Daniel is having an affair.[42] From this introduction to the affair, the audience understands that the anonymous caller is Daniel's wife, thus creating a link between the first two "chapters." The scenes of Daniel follow those of Octavio and Susana's infidelity, which aim to connect him with Octavio through his affair with Valeria.

El Chivo's presence in the second "chapter" also serves to connect it to the first. He would appear to have nothing in common with Valeria and Daniel, but the cuts to him create thematic links with all three stories. This is achieved by the development of the theme of the absent father. The most significant scene is that in which El Chivo is watching his daughter from afar, before breaking into her apartment and taking a photograph of her. In the picture, she appears with her mother and stepfather, and the audience later sees El Chivo replace the other man's picture with his own (first as a tramp and later with the new clean-shaven image of himself). As has been seen, Arriaga Jordán wrote the three characters as three stages of the same man, which leads to the interpretation that this desperate act of frustrated fatherhood prefigures Daniel's future suffering at the abandonment of his daughters.[43] Valeria also has a problematic relationship with her father, with whom she is not in contact. She refuses to let Daniel contact him following her accident, as "he is capable of saying that I deserved it." This, however, is not further developed.

Despite these links, the "chapter" has its own style and pace and highlights the differences in lifestyles among the classes in Mexico. In Iñárritu's words, "The second story is the most classical — the story moves slowly, and the two characters are more conventional, more boring" (Oppenheimer, 2001, 24). The emphasis here is on interiors, which provide a claustrophobic setting to bring out the tensions between the couple. Rodrigo Prieto, the film's cinematographer, spoke of the specific style cultivated here: the hand-held cameras of the first section and the emphasis on movement and action are replaced by more static shots, and the scenes are shot using cameras that give cleaner, crisper images (Oppenheimer, 2001). There is less use of cross-cutting, with only two cuts to El Chivo. In addition, fewer locations are used with almost all of the action taking place in the couple's apartment. There are only five scenes in two other (interior) locations, three in the hospital and two in Daniel's office.

The conventional nature of the couple and the focus on the intimacies of their everyday life serve to critique the star system and also to humanize Valeria for the audience. The famous, glamorous model and her boyfriend, the editor of a fashion magazine, are seen to be "just like us" through their arguments and frustrations and in the tensions that exist between them. It has been seen how the film humanizes El Chivo by focusing on his emotional point of view. It does the same with Valeria, a character on the opposite end of the social scale. Like El Chivo, Valeria initially appears to belong to another entirely inaccessible world; she is first seen on a poster for Enchant perfume, and is then seen on television, lying about her latest love. At this point, she does not appear to be a "real" person who could have anything to do with the lives of the other characters that we have seen. It is ironic, then, that Octavio and Jorge cause the accident in which this beautiful woman is badly injured. The irony is particularly harsh in Jorge's case, as he was admiring the model's looks just before he is killed in the collision with her.[44]

A key scene that takes Valeria from being an image on the screen to a "real" woman shows her in the television studio, as the program ends. The audience is initially given the impression that we are still watching her on television; however, the camera pans back to reveal her image on the monitor at the studio. When she leaves the studio with Andrés, and he takes her to the apartment that Daniel has bought for the two of them, it becomes clear that Andrés was posing as her lover. This shift from the television image to the "real" Valeria develops a central idea of the film: the universality of human emotion. The inaccessible celebrity is revealed as a flesh-and-blood woman, one who has the same feelings as the "common people."

Her accident further connects her to the world of the other characters, as it causes her to be dropped from the superficial worlds of fashion, beauty, and the entertainment industry. Her career is abruptly terminated, as is seen from the phone conversation with her agent who informs her that she has been dropped from the Enchant advertising campaign. The Enchant poster, which features Valeria in a sexy dress, revealing her long legs, becomes a motif in this section. The poster is first seen as Daniel is driving with his wife and children, suggesting that Valeria has enchanted him with her persona as a model. The poster is then seen triumphantly on the wall outside their new apartment, but it soon comes to mock Daniel and Valeria following her accident. In two separate scenes after arguments, the characters both stare at the poster, through the window of their apartment, as if reflecting on what they have lost.

The image of Valeria on the poster contrasts with the image she now presents; she is without makeup, although still beautiful, and confined to the apartment. She wears a leg brace and is forced to move around in a wheelchair or on crutches, until she has her leg amputated.[45] Her dog, Richie, which acts as a surrogate child and comes to symbolize the state of the couple's relationship, disappears through a hole in the floorboards, and tensions in Valeria's relationship with Daniel develop. The new circumstances they have to cope with are symbolized by the rats that she discovers living below the floor, which are biting Richie. This is used to suggest that even with their wealth and status, the couple cannot escape from the harsh realities of life in Mexico City.

Despite the thematic connections between this "chapter" and the others, here too there are important divisions between the characters in terms of class and politics. Valeria is not shown to have anything in common with the other female characters. Although the violence of Susana's world badly affects her, Valeria differs from Susana in the economic independence she and Daniel have, which allows them to set up home together, and in the fact that she does not risk physical violence through her infidelity. Although she could have been linked to Maru (Lourdes Echevarría), El Chivo's daughter, who was also rejected by her father, Maru is an entirely undeveloped character. Comparisons between the male characters are also limited. These have been made between Daniel and El Chivo, but El Chivo's motives for abandoning his wife and daughter are very different from those of Daniel, who is enchanted by the beauty and status of Valeria. Both revolution and model are seen to represent a false utopia, a failed promise of collective and personal happiness. Daniel's relationship with Valeria is seen to evolve once she can no longer work as a model, and he is forced to get to know her without the trappings of her success. Despite the growing tensions between the two, in their final scene he holds her, as she is looking at the space where the Enchant poster once was. Iñárritu has said that this shows that Daniel "assumes his responsibilities with dignity by staying with Valeria" and that what was a fragile, physical relationship now has "a spiritual, emotional and physical dimension" (Niogret, 2000, 26).

El Chivo, as has been seen, has failed in his revolutionary goals and has abandoned his political aims; he is reduced to carrying out meaningless, mercenary acts of violence. The film does not argue for El Chivo to return to his revolutionary beliefs; on the contrary, it suggests that political struggles are bound to fail, whereas personal relationships can bring fulfillment. The character can find redemption only by putting the violence of the past behind him, in order to deserve a relationship with his daughter. On the one hand, Daniel and El Chivo appear to be linked by the fact that it is suggested that they will find happiness through their relationships with Valeria and Maru. On the other hand, although in El Chivo's case there is a promise of a reunion with the daughter he abandoned, Daniel's relationship with his daughters suffers through his decision to remain with his lover.[46]

Gender: Representations of Masculinity and Femininity

Many of these commonalities and distinctions between the characters originate in the way that gender codes interact with class. Ramírez Berg (1989) argued that much recent Mexican cinema represents masculinity in crisis. He explained that just as female images have multiplied since the late 1960s,

> [m]en have been no less affected by the sexual revolution, and their screen image and role in society [are] in crisis as well.... Machismo has been shattered, leaving the Mexican male scurrying desperately about for an appropriate role model to take its place. (Ramírez Berg, 1989, 179)

Each of the male protagonists in *Amores perros* demonstrates this crisis in different ways. Daniel, as a besotted lover of a top model, is far removed from the representation of stereotypical machismo; nevertheless, his desire for Valeria is rooted in constructs of masculinity. A man who can "have" a beautiful, successful model is himself judged as successful in patriarchal societies and is more attractive than a family man with an aging wife. His frustrations with Valeria can be explained by the fact that, disabled, she is no longer the prize she was in terms of promoting his status, and that life with her after the accident can never be what he imagined it would be. El Chivo is seen to be following a masculine fantasy, that of "saving the world" through his guerrilla activities, but his failure to do this, his years in prison, and the absence of his family have led him to an emotional crisis.

Octavio, as the youngest of the three, is the character who best illustrates the conflicting masculine codes in Mexico at the end of the 1990s. In some respects, he clings to the idea of machismo to affirm his sense of self, but he also cultivates an identity of sensitive lover in opposition to his brother, Ramiro, who beats his wife, has a lover, and is living out a fantasy life as a criminal. Octavio's problems stem from these opposing identities, which make him unable to separate love from violence or power games. He wants to save Susana from his violent brother, but he also uses her as a weapon in the ongoing battle he has with his brother. Sexual desire becomes the language of a complex power game. If Octavio succeeds in taking Ramiro's wife away from him, he defeats him. Iñárritu has explained that Octavio's motives are not simply romantic; he erroneously seeks his mother's and brother's approval through his betrayal, by showing them that he has the power to win Susana (DVD, "Behind the Scenes").

This is demonstrated in a scene that shows Octavio and Susana making love while Ramiro is being beaten up, a beating organized by his brother through his dogfighting contacts. The scene is shot in the style of a music video, with images accompanied by the Spanish band Nacha Pop's "Lucha de Gigantes" ("Battle of the Giants"). The song's lyrics fit the scene well, as they speak in abstract terms of violence, existential struggles and fears, self-deception, and the fragility of people. Images of Susana and Octavio are crosscut with those of Ramiro's attack. The editing together of the scenes prevents the audience from enjoying the lovemaking. In the same way, Octavio cannot fully immerse himself in the act. He is facing the mirror, which can be seen to represent his conscience, while the audience is shown the consequences of his actions, the brutal beating of Ramiro by three men. Susana, aware of the risks they are taking, is also unable to fully enjoy their lovemaking, and she is shown looking worried.

The film critiques machismo and patriarchy by having the three male protagonists move on from the path that they chose to assert their masculinity. Daniel makes a commitment to the disabled Valeria, choosing love and care over lust and glamour; El Chivo gives up his life of violence for the promise of a paternal role; and Octavio keeps alive his hopes of a future with Susana, when his love for her can now be separated from sibling rivalry, following Ramiro's death. Although she rejects him after the death of Ramiro, he makes it clear that he will continue to hope that they will be together.[47]

If *Amores perros* shows masculinity in crisis, the women in the film are, to a large extent, victims of this crisis and, with the exception of Valeria, are not well developed. Susana is used in Octavio's power games and is a victim of her husband's violent machismo. The mother (played by Adriana Barraza) of Ramiro and Octavio also suffers at their hands; she provides for them materially and is refused money by them, even when they are flush with their illegal earnings. It should be said that she is an unsympathetic, marginal character caught up in a patriarchal value system. She always takes the side of her eldest son, even when he abuses his wife, and is unsympathetic to Susana when she needs child care. Her marginality and lack of a subjective position are emphasized by the fact that she is named only once, as Doña Concha, when she is offered sympathy at Ramiro's funeral. Maru is another marginal character; she is only ever seen from her father's perspective, and her point of view is never shown.

Valeria is, in fact, the only female character who is given a dominant point of view. She, as a model, is part of a patriarchal, capitalist system that uses women's looks to sell its products. Valeria is played by the Spanish actress Goya Toledo, who is tall, slim, and blonde, a form of beauty at odds with the appearance of most Mexican women. Valeria thus unwittingly endorses the inherent racism in the Mexican media, which judge lighter skinned women of European origin to be more beautiful than women of mestizo or indigenous origin. The end of Valeria's career is the result of the same patriarchal system that gave her success, as any physical imperfections clearly disqualify a model from working. This makes her enter into a period of reflection, as she is forced to acquire a new, less superficial, identity. In one shot, she is seen looking at childhood photographs and reconnecting with her premodel reality. Of this, Iñárritu has commented that, as a result of her accident, Valeria changes from a superficial model into a woman who "acquires an interior beauty" (Niogret, 2000, 26). It is worth noting that, although the film uses Valeria to comment on the superficial worlds of fashion and beauty, there is a paradox in that the beauty of the actress Goya Toledo clearly helps to sell this film.[48] Valeria's future is left open; it is not clear what her postmodel identity will be, and her "happy ending" is that Daniel has decided to stay with her.

Conclusions

Amores perros is a sophisticated film that presents diverse images of life in Mexico City from a range of perspectives. The writer and director seek to bring out the humanity in their characters and draw connections between those that appear to inhabit entirely distinct social worlds. Clever editing, the juxtaposition of key scenes, and thematic links create a coherent film from diverse stories. Nevertheless, the will to bring out a universal human condition leads to the downplaying of social factors that separate characters. As has been seen, the connections made between the characters do not always work for this reason.

The male characters in the film are linked by the need to redefine their masculinity, whereas the women are seen as victims of a patriarchal society and are often shown in marginal positions. Susana, Octavio and Ramiro's mother, and Maru are rarely given a point of view, and their feelings toward the male protagonists are not known. The film does critique machismo and patriarchy and succeeds in examining the complexities of heterosexual gender relations, unlike *Like Water for Chocolate,* which is a celebration of traditional femininity, with men only of interest as objects of desire.

The two films contrast on a number of other levels. Whereas *Like Water for Chocolate* creates a mythical, traditional, rural Mexico, *Amores perros* represents urban, modern lives in Mexico City at the end of 1990s.[49] The principal theme of each film is love; however, each deals with this theme in very different ways. Love in *Like Water for Chocolate* is in itself a simple, romantic affair, with two people destined to be together and to marry, with complications arising from outside. Love in *Amores perros,* in contrast, is always complicated and inseparable from other issues such as power, desire, violence, infidelity, politics, and money. In terms of characterization and gender representation, the films also take contrasting approaches. Arau's film filters its narrative through the perspective of a single heroine and highlights her suffering at the hands of her wicked mother, whereas Iñárritu's film refuses to rely on a sole protagonist. Each of the three "chapters" has its own protagonist, with none acquiring the status of hero or villain. The contrasts in the films demonstrate that there is more than one formula for commercial success and that images of Mexico do not have to be rooted in a folkloric romanticism to appeal to international markets. It is hoped that the success of *Like Water for Chocolate* and *Amores perros* will further open international markets to Mexican and other Latin American films that show a range of national images.

Notes

1. See *www.unam.mx/filmoteca/filna/temp25826.html* and *http://us.imdb.com/Tawards? 0103994.*

2. For more on Mexican cinema in the 1990s, see Rashkin (2001), Torrents (1993, 222–29), and Maciel (1999, 193–286). Films that have been associated with the mini boom of the early 1990s are *Bandidos* (*Bandits,* Luis Estrada, 1990), *Sólo con tu pareja* (*Love in the Tim of Hysteria,* Alfonso Cuarón, 1991), *Danzón* (María Novaro, 1991), *Angel de fuego* (*Angel of Fire,* Dana Rotberg, 1991), *La mujer de Benjamín* (*Benjamin's Woman,* Carlos Carrera, 1991), *Cabeza de vaca* (Nicolás Echeverría, 1991), *Cronos* (*Chronus,* Guillermo del Toro, 1992), and *Novia que te vea* (*Like a Bride,* Guita Schyfter, 1993) For a list of Mexican films made in the 1990s and early 2000s, see *www.mty.itesm.mx/dhcs/carreras/lcc/cine_mex/pelicula8.html.*

3. For more on the relationship between Mexican cinema and the state from 1970 to 1999, see David Maciel's excellent article (Maciel, 1999, 220).

4. For more on the Salinas regime, see Russell (1994).

5. In her article on *Like Water for Chocolate,* Nuala Finnegan examines the film in the context of Salinas's Mexico and the hostility toward Mexicans in the United States as a result of the North American Free Trade Agreement (NAFTA) (Finnegan, 1999, 312).

6. Filming also took place in Eagle Pass, Texas.

7. Figures show that the urban population of Mexico jumped from 42.7 per 2,5000 in 1950, to 50.8 per 2,5000 in 1960, to 72.8 per 2,5000 in 1990 (Tarrés, 1992, 27).

8. Arau made the comments as part of a defense against accusations that he had stolen funds from the Ministry of Tourism for a film project that was not realized (Segre, 1997, 45).

9. For more on the parallels between the Cinderella story and the film, see Shaw and Rollet (1994, 84).

10. Elsewhere, Arau has expressed a belief that, as a man, he would be unable to adequately express these "feminine feelings," but Laura Esquivel rejected all the women directors he suggested (Stone, 1997, 464), possibly so that her input would be greater.

11. Cast members included Ada Carrasco (Nacha), Sandra Arau (Esperanza), Yareli Arizmendi (Rosaura), Arcelia Ramírez (great-niece), and Claudette Maillé (Gertrudis).

12. The *federales,* unmentioned in the film, are identified as the "bad guys" of the revolution in the novel, capturing Pedro on the day his wife gives birth.

13. They are both *criollos,* Mexicans descended from the Spanish who have not intermarried with the indigenous population.

14. In her treatment of the indigenous characters, Esquivel is guilty of many of the faults of the *indigenista* novel of which Braulio Muñoz (1982)has written: "The characters, especially the Indians, are no more than caricatures and are represented totally from the outside, with little effort to explore their psychology" (69). Esquivel's Indians are folkloric, lovable caricatures occupying secondary roles in the narrative. For more discussion on Esquivel and Arau's treatment of the indigenous characters, see Shaw and Rollet (1994, 82–92). See also Lillo and Sarafati-Arnaud (1994, 487–88).

15. For more on the categories of melodrama and woman's film, see Gledhill (1987).

16. For an overview and analysis of feminist film theories regarding female spectatorship, see Thornham (1997, 45–66).

17. Other examples of Tita's powers can be seen in the mass melancholy and vomiting that she triggers through her tears, which enter the wedding cake at Rosaura and Pedro's (illegitimate) wedding, and the passion that her cooking generates at Alex and Esperanza's (legitimately romantic) wedding.

18. See Pérez Turrent (1994) for a selection of international reviews of the film. For a critique of the use of the term *magical realism* in international markets, see Martin (1989, 141–43).

19. See Scott (1990) and Riquer Fernández (1992) for a discussion of feminism of equality and feminism of difference; for a selection of essays that critique essentialist feminism, see Nicholson (1990).

20. For a variety of conceptualizations of feminist criticism in Latin America, see Mora (1989, 2–10).

21. See also Lillo and Sarafati-Arnaud (1994, 487).

22. Debra Castillo (1992) noted the ambivalence behind the siting of women's creativity in the kitchen. She writes, "The recipe serves as an index of female creative power; it also describes a giving of the self to appease another's hunger, leaving the cook weakened, starving. To have access to speech, to recipe sharing, she must feed others, often from her most intimate self" (xv).

23. On the idealization of the female characters in these films, E. Ann Kaplan (1987) wrote: "Their sphere was defined as the domestic, but this sphere was shown, in the manner of domestic feminism, to engender values higher than the male public sphere, which was implicated in consumer capitalism" (126).

24. One film critic talked about Leonardi's "plank-like performance" (Feay, 1993, 72).

25. Tita also has to feed Esperanza, Rosaura's daughter, as her mother is again unable to provide milk for her child or to seek alternatives. Tita decides not to try to breastfeed her after the pain of losing Roberto, but she follows Nacha's lessons by nurturing Esperanza on special teas.

26. Gertrudis's passionate nature and her natural rhythm are attributed to the fact that her biological father was a mulatto. For more on Gertrudis and the film's use of racial stereotypes, see Finnegan (1999, 318–20).

27. The score was written by the acclaimed composer Leo Brower, who also wrote the score for *Memories of Underdevelopment,* as well as scores for numerous other Latin American films. See *www.imdb.com* for more details.

28. For box office figures, see "Top 250 films" (2002).

29. For a detailed discussion of the problems with IMCINE from 1994 to 1997, see Maciel (1999, 220–27).

30. The other films are *Todo el poder* (*Gimme Power,* 2001) and *Por la libre* (*By the Free Road,* 2000).

31. Jordi Soler, a writer, broadcaster, and cultural attaché in Dublin, has spoken of his own experiences of persecution under the regimes of Carlos Salinas de Gortari, and Vicente Fox, and claims that cultural figures are given more freedom under Fox. He nevertheless criticizes Fox's regime for its lack of any cultural policy (speech given at the Annual Conference of Hispanists of Great Britain and Ireland at Cork University, April 11–14, 2002).

32. *Y tu mamá también* was given an over age eighteen certificate in Mexico (equivalent to an R rating in the United States), which the director fought, maintaining that the film was aimed at adolescents. See Feinstein (2002).

33. Critics have compared the film to Quentin Tarantino's *Pulp Fiction* (1994) in terms of structure (Barton, 2001; Lawrenson, 2001). Iñárritu claims that the film that most influenced him and Arriaga Jordán is *Smoke* (1995), another collaboration between a director (Wayne Wang) and a writer (Paul Auster) that also looks at interconnected stories (Niogret, 2000).

34. As an ex-disc jockey, Iñárritu is particularly interested in music. He directed one of the music videos included in the DVD version of *Amores perros* and coproduced another. In addition, the CD of the film has been released internationally. The double CD was produced by Gustavo Santaolalla.

35. Iñárritu does not quite manage to avoid all of these types; the corrupt cop makes an appearance in *Amores perros.*

36. For a detailed analysis of this film, see Rashkin (2001, 194–213).

37. The editing process took seven months (see DVD, "behind the scenes").

38. The fate of the two half brothers is unresolved in the film; they are left untied, with a single gun between them. In the original ending, the sound of a gunshot was heard, implying that one had killed the other; however, Iñárritu decided to leave this open, as it was against the message of hope and redemption that he wanted the film to have (see DVD, "Deleted Scenes").

39. His later union with Cofi is examined below.

40. His real name is Martín de Esquerra. The audience learn his surname in his wife's obituary; she is referred to as the widow of Esquerra. He only reveals his first name toward the end of the film, as he is leaving a message on his daughter's answering machine. It is only at this point, when he has renounced violence, that he is ready to claim his prerevolutionary identity.

41. When told that Gustavo Garfias wants him to kill Garfias's wealthy partner, El Chivo laughs and says ironically that he's a real proletarian.

42. On the first call, the caller hangs up when Daniel's wife answers, and on the second, Daniel takes the phone to another room and tells the caller that he loves her.

43. This is highlighted in one of the deleted scenes in the movie. Daniel is featured here visiting his children and sad at his separation from them. Iñárritu says that he left this scene out, thinking it would be confusing if he emphasized Daniel's point of view over Valeria's (see DVD, "Behind the Scenes").

44. His comment, "Me cae esta mujer," which literally translated means "This woman makes me fall," expresses this irony.

45. There might appear to be parallels with Luis Buñuel's *Tristana* (1970), but Valeria has none of the fetishist associations of the one-legged character played by Catherine Denueve in Buñuel's work. For an analysis of fetishism in *Tristana,* see Labanyi (1999).

46. Although this does not have to be the case, the fact that Daniel is never seen with his daughters in the final cut of the film seems to suggest this.

47. Susana tells Octavio that if you want to make God laugh, tell him your plans, and he replies that God may laugh, but he will continue to make his plans.

48. The same can be said of the way that violence is used in the film. On one level, the film critiques the macho world of dogfighting; nevertheless, the fights generate excitement, with the viewer manipulated into willing Cofi to defeat Jarocho's dogs.

49. The date, May 11, 1999, can be seen on a newspaper El Chivo is reading when he learns of his ex-wife's death.

3

Searching the Past for the Future

Justiniano's *Amnesia*
and Larraín's *The Frontier*

The Frontier (*La frontera*, 1991) by Ricardo Larraín (b. 1958) and *Amnesia* (1994) by Gonzálo Justiniano (b. 1955) are two of the most interesting films made in Chile in the 1990s, signaling the potential rebirth of Chilean cinema.[1] Although key Chilean directors such as Miguel Littín and Raúl Ruiz continued making films in exile (Mexico and France, respectively), the military regime of Augusto Ugarte Pinochet from 1973 to 1990 effectively destroyed the national film industry.[2] Despite the existence of a respectable number of filmmakers working in exile, films made in Chile had limited success in terms of distribution. The Chilean novelist and director Antonio Skármeta lamented this situation, commenting in an article written in 1988: "I do not believe there have been any Chilean filmmakers who have achieved recognition beyond professional circles, or outside the country where they live and where their films are financed" (Skármeta, 1997, 265).

This highlights the importance of both films in terms of Chilean national cinema. *The Frontier* has been one of the most successful Chilean films in terms of box office receipts and critical appraisal (Mouesca, 1997, 125).[3] In February 1992, it won the Silver Bear in the first film category in the Berlin Film Festival, and in March of that same year it won a Goya, the prestigious Spanish film award, for the best Spanish-language foreign film for films shown in 1991 (Mouesca, 1997, 125).[4] *Amnesia* also achieved critical acclaim, winning awards at the Havana Film Festival for best actor (Julio Jung as Zúñiga) and best cinematography (Hans Burman), as well as the Cuban Press Association's award for best film. It also won a Golden Kikito at the Gramado Latin Film Festival (*http://us.imdb.com/Tawards?0109105*). The film did moderately well in theaters in Chile, but it was more successful when shown on television seven months after its release, achieving the highest ratings after the film *Ghost* (García & Ricagno, 1995).

Despite the impact of these two films, it is important to highlight the diffi-culties of Chilean cinema when faced with the competition from Hollywood and European cinema and the scarcity of funding within Chile. In an inter-view, Ricardo Larraín spoke of the disappointment that followed the success of *The Frontier* and of the truth of a jury member's claims that, as a Chilean director, he would have few possibilities to make other films.[5] Larraín was still collecting awards for soft drink and beer commercials after winning the prestigious European film awards, unlike most other internationally success-ful directors. This is clearly a main source of income for Chilean directors, who cannot rely on making films to earn a living, highlighted by the fact that by 1998 Larraín had made over 700 commercials.[6]

Gonzálo Justiniano, the director of *Amnesia,* spoke of the difficulties of making films in Chile, claiming that "films have been made by suicidal mad people who took risks" (García & Ricagno, 1995; my translation). He attributed his relative success to the fact that his films have been coproduced with European companies and distributed in Europe, although *Amnesia* itself was funded by the Chilean production company *Cine Chile. The Fron-tier,* however, could never have been made without European funding: it was coproduced by the Spanish national television company Televisión española after Larraín and the Argentinean Jorge Goldenberg won the prize for best (yet to be filmed) screenplay at the Havana Film Festival in 1989.

Both *The Frontier* and *Amnesia* take Chile's recent past as their subject. This is not surprising considering that Chileans living in their country were unable to make films addressing contemporary political issues for seventeen years. Suppressed stories need to be told in a public forum, and, as B. Ruby Rich has argued, the most effective therapy for victims of the regime is democracy, as it creates the spaces for these stories.[7] Both films argue that unless dark forces of the past are examined and understood, the country can never be at peace with itself, and Chileans will not be able to construct a present and a future. It is also interesting that both films have extreme geographical settings. The frontier land is at risk of tidal waves, subject to periods of intense rain, and the prisoners and soldiers in *Amnesia* have to endure the harsh climate of the desert. The full metaphoric potential of the geography is used in the films, as will be seen; however, these settings are also grounded in realism, as both prisoners and those forced into internal exile were sent to the most inhospitable parts of Chile during the Pinochet years.

Despite these shared factors, each film has its own agenda and approach. *The Frontier* was made in 1991, three years before *Amnesia,* and possibly for this reason it is more cautious in its attack on the Pinochet regime. *The Frontier* tells the story of the internal exile of Ramiro Orellana (played by

Patricio Contreras), a former math teacher. It is set in 1985, the final period of the Pinochet dictatorship, and Ramiro has been sent to an unnamed frontier town because he signed a letter of protest at the arrest of his colleague, Oscar Aguirre. A man who is neither an activist nor a member of any party is, through a simple act of solidarity, made into a political prisoner.[8] In *The Frontier,* the national issue of exile, which affected a generation of Chileans, is seen through an individual. Audiences travel with Ramiro, witnessing his initial alienation and the way he gradually adapts to circumstances. References to the military regime are veiled, and criticism is directed at the two officials of the town who control Ramiro's movements in exile, officials who are ineffective and stupid, rather than sinister or violent. The film is more interested in the theme of personal recovery from trauma than in directly denouncing human rights abuses.

In contrast, a denunciation of the military regime is the main objective of *Amnesia*. The film has two time frames, the beginning of the dictatorship (1973) and the transition to democracy (sometime after 1990 — the exact year is not specified). The use of flashback, which takes the audience to a prison camp in the desert, challenges the transitional government's neglect of the country's recent past, and the abuse of power by certain members of the military establishment and the murders and imprisonment of innocent civilians are condemned. Also under attack are the entire workings of an army that turns conscripts into murderers, ignores the doubts of highranking officials, and prizes the following of orders above the value of human rights. *Amnesia* thus deals directly with many of the principal political and social issues confronting contemporary Chileans, whereas *The Frontier* focuses on the emotional effects of exile, avoiding direct confrontation with the military. For these reasons, the chapter begins with an analysis of *Amnesia,* as it is necessary to provide a historical and political context in any discussion of the film, a context that will also be useful in a reading of *The Frontier.*

Past and Future in *Amnesia*

Amnesia was the fourth film made by director Gonzálo Justiniano.[9] As the title suggests, the film focuses on issues of memory and amnesia in contemporary Chile, reflecting political debates bubbling under the surface in the 1990s and continuing into the twenty-first century, as Chile makes its transition to democracy from dictatorship. The film suggests that personal and national recovery from the traumas of the dictatorship years can only come with an end to officially endorsed amnesia. The following discussion places the themes of memory and a denial of the past in a social, political, and historical context. Flashbacks are used to represent memory in the film. In the following discussion, after analyzing the function of these flashbacks, key sections of the narrative present and past will be examined in detail to highlight the particular composition of the memories and the issues raised by them.

Memory and Denial: The Political Context

The emphasis on memory is to be expected in a country emerging from the long years of a dictatorship that silenced opposition groups and murdered and tortured citizens, then passed over the running of the state to elected parties on the condition that there would be immunity for the perpetrators of the crimes and that the armed forces would retain their autonomy.[10] Critics of the transition have argued that memory was sacrificed in the consensus politics of the late 1980s and 1990s.[11] Chilean cultural theorist Nelly Richards has argued that the official consensus of the transition rejected private memory (Richards, 1997, 29). In his critique of the transition, Chilean political scientist Alfredo Jocelyn-Holt Letelier states that, "more than one generation of Chilean politicians ended up turning its back on history" (Jocelyn-Holt Letelier, 1998, 225). The notion of a consensus in a Chilean context depends on a silencing of discord and a disavowal of the violence of the very recent past. The pact to pass from dictatorship to democracy in exchange for immunity for the military was made with political parties, not with citizens, and, what is more important, not with the victims and the families of the "disappeared" (*desaparecidos*).[12]

The regime and its supporters predictably emphasized the need to ignore the past and to secure their own positions. They had begun to protect themselves from future prosecution while in power, passing the Amnesty Law in 1978, which granted immunity to all those who committed crimes from September 11, 1973, until March 10, 1978, when the state of national emergency was lifted (*www.derechoschile.com/eng/about.htm*).[13] In a speech made two days after the twenty-second anniversary of the coup, Augusto Pinochet publicly called for the nation to forget the actions of his regime and for him and his allies to be free from prosecution:

It is best to remain silent and to forget. It's the only thing that to do. We must forget, and forgetting does not occur by opening cases, putting people in jail. FOR-GET, this is the word, and for this to occur, both sides have to forget and continue working. (*www.derechoschile.com/english/about.htm*)

Pinochet's declarations are also veiled threats, particularly as he was still the commander in chief of the armed forces when he made this speech.[14] These barely disguised threats surfaced just after the creation of the Comisión Nacional de Verdad y Resolución, (National Commission of Truth and Resolution), created in 1990 by Patricio Aylwin's government to investigate the murders carried out by the Chilean armed forces during the dictatorship years. One month after its establishment, an army major visited the head of the commission, Raúl Rettig, on Pinochet's orders, to express his concerns that the commission would be used as a political tool to discredit the armed forces. Aylwin's government, in response, assured the military that the report had no judicial powers. Once produced, the report disappointed opponents of the regime, as it examined only those cases in which the victims had died, thus ignoring the enormous number of cases involving torture. In addition, the report apportioned blame in very general terms, concluding that the state was guilty of excesses against human rights. As long as the Amnesty Law still stands, the Rettig report can achieve little in terms of justice for the victims.

An in-depth investigation into the past, with individuals accountable for their actions, has been rejected by the state as an impediment to the construction of the future. The response of national human rights groups to this denial of recent history has been to insist on the importance of memory, engaging in exhaustive work to find bodies and search for evidence to ensure that victims of the Pinochet regime are not forgotten, and to call for the punishment of the guilty (Richard, 1997, 41).

Justiniano's film dramatizes the two concepts of memory and denial, which determine how to interpret contemporary Chilean history. In *Amnesia*, cinema works alongside human rights groups to unearth history. As a medium, film can bring the dead back to life and present its own version of the truth through images of the past. The film can be located within the discourse of human rights activists, for whom the insistence on memory is not only a therapeutic means of invoking the presence of the "disappeared" but also a call for justice for those who have been tortured and lost their lives. In the words of Sola Sierra, president of the Association of Relatives of the Disappeared (Agrupación de Familias de Detenidos y Desaparecidos):

Remembering helps the people of a country avoid committing the same crimes, calling things by their name; a criminal is a criminal.... The worst thing that could happen in Chile ... would be for oblivion to do away with this problem. (*www.derechoschile.com/english/about.htm*)

Amnesia illustrates this view and condemns a culture of political consensus, in which selective amnesia is cultivated to ensure that military leaders go unpunished and that allies of the dictatorship will maintain their influence in the democracy.

Justiniano demonstrates the importance of memory by creating a protagonist, Ramírez (played by Pedro Vicuña), a former private in the Chilean Army who is unable to function in the present until he begins to explore his past. Only by coming face to face with his tormentor and superior in the army, Sergeant Zúñiga (played by Julio Jung), can he unlock the past and turn it into a narrative through memory. It is left to individuals to seek out the perpetrators of past crimes, to reconstruct their actions, and to punish them. In this climate, issues of justice and revenge become intertwined as there is no state apparatus to provide moral or legalistic guidance.[15]

These issues are additionally problematized in the film through an examination of the relationship of the individual to power structures. In this way, Justiniano adds a universal ethical dimension to a specific Chilean social issue. Military men are subject to conflicting moral systems: that which requires obeying orders from superiors in the hierarchy and that which calls for the respect of life. How each character responds to these systems is the key to determining the moral code of the characters and the film. What is particularly interesting is the ways in which *Amnesia* creates multiple levels of allegiances between prisoners and soldiers, all captives in the desert.

The Role of Flashbacks in Amnesia

The issues of memory, ethics, and bonds between men and women are raised in the film through the use of flashbacks. Ramírez is initially seen to be suffering from a form of mental illness; he is dependent on his wife to help him perform simple domestic tasks and is obsessively engaged in the search for Zúñiga, to the point that his obsession has previously resulted in his imprisonment. We learn this from his wife, who acts as if her husband's sudden disappearance from a bus when he thinks he has found Zúñiga is a regular occurrence.[16] It becomes clear that Zúñiga holds the key to Ramírez's memory, because once Ramírez meets Zúñiga, the flashbacks flow, telling the story of their time in the desert.

It has been argued that when official discourses fail to engage with recent history, it is left for individuals to construct personal histories through memory. The flashback is an ideal narrative form, because in the words of Maureen Turim, "[it represents] a privileged moment in unfolding that juxtaposes different moments of temporal reference. A juncture is wrought between present and past and two concepts are implied in this juncture:

memory and history" (Turim, 1989, 1). The use of flashback represents a psychological journey for Ramírez, as an exploration of his memories allows him to make sense of his past and construct a present. Turim explains that flashbacks often have parallels with psychoanalytic processes, with the "cure" located in the narration and interpretation of personal history (Turim, 1989, 18). In *Amnesia,* the past has to be unlocked and recounted through personal memory for Ramírez to be able to continue with his life. His psychological illness can be traced to the fact that he has been forced to kill an innocent man and woman and to bury other prisoners of the regime, killed by Zúñiga, while in the desert. Through sustained sequences of images of the past, which dominate the narrative once he has found Zúñiga, Ramírez understands the control that his superior has held over him, and is thus able to regain control over his enemy and over his actions in the present.

The flashbacks, as well as acting as a form of therapy for the protagonist, allow the viewers to make sense of the film. Ramírez initially appears disturbed, even slightly sinister, and his obsession with Zúñiga could be seen as psychotic. From the use of flashbacks, the audience learns to understand the protagonist and sees that he has been traumatized by his experiences in the desert. In this way, private individual memory becomes collective public memory, as personal images are projected onto the screens in movie theaters or on television. Through visual representations of memory, the film effectively challenges official rejections of the past.

The time of memory structures the narrative. Carrasco says to Ramírez when pleading for his life, "You don't know what it is to kill a man. You'd never forget," and Ramírez and Zúñiga, the two men who have killed, are never allowed to forget. Zúñiga has forced Ramírez to bury the dead in the desert; now private and sergeant unearth their memories, relive their actions in the desert, and give back life to the murdered. Viewers are given the illusion that they are directly witnessing the characters' past. Memories are represented as film, with the characters Ramírez and Zúñiga becoming the directors of their past, as they reconstruct the images. In this way, the flashbacks create a closer link between characters and viewers, as both are remembering/watching the same images.

Ramírez's journey back to the past is filled with infernal allusions, as it is a dark history, which has to be sought out if he is to create a new life. In his search for Zúñiga, he passes through an unlit alleyway and is told to go to hell by a solitary vagrant. There is a close-up of his face, but it has been obscured by the darkness of the night. He walks up a labyrinthine circular staircase, reminiscent of Jorge Luis Borges's images, and as he approaches an open fire, his shadow looms on the wall, conjuring up the self who hides in the past and eclipses his present realities.[17] The circular labyrinth here suggests the psychological journey that Zúñiga and Ramírez will have to face, as the past forms a circle with the present. This is followed by the appearance of the woman who leads Ramírez to Zúñiga (in exchange for money); she offers him a clove of garlic, an age-old symbol of protection against the devil. The search for garlic is linked to the search for Zúñiga, as Ramírez tells his wife he has gone out to buy garlic for their anniversary dinner. Paradoxically, to protect himself from evil, he has to seek out evil, to exorcise its effects. The hellish images continue when the audience learns that the location in the desert was known as the Ruta del Diablo (or "Devil's Route").[18]

The journey to the past, then, is represented as a descent to hell, to regain memory and to be able to cope with the present. Chilean director Pablo Perelman, speaking of the loss of memory caused by psychological trauma, claims that that there is amnesia if one is trapped within pain, but that if one overcomes that pain and turns it into something else, memory returns and life can continue.[19] This is the case with Ramírez, who has blocked out the past, until he transforms his pain into a possibility of seeking a personal form of justice/revenge, by making Zúñiga accountable for his actions.

The title of the film might appear to refer only to Zúñiga's choice to embrace a form of self-regulated amnesia that he has attempted to cultivate, to protect himself from his conscience. Nevertheless, it can be argued that Ramírez is also suffering from involuntary amnesia. In a classic Freudian sense, he has unconsciously repressed his memories of the desert, as they are too painful to accept. At the beginning of the film, there is a single eight-second flashback of a man sitting in the desert as a tower burns behind him. The scene seems coded and has no coherent meaning for the viewers. It is revealed in the last flashback of the film that this is a vision of the final moments in the desert, of Captain Mandiola (played by Nelson Villagra), sitting alone as the soldiers abandon the burning camp. The hermetic nature of the opening flashback suggests that Ramírez is trapped in a single memory, unable to live in a present without a past. Once he meets Zúñiga, however, amnesia, whether cultivated or involuntary, is impossible for either man. Ramírez is seen to be the focalizer of the first flashbacks, yet as they continue, it becomes increasingly difficult to determine whose personal history is represented, as both embark on a journey of shared memories. No one character is behind the eye of the camera, and the flashbacks are shot with the camera taking the role of literature's third-person omniscient narrator.

Memory is kept, in the context of the film, through the writings of one of the prisoners, Alvear (played by José Martin). Fearful of his imminent death, Alvear secretly writes his thoughts in a notebook, which passes to Captain Mandiola, then to Ramírez. Alvear's book comes to represent a counter-history; his words become a guide to a reading of the film, repeated by Mandiola, reread by Ramírez, and used indirectly by the director to explain the function of the flashbacks. These words are "Who understands men? One day perhaps after my death when these signs are the only testimony repeated by the mouths of the dead." The seemingly impossible image of the dead repeating words can only work through memory. The film gives those murdered back their voices by rescuing their testimonies. The key to the past lies with them, and attempts to silence their voices and forget their lives must be fought.

An analysis of the structure of the flashbacks and an examination of the links between the narrative present and the images of the time in the desert can provide a key to understanding the function of memory in the film. *Amnesia* is a carefully constructed film, with precise editing of the composition of the segments of the past and those of the present. There are seven sections of the film that form the narrative present and six flashbacks. The table on the following page presents a breakdown of the film's composition.

This listing shows that the film initially devotes more time to the present, in order to set the scene, until the past begins to direct the narrative. Nevertheless, until the flashbacks begin to flow, the film deliberately raises a series of unanswered questions: why has Ramírez not been able to manage by himself? Who is Zúñiga, and why is the protagonist engaged in an obsessive search for him? What is the book in Ramírez's drawer that he consults, and why is there a gun beneath the book? What is the memory that comes to him? So, although the narrative present initially dominates, it makes no sense without the past. This idea of Ramírez trapped in a meaningless present is illustrated when he tries, unsuccessfully, to see his reflection in a plate. The image is distorted and unclear, as he is a man without access to his past.[20]

The narrative structure of the film gives form to a key Chilean social issue: the present precedes the past, reflecting Chile's attempt to turn its back on its history and to build a future from the present. Yet the film is dependent on the flashbacks for meaning, an obvious parallel to the country's need to analyze its history. Once Zúñiga and Ramírez come face to face in the present, the past begins to dominate the narrative, with flashbacks two or three times longer than any of the scenes in the present. During the first three long flashbacks, made up of Ramírez and Zúñiga's memories, the focus on

Narrative Present	Flashbacks
1. Ramírez and his wife at the market and his search for Zúñiga (5 minutes, 30 seconds)	1. Man sitting by burning tower (8 seconds)
2. At home, Ramírez searches for garlic and meets Zúñiga (5 minutes, 46 seconds)	2. In the desert, shooting and burial of prisoners (11 minutes, 15 seconds)
3. In a bar with Zúñiga (1 minute, 10 seconds)	3. Ramírez reaches camp; encounter between Captain Mandiola and Alvear; soldiers and prisoners build camp(13 minutes, 48 seconds)
4. In a bar with Zúñiga (1 minute, 32 seconds)	4. Marta (one of the female prisoners) loses baby, shot by Zúñiga (2 minutes, 49 seconds)
5. On a street and at Zúñiga's job (night watchman) (4 minutes, 26 seconds)	5. Alvear finds water; López (one of the soldiers) and Gajardo (one of the prisoners) escape; Captain Mandiola breaks radio (3 minutes, 58 seconds)
6. On a bus with Carrasco (1 minute, 41 seconds)	6. Final scene of destruction of camp, murders of Alvear and Yolanda (one of the prisoners); Captain Mandiola sitting by burning tower (2 minutes, 50 seconds)
7. Zúñiga's ordeal and dinner (6 minutes, 13 seconds)	
Total time in present: 25 minutes, 18 seconds	Total time of flashbacks: 34 minutes, 48 seconds

the present is dramatically reduced, with brief cuts forward to the two characters in the bar. It is only once they have begun to significantly reconstruct key moments in the desert that the story in the present is able to unfold. A new plot begins at this point, that of Ramírez and Carrasco's plan to murder Zúñiga, and for a moment the past and the present occupy similar proportions of the film in terms of time (see no. 5 in the table above). In a classic psychoanalytic breakthrough, movement forward is possible once the traumas of the past have been faced. It is interesting to note that once the final scene in the desert has been projected, there are no more flashbacks, and the plot in the present can be concluded, suggesting closure and personal healing.

The images of the desert are chronological; memory is made into narrative as the events of this time period are pieced together and explained. It is never specified exactly when the events take place. We know from Captain Mandiola's final declaration that 183 days have passed, half a year, but he is unaware of the date: he marks the passing of time, as prisoners do, but loses sight of the precise dates, as there is little to distinguish one day from another. We can assume that the action takes place in the early years of the Pinochet coup, as the rules are still being written: the privates and the captain are shocked at the orders they receive to kill the prisoners, and the aging techniques used for the characters, such as Zúñiga's gray hair in the present, suggest that a significant number of years have passed.[21]

All flashbacks refer to the same period of time and the same place, and no other timescale in the past is referred to. It is not known what events occurred in any of the characters' lives from the time in the desert to the narrative present; for example, it is never explained how Ramírez met his wife. This is because the protagonists are all trapped in the time and space of the desert, the hostile environment where their humanity was under attack. The smooth editing by Danielle Fillios from the scenes of the present to those of the past and back highlight the close connections between the times. Zúñiga's words in the present are heard as they are transported to the past (see no. 3 in table); a bottle of whiskey thrown to Ramírez becomes a water canteen in the desert (no. 5 in table); Zúñiga shown face down after falling from the bus, cuts to a temporarily defenseless Zúñiga still asleep and in pajamas as Captain Mandiola takes control (no. 5 in table). A solitary, primitive swinging lamp also connects the two times; it is shown in the streets of the present and in the desert camp, with light symbolizing memory.[22]

A Reading of Key Scenes

Now that the function of flashbacks within *Amnesia* has been examined, a closer look at the content of some key scenes can bring to light a number of important themes. I will next examine the narrative present and the flashbacks in the last part of the film here, as this is where the audience sees the longest sequence in the past and the shortest in the present (see the table above). It also serves to illustrate the intention of the film to rescue history.

Key themes are established here of direct relevance to a postdictatorship society: principally, the question of individual responsibility for human rights abuses and the role of the imagination in constructing alternatives to hegemonic laws. Flashback 4 and the switch to the present are also discussed: here, Zúñiga's memory betrays him and forces him to let go of his selective amnesia and confront his conscience. This discussion concludes with an analysis of the final scenes in the present: Zúñiga's "trial" by Carrasco and Ramírez and the anniversary dinner. The characters' examination of the past has led to a form of personal justice and a resolution of trauma, and it is suggested that by confronting his tormentor, Ramírez has found a way forward.

In the third scene in the narrative present, the two men are in Zúñiga's drinking club, an underground world for ex-military men. It soon becomes apparent that images we have been witnessing are those of the story Ramírez has been telling Zúñiga of Carrasco's escape. Zúñiga attempts to justify his actions when asked by Ramírez why they had to kill him, by arguing that they were only following orders, someone had to clean up the world, and it did not matter now, as it was all in the past, a distant memory. Zúñiga is in a difficult position, as he needs certain memories to maintain his status. In the narrative present, he is living underground, emerging in the dark to work as a night watchman, with a false Uruguayan identity, and renamed Alcántara. His new name has symbolic value, as it is extremely close to *alcantarilla* (meaning "sewage"). In the world of the bar, he can reclaim his former identity as a sergeant. Nevertheless, his conscience has clearly been troubled by the acts of murder he has committed. As he tells Ramírez, a friend has helped him (and others) develop the theory of selective amnesia, "amnesia you control," a self-help therapy technique, whereby he remembers what makes him feel good and discards anything painful. The national parallels are clear.

His meeting with Ramírez destroys this selective amnesia and forces Zúñiga to confront his most painful memories. After the recounting of the events of Carrasco's escape, Zúñiga claims: "Time erases everything. Who'd have thought that it would all be just a memory, as if it had never happened?"

Yet, as he is speaking these words, flashback 3 begins. As the two timescales merge for a moment, the images directly negate Zúñiga's own negation, as both men are transported back to the desert. The flashback picks up where the last one left off, with Ramírez's return to camp after he has buried the bodies of the prisoners killed by Zúñiga. The burial and the long trek back to camp are his punishment for refusing to shoot the prisoners. The story has a dynamic of its own; the two men have started to relive their time in the desert, and the story must be concluded. The past moves forward until it can reach the present.

Within the flashback itself, important themes are raised, issues that can only be examined once memory is regained. One of the main concerns of the film is the conflict between obedience of orders and personal integrity. The military men are put to a moral test in the desert, a common biblical location for testing moral strength. Not only is the desert an effective metaphor for the harsh nature of dictatorship, signifying isolation from humanity, physical and emotional deprivations, and an absence of life and fertility, it is also a historically accurate location, as has been seen. Ramírez passes the first challenge in the previous flashback, in his first failure as a soldier, when he refuses to shoot the prisoners. There are clear parallels in Captain Mandiola's refusal to kill Alvear as ordered.

Captain Mandiola is a military man of the old school; his forefathers were in the army at a time when territorial wars were fought with neighboring countries. The fact that the film is set in the desert where wars with other republics were once fought shows the degeneration of a military waging war on its own people.[23] The absurdity of the situation is highlighted in the film by the ridiculous marching in the desert and the soldier who, night after night, looks through binoculars for imaginary enemies, seeing nothing but darkness. Mandiola is clearly unhappy at the role he is expected to play in the desert. As he tells his superior Marambio, "I don't even know what war we're fighting now." He communicates via the military radio with Marambio, who gives him orders at various points to kill the prisoners. Marambio is a faceless, disembodied voice, known by his code name, Fish Head (Boca de Pescado). Those who give orders never have to confront their victims, as Mandiola protests in their radio exchanges, while their hidden identities guarantee their immunity in the future. It is worth noting that the man who gives Zúñiga the orders to murder the prisoners on the road never reveals his name and has his face covered, while he too has received his instructions from nameless officials, all to prevent senior military men from being held responsible for murder.

During the radio exchanges, Mandiola is known by his code name, Fish Mouth (Boca de Pez). The meaning of the Spanish is lost in the English translation, as *pez* denotes a live fish, whereas *pescado* denotes the dead fish to be eaten. Marambio, as the head of the dead fish, gives the orders to kill, whereas Mandiola is the voice that gives life, refusing to kill Alvear, a Spanish journalist, and finally declaring unilateral peace and the freedom of the two remaining prisoners. This is overturned in the final flashback by Zúñiga, who has heard Marambio's orders to destroy the camp and the prisoners. Ultimately, no life can come from the head of the dead fish, and fish cannot live in the desert without water.

Significantly, Alvear finds water just as Mandiola rebels against Marambio, throwing his wireless valve to the floor when he receives his orders. Water in the desert represents the possibility of constructing a new world. Alvear excitedly tells the soldiers that they can now build a city stretching to the sea, where all will be equal and where they will live in harmony with nature. His utopian plans, however, coincide with Marambio's orders to have the camp destroyed. The message is clear: groups imprisoned by the regime are prevented from building their new world by forces of destruction.

Like Scheherazade in *A Thousand and One Arabian Nights,* the book Alvear is reading that is confiscated by Captain Mandiola, Alvear takes the role of the storyteller. He nurtures the imagination, telling both the soldiers and the prisoners of the possibilities of a better reality, with equality for all. Although Alvear is not always present in the flashbacks, and since his cannot be the gaze that controls the images, as he is dead, he can be seen to represent the director's voice. He is the one to tell Captain Mandiola that literature is as "harmful" for prisoners as for jailers, as they are all captives of the totalitarian regime, and literature, he implies, can help to free the imagination. As with Manuel Puig's *The Kiss of the Spider Woman,* freedom can be found within imprisonment, by creating alternative possibilities to hegemonic laws. Alvear, as a homosexual, has lived his life in opposition to societal gender codes, and it is significant that he is the one to show Mandiola that he can create new relationships and resist the brutal militarism represented by Marambio.

Mandiola initially attempts to assert his authority over Alvear, claiming he has power over Alvear and can destroy him at will, while Alvear is insignificant. All of this is negated by the fact that Mandiola is unable to kill Alvear. Moreover, the prisoner has moral authority over Mandiola and soon begins to influence the Captain's behavior: subsequent flashbacks reveal him growing obsessed with the wind, the symbol of freedom and imagination in the desert, and detaching himself from the realities of the prison camp. In the first flashback, the tension between thought and action was established as Ramírez chants, "don't think, just dig," to prevent himself from thinking about the fact that he is burying the dead. In an inverse replaying of this scene, Mandiola begins to think and can no longer carry out actions dictated to him. He writes while Marambio's voice is ignored in the background: "Just like the wind the silence eats away at my mind, and my thoughts. Why have doubts? Man has had to kill to survive from ancient times." Mandiola knows that the killing of innocent men and women has nothing to do with survival, and this fuels his doubts. His writing has a surreal frame: he is seen in the window of his headquarters, clouds reflected, symbolizing his thoughts, accompanied by opera music, representing his imagination escaping from the sordid reality.

Alvear and Captain Mandiola are destroyed by the military, yet through their memory they come to represent the possibilities for change. The writings of the two in Alvear's notebook offer personal histories of thoughts and feelings to counter the army's official version of the salvation of the country from dark communist forces. Mandiola initially tries to brush off notions that the military will have to face future accusations, claiming: "History has always been written by the winners, and the rest fall by the wayside." He is clearly referring to the military hierarchy as the winners, yet this is less clear in the context of the film. This history is written from the perspective of the moral victors, the prisoners, Captain Mandiola, and Ramírez. Once again, the film counters the suggestion that amnesia will protect the military. Ramírez becomes the keeper of history; the notebook is now in his possession and comes to symbolize the story in the desert, which his memory recaptures.

The flashbacks establish the ethical code of the film. Within the military, Captain Mandiola and Ramírez are both prepared to disobey orders that conflict with their own moral systems, showing the potential for change at the top and bottom ends of the military hierarchy. Mandiola could simply pass Zúñiga the orders to kill that he receives, who in turn would give the order to one of the privates, following the expected chain of command. However, Mandiola refuses to abdicate responsibility, and through this he becomes an unlikely hero of the film. By making a hero of a captain of the dictatorship, Justiniano has a clear position on the classical ethical dilemma of whether one is responsible for murder when one is following orders.

Zúñiga, the man in the middle, connects to the top of the military hierarchy by ensuring that Marambio's orders are carried out and has Ramírez murder the prisoners with a gun pointing at his head. The flashbacks constitute the evidence for Zúñiga's trial and, as shared memory, also force him to examine past actions that he has tried to bury in selective amnesia. He is most troubled by his murder of the prisoner Marta (played by Marcela Osorio) after she has lost her baby. The events — the miscarriage, Ramírez's support, Zúñiga's intervention, Marta's suicidal defiance, and the shooting — constitute the entire memory sequence. This is the only case

Zúñiga (Julio Jung) threatens Ramírez (Pedro Vicuña) in *Amnesia*.

where a single narrative fills the scenes of the past, highlighting the pivotal position of this event in the memories of both characters. The impact this has had on Zúñiga is seen when flashback 4 ends with a close-up of Zúñiga looking shocked as he comes out of the memory, as if waking from a nightmare. He takes refuge from his conscience by hiding behind his now forbidden military identity. He tries to block out the memory by whistling a military tune, shouting at Ramírez to march and sing with him, and shouting at a passerby to go home while declaring, "We are the army of the shadows."

Zúñiga has never had to face the consequences of his actions in the army and has shunned individual responsibility, hiding within the collective and in the underground world of secret identities and mutual "back scratching," as networks are created to protect ex-military men. He thus has never had to examine his behavior and remains the same man, in terms of values, as he was in the desert. This is made explicit when he makes frequent references to the good old days (when he had power) and tells Ramírez that they would do it all again if they had to. There are direct comments here relating to the contemporary situation in Chile: Zúñiga comments bitterly that he has been forced to go underground, whereas those who gave the orders are still in positions of power and are seen on television shaking hands with those who were formerly their prisoners. The point is that these men have not been called to justice and put on trial.[24]

Carrasco and Ramírez have a long-standing pact to execute their own form of personal justice/revenge, in the absence of national justice. They do not intend to allow Zúñiga any defense, as they know he is guilty; they intend to murder him. His crimes are many: he humiliates his inferiors, he kills with ease, he subverts Captain Mandiola's attempts to create a new peaceful order, and he finally succeeds in turning Ramírez into a killer. These crimes that condemn him are the actions that make him an exemplary soldier of the dictatorship. In this way, Zúñiga's trial is that of the military regime, his guilt is their guilt.

The final memory of the desert reveals the principal cause for Ramírez's illness, as it is here that audiences see Zúñiga aim a gun at Ramírez's head, insisting that he shoot Alvear and Yolanda (played by Myriam Palacios), the two remaining prisoners. Ramírez and the audience now have a series of images of the events and are able to see that he was turned into a killer through violence. He initially believed that he could gain revenge on the man who made him act against his principles by murdering him; however, he comes to understand that he can regain control over his actions by refusing violence. Zúñiga believes that if he asks Ramírez, the incapable killer, to shoot him, he has a chance of surviving. The audience is initially led to believe that Ramírez will shoot Zúñiga, as, following a close-up of the gun, he releases the safety catch and recites with a sinister smile, "It was hard, but I learned." There is a cut to the next scene, and suspense is maintained as the audience sees an unknown hand chop off the head of a fish, and witnesses Carrasco, Ramírez, and his wife at the dinner table. After focusing on the decapitated fish, the camera pans out to reveal a sniveling Zúñiga in the corner, his face contorted from being hanged by the other two.

The focus on the fish, a symbol used throughout the film, is significant. The symbol is first used at the beginning of the film, when a crate of dead fish is overturned as Ramírez is searching for Zúñiga, showing the obstacles he has to face in his journey to recapture his past in a country with collective amnesia. Just as Mandiola (code-named Fish Mouth) defied Marambio (code-named Fish Head), Ramírez and Carrasco take the power away from Zúñiga. If his trial can be seen to be that of the military regime, then this ending suggests that revealing the acts of violence and murder and forcing the guilty to acknowledge their crimes can remove their power. The head of the fish has been cut, suggesting not Zúñiga's death, as it initially appears, but the end of his control over his victims.

In a country with a legal system unwilling to try all the Zúñigas of the dictatorship years, Justiniano creates a dramatic trial: the flashbacks provide the evidence, and Zúñiga's punishment is to know the fear experienced at the point of murder and to be confronted with the memories he has tried to bury. Ramírez has made the former sergeant understand his own murderous actions by placing him in the position of his victims. The label "pig" that Ramírez and Carrasco put around Zúñiga's neck may initially appear childish; however, it represents an important reversal of the power relations. Both soldiers and prisoners have been dehumanized by Zúñiga in the desert, and he now experiences this treatment. Amnesia has been defeated; Zúñiga will never forget his actions, as he has shared his victims' fear, and Ramírez has recovered his time in the desert. By sparing his former sergeant's life, the man who forced him to murder, he is free of his control, no longer a submissive soldier of a dictatorship, but a citizen able to reconstruct his life.

Exile, Frontiers, and New Worlds in Ricardo Larraín's *The Frontier*

The Frontier can be seen as the film of the transition, marking the return of cinema to Chilean screens after years of exile.[25] It is fitting, then, that it takes the theme of exile as its subject. *The Frontier* is set in 1985 and examines the experiences of a *relegado*, an internal exile, in the later years of a dictatorship that, although alluded to, is never directly mentioned. As with *Amnesia*, historical reality is fictionalized to comment on contemporary Chilean society. Internal exile was a common measure taken by the Pinochet regime. People were sent to the most inhospitable parts of Chilean territory, such as the Dawson Islands in the Strait of Magellan, Pisagua, and Quiriquina Island in Talcahuano Bay. Many others went into exile abroad: by the end of the 1970s, there were hundreds of thousands of Chileans in western Europe (Collier & Sater, 1996, 360).

This film is set in an isolated town known only as The Frontier, cut off by the sea and prone to tidal waves.[26] In this way, the dissident protagonist, Ramiro (played by Patricio Contreras), is marginalized from the political capital, where it is believed that he will be forgotten. Nevertheless, Larraín takes the territory of the exile and places it center-stage, telling a story of a displaced nation through an individual. Exile, both internal and foreign, has become an intrinsic part of the national experience, and notions of home and a secure identity have been shattered by political and personal upheaval.

The Frontier plays out in fictional form real experiences and emotions of the dictatorship years, blurring the boundaries between fiction and reality. Ramiro's individual story clearly has national parallels and could help to explain the success of the film both at home and abroad.[27] A generation of Chileans have had to cope with the loss of their families, with torture, with internal and external exile, and with the return "home" to changed worlds. The film offers a representation of Chileans' ability to adapt to circumstances and of the possibilities of renewal after loss. Audiences are able to relate to Ramiro's experiences in a poetic, allegorical interpretation of Chilean history, without having to relive the most distressing events of the 1970s and 1980s. The coup of 1973 is never directly mentioned in the film, no murders or tortures are witnessed, and there are no brutal military men, only incompetent officials. In this way, the film contrasts with *Amnesia,* which focuses on the early 1970s in order to highlight murders committed by the military.

It is not surprising in a land caught between democracy and dictatorship that this is a film about frontiers. The notion of the frontier normally implies a crossing from one point to another, a bridge to be crossed on the journey to a destination; however, this film remains in the borderland. Set in the spaces in between, *The Frontier* is a film without certainties, where dichotomies are blurred. It represents a world where, as in *Amnesia,* the past is part of the present and the future, where sea invades land, where madness and sanity are relative terms, as are freedom and imprisonment, where everyday life is lived out on the margins of a tired dictatorship, where the heroes are the ordinary people, where the powers that be are impotent, where Catholicism and Mapuche beliefs live side by side, where national and personal histories converge, and where the political can only be understood through the personal.

It is in this world without fixed boundaries that Ramiro is able to reconcile his individual identity with his role in society. Reconstruction is possible precisely because this is a frontier territory. His personal struggle is a political struggle, and his individual search for a new identity after violent change is a national search. Ramiro, like the land he now inhabits, is in a fluid state of being; wrenched from his previous life, he has to adapt to create a new reality. Chileans watching this film in 1991 were also in the borderland between dictatorship and democracy, attempting to build a democratic society with Augusto Pinochet still head of the armed forces. The main point of the film is that new identities can be constructed in the wake of devastation through solidarity and friendship and by learning to understand the past in order to find strategies to live in the present and rebuild the future.

The fact that Ramiro is represented as an ordinary man is significant in this context because, although his experience is highly personal, audiences are invited to relate to his sense of alienation and gradual ability to adapt to new circumstances. Ramiro Orellana is not handsome, strong, or charismatic, nor is he ugly, weak, or dull. He has no exceptional qualities; the circumstances in which he finds himself are remarkable, but he is not. He is the victim of a dictatorship that cannot accommodate dissidence of any nature. His goals are those of most people: to find companionship, love, and an occupation. In an interview, director Larraín confirmed that this was his intention: "The film gives an image of an ordinary country, of the suffering of ordinary citizens rather than that of great heroes, or great political personalities" (Rodríguez, 1993, 31). Through this focus on the ordinary nature of the protagonist, *The Frontier* suggests that, in the wake of tortures, disappearances, and exile, it is the common man who has to create a social and political role for himself, to help rebuild a new community, to see himself as an agent, not a victim, of history.[28]

The geographical setting of the film is the perfect stage to play out the drama of the film. Ramiro can reinvent himself away from the metropolis and his life there as a teacher. The metaphor of the tidal wave captures violent periods of history (in this case, the Spanish Civil War and the Chilean military coup of 1973) and the traumatic effects of these events, and the watery feel to many of the images is significant. All of the opening scenes are accompanied by rain, and the panoramic shots of Ramiro's entry to the town blur the distinction between the land and the sea. There is a liquid texture to the images, which suggests the fluidity of identity of the exile and the flow of time with its constant changes. Internal exile is a paradoxical state, as Ramiro is both an outsider and in his own country. Once again, he is in the borderland, neither home nor abroad.

Ramiro

Ramiro arrives in the town lonely, without money, shelter, an occupation, or any idea of what awaits him. He is handed over like a piece of merchandise to the local officials, who have to sign a form confirming that they have received him in "perfect condition." The irony that a man separated from his home, family, friends, and job should be in perfect condition is wasted on the local officials, obsessed with following orders that never come. Ramiro has been wrenched from his former life and is momentarily deprived of all the elements that constitute selfhood. This is clearly part of his punishment. His internal exile is meant to be a form of imprisonment: he is unable to leave, as there is no escape from the town, and he has to sign his name several times a day at the office of the town's delegate (played by Alonso Venegas). However, on entering the frontier territory, Ramiro has been freed from the trappings of a fixed identity.

As with many journey narratives, there has to be a period of defamiliarization and disintegration of identity for the protagonist to be prepared to reinvent himself or herself within the new world he or she is entering. Ramiro's journey begins with a descent, typical of an entry into a hellish world, as he driven down a steep hill to the center of the town in the delegate's car. Scenes of desolation accompany his arrival. The rain-soaked land and a solitary skeletal tree speak of a harsh terrain, while the melancholic single trumpet chosen for the music adds to the sense of desolation and loneliness. In the first few scenes, a blue light indicates both day and night, as the relentless rain allows for no daylight. Ramiro is initially trapped in darkness that appears endless. The absence of a clearly defined new day indicates that he is in his own frontier land, caught between his past and his present.

The first local character he comes across is the drunken diver's assistant (played by Eugenio Morales) on the makeshift ferry, who mumbles something unintelligible about a big hole. This immediately suggests the initial lack of communication and emotional emptiness of this new world. The significance of this is only apparent later, when Ramiro begins to help the diver (played by Aldo Bernales) in his quest to fill the hole. Just as a new day eventually dawns, Ramiro becomes part of the project to fill the hole, the symbolic cause of destruction in the film. However, before he is able to build a new life for himself, he has to be open to admitting a new identity. This is symbolized in the film by the fever that almost kills Ramiro, just after his arrival. The fever can be seen as a physical manifestation of the trauma experienced as a result of being taken away from his previous life, and the subsequent treatment prepares him to be able to accept his new world. His illness and cure are a form of death and rebirth.

It is significant that Ramiro is cured by Hilda (played by Griselda Núñez), the Mapuche healer, while the officials are unable to do anything, and the priest, Father Patricio (played by Héctor Noguera), is tellingly absent. Hilda takes over the room in the parish, a pagan entry into a Christian space. She prays to the universal mother and father, male and female energies that rule the universe, watched over by a powerless figure of Jesus. Several readings are possible from this scene: it could be argued that Christianity and Mapuche beliefs unite to ensure Ramiro's recovery, or that Christianity is unable to bring about positive change. From the generally unsympathetic representation of the priest, seen in his hostility to Ramiro, the lack of spiritual guidance offered, and his failures to listen to Hilda's warnings of the tidal wave, it can be argued that there is a negative representation of Christianity in the film.

Hilda's cure is achieved through herbs and prayer, symbolizing a union between the spiritual and the physical worlds. Hilda tells the protesting officials that they have to give Ramiro the medicine, as she is too busy. The town officials obey her because Ramiro will die without the medicine, which would bring them problems with the higher authorities. This clearly shows that in the hierarchical system of the film, Hilda is the spiritual leader of the community and has a natural authority over the officials. The same point could be made regarding Maite (played by Gloria Laso), who is clearly shown to be the most able member of the community. Maite is a highly respected resident of the island; she is the daughter of the Spanish exile Don Ignacio. When Ramiro first arrives, she organizes his stay in the parish when faced with the incompetence of the town delegate and his secretary, who do not know what to do with him. Both Hilda and Maite are presented as the rightful lay and spiritual leaders of their communities, but they are victims of a dysfunctional system, where patronage appears to rule over merit.

Nevertheless, this is a land far from the military dominance of the capital city of Santiago, and the power of the delegate and his secretary never goes beyond the surface. Although they can make Ramiro sign his name every few hours, a ridiculous act in a land cut off by the sea, they never manage to have full control over Ramiro. Hilda, as the indigenous inhabitant of the land who understands its healing properties, is the one to prepare Ramiro spiritually and physically for his journey. Placing Hilda center stage is significant, as she belongs to a discriminated group. The Mapuche lost most of their lands in the southern third of the country in 1882 and were forced by the army to live in tribal reservations.[29] Their language, Mapudungun, was not recognized until 1993 by President Aylwin's government, and, according to a national census carried out in 1992, 90 percent of Mapuches were living in poverty.[30] Larraín claims an important place for Hilda by making her the benign force in the film and by representing her language as endowed with a mystical power. It is she who provides the main belief system in her prayers for the need for balance between people and the earth and the union of male and female energies.

These energies come together in the characters of Maite and the diver. Ramiro, the stranger, arrives in this town caught between the sea and the land and finds guides to the land in Maite and to the sea in the diver. The relationships are mutually supportive, as he too brings love and companionship to Maite and assistance to the diver in his search for the elusive hole. Maite, like so many Chileans of her generation, has lost her family to the tidal wave, a symbol of political violence, while the diver searches the sea for the causes of the wave, of the violence. They both teach Ramiro the importance of understanding personal and national history and his place in it if he is to be part of the project to build a better future.

Maite

Maite is the first person with whom Ramiro has any intimate contact, and from the outset of their friendship, she makes the connection between personal and national histories. She links her exile from Francisco Franco's Spain following the fascist victory in the civil war of the 1930s to her abandonment by her partner, the father of her child, to the tidal wave in which her mother and son died, to the Chilean military coup of 1973. The coup is not directly mentioned, but by telling Ramiro, "And then we lost again," Maite indicates that she shares in the collective tragedy that transcends Ramiro's particular circumstances. Maite's mother and child, lost at sea in the tidal wave, become metaphors for the "disappeared" generations following the coup, whose bodies, in many cases, have never been found.[31] She says all this to Ramiro as they are eating lunch next to Maite's family home, destroyed by the tidal wave: a shared act takes place in the ruins of the past, as they sit by the sea, which can be seen to represent time. Past, present, and future converge in this scene; by sharing stories of the past, Maite is laying the foundation for a relationship that can bring solace to both of them.[32]

It is significant that the two first make love after Ramiro brings Maite a doll paperweight, her child's toy that the diver has rescued from the sea, suggesting that he can only love her once he has accepted her past, and she can only love him once she is able to share her grieving. Maite has been unable to bury her mother and son because they are lost at sea, and the doll is at least a physical presence that she can relate to her child. There are hints at national parallels here, with relatives and friends unable to bury the bodies of their murdered loved ones, and thus unable to complete the grieving process.[33]

On a poetic level, Maite's tears suggest a union with the sea, which has, as the diver says, given back what it has taken. The union with nature would have a symbolic completeness with Ramiro's semen entering her. Nevertheless, their lovemaking is interrupted by the town officials, hysterical because Ramiro is late signing his name in the book they use to keep control of his movements. Neither character can build a successful present and immediate future, because, despite their union, they are still living on the margins of a despotic society where their leaders are incompetent, controlling, and out of

Maite (Gloria Laso) holds her dead father (Patricio Bunster) in *The Frontier.*

touch with, but in fear of, the centralized military leadership. Maite rejects a future with Ramiro, refusing to leave with him for Santiago and choosing death over life in the second tidal wave. Once again, the implication in national terms appears to be that the country cannot build a successful future until it finds and buries its dead. It is tempting to add that the film is calling for the perpetrators of the crimes to be brought to justice, but all is allegory, and there is no direct reference to the executors. The emphasis in this film is on the survivors and their strategies for coping.

Ultimately, Maite has been too scarred by her personal history to cope with the second tidal wave. The final shot of Maite is of her holding her dead father in her arms, humming to him a child's lullaby, deaf to Ramiro's pleas for her to leave with him. Her mother and father represent her past; her child, her truncated future. They have now all been taken by the tidal waves, and she is left without a present. She finds her future in her choice to stay with her father and seeks her liberation in death. The audience is never shown her drowning or suffering, and her death is thus represented as peaceful deliverance as she prepares to step out of time.

The Diver and the Sea

The sea in *The Frontier* is the symbol that gives the film a poetic unity. It is both an unruly force that unleashes its power in the form of tidal waves and a nurturing force that sustains the land, provides its beauty, and feeds its inhabitants. The sea represents the waves of time that make up history, reflecting constant change with its periods of calm and periods of violence. The tidal wave is at once a literal and symbolic means of representing violence, brutality, and the disharmony between humanity and nature. If the sea represents time, then Ramiro's work with the diver, exploring the sea and searching for the hole, can be seen as a metaphor for his entry into history. Together they attempt to unlock the mysteries of the past and restore balance to the world they inhabit.

The diver is a mythological figure who inhabits the spaces of land and sea: he is given no name and is never seen in any clothes other than his diving suit. Nothing is known about him beyond that which pertains to his occupation. A realistic reading would perhaps search for clues to his obsession with tidal waves by assuming that he has lost family and friends in the previous tidal wave; however, this could be no more than conjecture, as no clues are given. Whenever Ramiro accompanies him on his boat, the sun is shining and the sea is calm and blue. This is in clear contrast to the dark, rain-soaked scenes of Ramiro, the delegate, and his assistant. The diver provides the optimism of the film. He has dedicated his life to understanding the cause of the tidal waves and attempting to prevent further devastation.

Ramiro first comes across the diver as he is forced to beg for some food on credit in the local bar, because his money has not arrived. He overhears a monologue, heavy with symbolic meaning, directed by the diver to his alcoholic assistant. He is trying to alert his partner to the dangers occasioned by his drinking, as his job is to pump air to the diver when he is under water. As the diver is telling his assistant that his life depends on him, the assistant dies, clearly unable to even sustain his own life. Just as the diver depends on his assistant, Ramiro depends on the goodwill of the waitress in providing him the with food. This scene reveals the inability to survive alone and introduces one of the key messages of the film: the need to work collectively in the search for a better future.

The diver's assistant has poisoned and destroyed his own body, just as the Mapuche healer claims the colonizers have poisoned the veins of her land. Man and sea as part of the natural world can work together only when they have a respect for each other and themselves. This is why the sea reveals its secrets to Ramiro and the diver and allows them to find the statue of the country's independence leaders, along with the locals' possessions lost in the last tidal wave. The diver's union with Ramiro is significant as both in their own way are resisting the forces of destruction that have fallen upon their country. Ramiro has sacrificed his "freedom" by acting in solidarity with a colleague, and the diver is attempting to secure the town's safety.

Through his research, the diver has come to believe that there are two seas with a hole connecting them. He explains to Ramiro that the water under the lower sea heats up and rises up the hole. The intense volume of water is the cause of the tidal wave. It is never clear how finding the hole will solve this problem; however, as with most romantic searches, reaching the destination is all that occupies the imagination, not what happens when the destination is reached. It is interesting that the diver reads of the Mapuche myth of Tentén-vilu, the goddess of the land who fights to overcome Coicoi-vilu, the sea serpent who caused the waters of the sea to rise in order to destroy all living creatures on the land. Tentén-vilu succeeds in raising the land and saves people by turning them into birds or enabling them to fly. Nevertheless, the waters never returned to their original limits, and the archipelago of Chiloé was created.[34] In a sense, the diver takes on the role of the goddess of the land, attempting to find the hole, another version of the sea serpent.

The diver, however, is working in isolation, caught between myth and science, attempting to translate back issues of *National Geographic* without understanding much English, and lacking an assistant. This isolation and a lack of communication with others in the field lead to his mistaken views on the causes of tidal waves. He is a victim of the underdevelopment in which he finds himself.[35] Nevertheless, the diver's search has to be seen in a symbolic/mythical light, as indicated by the way in which it is represented in the film. As the diver tells Ramiro of his theories, they are on top of a hill overlooking the land and sea. The diver circles Ramiro, and the use of a close-up shot makes him look larger than he is. He is in the center of the frame and almost appears to be rising from the sea, like a mythical sea-creature. A large rainbow covers the land and sea, suggesting, in biblical imagery, that they have not been forgotten, that there is still hope for a better future. The music in this scene also creates a sense of wonder and awe at the mysteries of the sea. One synthesized chord held throughout generates suspense, while three notes repeated over the chord here and at other key moments of the film produce a watery, haunting sound.[36]

The hole is a dystopian symbol for all that is wrong; it can be seen to represent lack, disharmony, emptiness, the forgotten past. The urge to find and fill the hole takes on a mythical dimension and can be seen as part of the history of the search for the utopian dream. In an inverse reworking of the biblical myth of the Promised Land, the search here is for the causes of destruction, to find peace and harmony to create a new land. In one of the key scenes of the film, the hole is linked to the search for the past in order to find the future. This is when Ramiro finds "El Abrazo de Maipú," the statue of the embrace of José de San Martín and Bernardo O'Higgins, the heroes of the struggle for Chilean independence.[37] This event is marked by a poetic intensity, as it is also Ramiro's first dive, suggesting that his apprenticeship is over and he is now ready to enter the mysteries of the sea. The significance of the dive is highlighted by the preparation: Ramiro is naked as though ready for a new beginning as his friend dresses him in his diving suit; he then carefully and slowly places his helmet on Ramiro's head in a ceremonial manner. As Ramiro plunges into the water, the camera takes the viewer down with him to share his wonder at this new world. This is the first time viewers have been in the sea, as we have always stayed with Ramiro on the boat during the diver's descents. Once on the seabed, Ramiro appears as a barely perceptible shadow amid the deep blue. The synthesized music accompanying the dive is mystical and otherworldly and interprets the sounds Ramiro is hearing through his helmet. The same three notes heard when the diver is explaining his theories of tidal waves are repeated, providing a sense of thematic unity.

Ramiro declares in awe as he and the diver lift the statue, "The founding fathers of the nation on the bottom of the sea." This is particularly significant because the diver had informed Ramiro as he was about to dive that they were close to the hole, the hiding place of history that has taken their past from them. The message is implicit: Chile has been left without any valid leaders following the coup and has to look to its buried past for inspiration. The lessons of history are there for those who know how to find them, and by working together and with nature, Chileans can find a way to recover their independence. It is striking that Ramiro is declared free just after he has erected the statue of the liberators, suggesting that knowledge of the past can lead him to a form of personal freedom. Once again, the scene plays out the interconnected nature of the personal and the national, the past and the present. The nature of freedom is, of course, questioned in the film. Was Ramiro any freer in Santiago, living under the dictatorship, and would a return to his former life be possible now that he has lived a different reality? The fact that Ramiro does not know if he wants to return to Santiago hints at some of these complexities.

The diver, like Maite, finds death and a form of liberation in the second tidal wave. As everybody is running to the hills for shelter, he is seen enveloped in a blue light, in his diving suit costume and helmet, walking into the sea. The illuminated blue, the triumphal music, and the farewell wave he gives the priest, who is trying to make him stay, suggests that this is his time of deliverance. There is the sense as he walks into the sea that he is returning home. He is a diver looking to fathom the mysteries of the tidal wave, and this is his chance. He sacrifices his life in the belief that he is pursuing knowledge that can save his community.

Endings and New Beginnings

The final scenes of *The Frontier* are interesting in that the second tidal wave would be expected to be catastrophic. Nevertheless, as seen in the representation of Maite's and the diver's assumed deaths, there is a sense of relief and even celebration in this cataclysmic occurrence. The film takes on an otherworldly quality as the effects of the sea's invasion of the land are shown. A mystical impression is created as people running to the cemetery are filmed in slow motion, accompanied by haunting music. The people are silhouetted against a blue illuminated light, like beings entering a new world. Later, the camera merges with that of the national television crew come to film the aftermath of the tidal wave. The camera shows the view from the helicopter and highlights the landscape in an impressive piece of cinematography (by Juan Carlos Castillo), as the beauty of the scene is shown in shots reminiscent of nature documentaries.

As has been seen throughout the film, the metaphoric potential of the tidal wave has been well exploited. Parallels have been drawn by Maite and Don Ignacio between the first wave and Franco's dictatorship in Spain and Pinochet's coup in Chile. The second wave occurs in 1985, and the celebratory tone of these scenes suggests societal changes taking place. The 1980s have been described as a period of "the renewal of politics," as political movements grew and resistance to the dictatorship became more vocal, culminating in the transition to democracy by the end of the decade (Collier & Sater, 1996, 378). Although none of these events are mentioned in the film, and indeed some took place after the time period covered in *The Frontier,* the screenplay (by Larraín and Goldenberg) for the film was written in the late 1980s and was first shown in 1991, and the sense of renewal felt in the country is echoed in the final scenes of the film.

The day after the tidal wave, viewers witness the first full sunrise, as golden orange fills the screen, suggesting the dawning of a new era. Forces of history can bring times of violence, as represented by the first tidal wave, as well as times of peace and there is hope that the next period will be one of peace. Women, children, and men reach a new equality in their bid to survive; the priest and Hilda share a space for their prayers. The previously useless town officials are shown helping people to reach the hills. The last scenes appear to suggest that the tidal wave has cleansed the people of the frontier town and offered them the possibility of reforming social relations. Hilda's voice is heard over the priest's calling for the union of male and female energies that govern the earth to redress the imbalance caused by the patriarchal misrule of her land. She has known how to read the signs of nature warning of the tidal wave, while the priest has been blind to the evidence of the world around him, paradoxically begging Jesus for a sign to guide him. It is also significant that the people flee to the cemetery to escape, reinforcing the message that they can learn the lessons of their future from their ancestors, and life and renewal can follow death. The final scenes of the film thus provide a message that is historical, collectivist, and ecological: people in the new Chile have to listen to the past and work together and in harmony with nature to construct a better world.

Ramiro ends the film as a man with a new political and personal consciousness. He has lost his lover and his friend to the tidal wave and is connected to the grief of his country's victims of the years of violence. Yet, each of his friends has had a part to play in Ramiro's development during his time in exile: Maite provides Ramiro with an emotional home and insights into personal history; the diver gives Ramiro a role within his new community, and together they search the sea for clues to the past and the future; and Don Ignacio teaches him the value of political resistance. At the start of the film, Ramiro is unaware of the societal role he has to play and sees his defense of his colleague as a purely individual act of friendship. When Don Ignacio tries to convince Ramiro of the subversive power of his action, he denies that it has any importance, and he seems unwilling to connect it to a national context. It is interesting that it takes a man living on the border between sanity and madness to make this important connection. Once again, Larraín highlights the creative potential of the borderland. Ramiro's second defense of his colleague, in which he names him in front of the television cameras, is a conscious political act.[38]

The film ends with Ramiro's appearance on television. Fiction and fictionalized documentary merge for a moment, placing Ramiro's story in a national context. The arrival of the television crew hints at the potential role of media communication in this new world: to inform people of the personal histories of those who have been victims of the dictatorship. The program makers know that Ramiro's comments are unlikely to pass the censors; nevertheless, stories are there waiting for the right moment to be told. The right moment is in fact five years later, when this film was made.

The final scene suggests that, despite the trauma faced by the loss of Maite, Don Ignacio, and the diver, Ramiro will have a place in the new Chile. All these characters have crossed over their borderlands to death, or to new life, in Ramiro's case. The film has not witnessed the birth of a superhero ready to single-handedly defeat the forces of evil, nor a new prophet, ready to lead his people out of oppression. However, thanks to his friends, Ramiro has learned to work within a community, and to love again. He is also a newly politicized man who has accepted the role that his fate has given him.

Conclusion

Both *The Frontier* and *Amnesia* search for a direction for the future of their country through an exploration of the past. Ramiro and Ramírez embody different national issues, each of particular relevance to contemporary Chile. *The Frontier* explores the condition of the exile; *Amnesia*, the condition of a man traumatized by the violence of the dictatorship years. Ramiro learns lessons relating to nature and relationships, and he discovers how to read the past from his present circumstances. He becomes a new man in the frontier land, able to take an active role in a Chilean democracy. In *Amnesia*, the characters are held captive by the dictatorship that controls their present and past. Ramírez cannot belong within the time of the present until he meets his tormentor and is able to force Zúñiga to examine his actions and their consequences. There is an underlying call for national justice throughout the film, and its absence leads to a form of revenge/personal justice. In contrast, *The Frontier* does not demand retribution, does not name the guilty; rather, it tells of personal survival and the importance of solidarity between the victims of the forces of violence.

Each film, then, employs different strategies to examine recent history. Nevertheless, both *The Frontier* and *Amnesia* dramatize the need to confront the past and to tell stories that have been silenced and denied. They call for the past to be brought into the present to allow progress and the creation of a future free from violence and oppression.

Notes

1. Paul Julian Smith writes that *La frontera* celebrates "the survival of a national cinema" after years of dictatorship and notes that the Chilean president, Patricio Aylwin was at the film's premiere in Santiago in 1991 (Smith, 1995, 46). The appearance and success of *Amnesia* three years later helped to consolidate the newly emerging film culture within the country.

2. For an analysis of Chilean cinema during the Allende years and in exile, see King (1997, 397–419). For further analysis and a comprehensive list of directors working abroad during the Pinochet years, see Pick (1997, 423–40).

3. I am grateful to Chris Perriam for this source.

4. For other prizes won by *The Frontier*, see *http://filmo.cl.Pages/LARRAIN.HTM.*

5. According to Larrían, "*The Frontier* generated many expectations and things didn't work out like that. When I received the prize in the Berlin Film Festival, a jury member said to me, laughing: 'If you lived in Europe, you'd have your next three films guaranteed, but you're going to return to your country, where there's no cinema, and this prize will mean nothing in concrete terms.' And it's true" (*www.filmo.cl.pages/LARRAIN.HTM*, my translation).

6. See *www.filmo.cl.pages/LARRAIN.HTM*. Larraín's latest film, *El Entusiasmo* (*Enthusiasm*), a Spanish/Chilean coproduction, opened in Santiago in December 1998. However, it did not achieve the same success as *The Frontier* and has not been widely distributed, beyond Spain, Argentina, and Mexico. The film, also cowritten with Jorge Goldenberg, tells the story of three young friends and their progress through life in contemporary Chile; it looks at the conflict between utopian ideals and market forces and personal greed. For more on this, see *http://secure.catalog.com/film/cannes99/html/quinzaine24.htm.*

7. Rich (1997) cites an article in the *New York Times* (unsourced), discussing the therapy methods used to ease the pain of traumatized children of "the disappeared." The article concludes that "the telling of secrets necessary to drain the political — and emotional — wounds" has been the most effective form of therapy (283). Rich clearly means to apply this conclusion to filmmaking in postdictatorship societies.

8. Ramiro's wife had been more involved in the political struggle and has just returned from exile in the Netherlands with their son, who is caught between a Chilean and Dutch identity. Ramiro's lack of interest in her political activity is brought out as a reason for their separation when she comes to visit him.

9. Justiniano's three feature films made before *Amnesia* were: *Hijos de la guerra fría* (1986), a French coproduction in French and Spanish, which won a number of international awards; *Sussi* (1987), a film that ridicules Augusto Pinochet and his supporters' campaign to win the 1989 plebiscite; and *Caluga o menta* (*Candy or Mint,* 1990), a film about marginalized young people in contemporary Chile. His latest film is *Tuve un sueño contigo* (1999).

10. Augusto Pinochet remained as commander in chief of the armed forces and declared himself senator for life. On March 11, 1998, he took his position in the National Congress, after ensuring that a law was passed that stated that any leader who served for a minimum of six years had parliamentary immunity. He was sworn in in front of supporters, as well as opposition politicians who had been in exile and persecuted. Safeguards to ensure his immunity from prosecution were tested when the Spanish judge Baltasar Garzón insisted in 1999 that Pinochet be detained while on a trip to England and extradited to face charges of crimes against humanity in Spain. The extradition requests were finally turned down in March 2000 by British Home Office Minister, Jack Straw on grounds of mental health. On July 1, 2002, the Supreme Court in Chile also ruled that Pinochet was mentally unfit to stand trial there, and on July 4, in response to this, Pinochet stood down as senator-for-life.

11. Opposition groups famously won the plebiscite of 1988 to vote on whether or not Pinochet should stay in power. By 1989, the democratic coalition, the PDC (Concertación de los Partidos por la Democracia), had won the elections, and by 1990, Patricio Aylwin had been elected president of the country. For more on this, see Collier and Sater (1996).

12. The term *disappeared* (*desaparecidos*) is used principally to refer to those unaccounted for, and assumed to have been murdered, during the military dictatorships in Argentina, Chile, and Uruguay.

13. The Amnesty Law was drafted by Mónica Madariaga, justice minister from April 1977 to February 1983. From the time of the transitional democratically elected government in 1990,

human rights defenders have fought to have the law repealed or amended, but they have had no success.

14. Ricardo Zurieta, Pinochet's successor as commander in chief of the armed forces in 1998, also emphasized the need to disavow the past in the Chile of the transition. In a speech made on May 27, 1998, he said, "We have to protect the previous Army leadership.... And in my personal opinion I do not think it is advisable to look back at things that happened in the past.... These situations must be analyzed by history itself because it is not convenient to get into situations that will provoke confrontation in this country" (*www.derechoschile.com/ english/about.htm*).

15. In his play *Death and the Maiden* (*La muerte y la doncella,* 1995), Ariel Dorfman also dramatizes the inevitable confusion between justice and revenge when there is no legal system in place to defend the victims of the military dictatorship. There are other parallels between the play and Justiniano's film, as the protagonist, Paulina, can only begin to explore the torture she experienced once she comes face to face, fifteen years later, with the doctor who supervised the torture and raped her. See also the film of the play, Roman Polanski's *Death and the Maiden* (1994).

16. Ramírez dramatizes a widespread psychological problem, clearly linked to the traumas of the previous years. According to the World Health Organization, in 1994, (the year the film was released), Santiago, Chile, ranked number one as the city with the highest recorded percentage of its population with mental health problems (Jocelyn-Holt Letelier, 1998, 287).

17. Circular labyrinths feature in Borges's writings, particularly in his collection of short stories, *Fictions* (*Ficciones,* 1992). They symbolize the impossibility of finding the truth through metaphysical searches.

18. The exact location in the desert is never specified. It is worth noting that Pinochet's regime founded prison camps in the Atacama Desert. See *Inside Pinochet's Prisons* (1974), a fascinating TV documentary about the existence of two camps in Chacabuco and Pisagua, made by an East German film crew using 16mm black-and-white cine cameras. The film was allowed to be made as the crew posed as West Germans sympathetic to the regime. It was broadcast on Channel 4 in Great Britain in 1999, at the time of Pinochet's detention in London. Chacabuco was an isolated camp about 110 kilometers (68 miles) from Antofagasta in the middle of the Atacama Desert. Between 600 and 1,000 prisoners were sent to Chacabuco between 1973 and 1975. For more on this, see the Web site *www.derechoschile.com/english/chacabuc.htm.*

19. Quoted in *Chile: la mémoire obstinée* (*Chile, Obstinate Memory,* directed by Patricio Guzmán, 1997), a powerful documentary about the importance of memory in the Chile of the transition.

20. Mirrors are used at various points to symbolize the characters' relationship with their past or with their conscience. Captain Mandiola's reflection is distorted by a crack in the mirror when the audience first sees him. In the final scene in which he appears, the crack has disappeared from the mirror, significant because he has regained the military tradition to which he belongs, is fully dressed in uniform, and has decided to disobey his superior's orders.

21. As is common with fiction and film made about the dictatorship years in Chile, there is little emphasis on dates or names of historical agents. See Ariel Dorfman's *Widows* (1997) and *Death and the Maiden,* Isabel Allende's early novels, and *The Frontier* (1991). In the latter, the coup itself is never referred to, nor are any political or military figures named. This helps to make universals from specifics and turns history into allegory.

22. I am grateful to Mónica Riera for this point.

23. Border disputes dominated Chilean foreign affairs throughout the nineteenth century. The War of the Pacific (1879–1983) is an example of a border dispute between Bolivia, Peru, and Chile that degenerated into war. At stake were the rich mineral deposits found in the

Atacama Desert. The Chilean Army was felt to be successful in this conflict, as it was less political and more professional than the armies of Peru and Bolivia. This is the tradition to which Captain Mandiola belongs.

24. Gonzálo Justiniano has spoken of how nobody dared talk about military culpability until the Contreras case. Manuel Contreras Sepúlveda was the director of Pinochet's security forces, the DINA (Dirección Nacional de Inteligencia). He was given a seven-year prison sentence for his role in the murder of Orlando Letelier, the minister of defense under Allende, and Letelier's North American assistant, Ronnie Moffit, in Washington, D.C. These are crimes that are not covered by the Amnesty Law because they were committed in a foreign country. See the Web site *www.derechoschile.com/complices.htm.* The Contreras case came to light just after the release of the film (García & Alejandro Ricagno, 1995).

25. *The Frontier* is described as the film of the transition in "Interview with Larraín" (*www.filmo.cl.pages/LARRAIN.HTM*).

26. *The Frontier* was filmed in Puerto Saavedra, an isolated town cut off from land by the tidal wave of 1961 and Nueva Imperial, a neighboring town, both in the Ninth Region. The region is known as The Frontier, as it borders the Mapuche lands, which were not incorporated into the national territory until 1882. Fiction and reality merge here in the selection of the location and the themes of the film. Puerto Saavedra has 200 inhabitants, a number of whom were used as extras in the film (Castrillón, 1993, 26).

27. *The Frontier* was particularly successful in Chile, where it was shown in one theater for eight months in 1992. It had the highest box office receipts for a Chilean film in twenty-five years (Rodríguez, 1993, 33).

28. The emphasis on *man* here is deliberate. As Chris Perriam has pointed out, the film follows traditional Western narrative, "underpinned by the assumption that it is men who have destiny problems, men who have destiny" (Perriam, 1996, 6). He argues that the women in the film take more supportive, healing roles.

29. For more on Mapuche history, see Pablo Mariman Quemenado *Elementos de historia Mapuche* (available at *www.xs4all.nl/~rehue/art/mariman.html.*)

30. See the Web site dedicated to human rights in Chile, *Perfil de Chile hoy* (available at *www.derechoschile.com/espanol/perfil.htm*).

31. I owe this observation to students in my Latin American Literature and Film course at Portsmouth University.

32. B. Ruby Rich's comments on the therapeutic importance of telling of secrets in Latin American films of the newly democratic societies in the 1980s, "to drain the political — and emotional — wounds," are also relevant here (Ruby Rich, 1997, 283).

33. See Ariel Dorfman's play *Widows* for a dramatic representation of this theme (Dorfman, 1997).

34. See the Web site *www.geocities.com/Athens/6928/tenten1.htm.*

35. The diver is reminiscent of one of Gabriel García Márquez's male characters in *One Hundred Years of Solitude,* whose discoveries have been made at times centuries before, but who, because of his isolation and underdevelopment, is ignorant of knowledge beyond time and space.

36. The other key moments are Ramiro's first dive and the diver's entry into the sea to certain death during the last tidal wave.

37. José de San Martín (1778–1850), the Argentinean independence fighter, joined forces with the Chilean Bernardo O'Higgins (1778–1842), Commander in chief of the patriot cause, against the Royalists, in the fight for Chile's independence against the Spanish colonialists. The Maipú embrace refers to the famous battle on the plains of Maipó in April 1818, when O'Higgins secured victory for the patriots by coming to San Martín's rescue with reinforcements (Collier & Sater, 1996, 38). The use of O'Higgins as a symbol is interesting, as he was

taken as a national hero by the Pinochet dictatorship, while his compatriot, Manuel Rodríguez, has become an important figure for the revolutionary left-wing opposition. The film, through Ramiro, is effectively reclaiming a national hero for the opposition. I am grateful to Ann Matear for this point.

38. Naming the "disappeared" is a way of remembering them and an important form of opposition to the military, who have tried to literally disappear their murdered victims to secure their impunity. See the wall of the dead, which lists the names of the "disappeared,"in Patricio Guzmán's film *Chile: la mémoire obstinée* (*Chile, Obstinate Memory,* 1997).

4

Representing Inequalities

The Voyage by Fernando Solanas and
I the Worst of All by María Luisa Bemberg

Fernando Solanas (b. 1936) and María Luisa Bemberg (1922–1995) are the best-known Argentine directors of their generation and are highly respected in national and international critical circles.[1] Both directors see filmmaking as a political enterprise and use their films to highlight specific injustices and to suggest solutions to inequalities, with Solanas promoting a socialist view of society and Bemberg advocating feminism. Solanas's *The Voyage* (*El viaje*, 1991) and Bemberg's *I the Worst of All* (*Yo la peor de todas*, 1990) are good examples of committed, socially engaged films, although each has its own approach and focus. *The Voyage* is an ambitious film that locates all of Latin America's ills in political and economic failures, whereas *I the Worst of All* is concerned with institutional misogyny, and uses the historical figure of Sor Juana Inés de la Cruz to make a feminist appeal for equality of opportunity for women and men. Through an analysis of the creation of heroes, heroines, and villains, representations of class and gender, and interpretations of history, this chapter examines the ways in which each film promotes its political and social vision.

Heroes, Villains, and Women:
Representations of Latin America in *The Voyage*

Written and directed by Fernando Solanas, *The Voyage* (1991) is the story of a young man's journey through Argentina, Bolivia, Peru, Brazil, and Mexico in search of his father and a Latin American identity. Solanas uses his hero's voyage of self-discovery to present his own vision of Latin American realities. *The Voyage* is a didactic film, with the lessons the protagonist Martín Nunca learns directed at implied audiences. He discovers the devastation caused by neoliberal economic policies and corrupt politicians who sacrifice national sovereignty to foreign, principally U.S., interests.

This section, through a close study of *The Voyage*, Solanas's most ambitious film to date, explores an example of oppositional cinema in the 1990s and examines the ways in which the director uses a range of approaches to represent Latin American social and political conditions, including cartoons, satire, a grotesque form of the absurd, and social realism, all combining to produce an epic text that seeks to be a model of Latin American filmmaking.[2] The section presents Solanas's views on filmmaking and his opposition to what he sees as Hollywood aesthetics and examines *The Voyage* in light of these views. It argues that although it is intended to be an explicit example of an anti-Hollywood film, the director's attempt to create a Latin American form of filmmaking results in representations that depend on some of the Manichean notions of good and evil of which the director is so critical in his characterization of North American cinema. In addition, despite the film's call for a return to leftist politics to address Latin American poverty, violence, and inequality in an age of globalization, *The Voyage* is disappointingly conservative in its gender politics, seeing the hero's quest in patriarchal terms and marginalizing the female characters.

Solanas's Theories of Filmmaking

Solanas is well known as a writer on Latin American film. He is best known for his influential ideas about Third Cinema developed with Octavio Getino in the late 1960s (Solanas & Getino, 1997). In their seminal essay "Towards a Third Cinema: Notes and Experiences for the Development of a Cinema of Liberation in the Third World" (1997), Solanas and Getino lay out their definitions of First, Second and Third Cinema. First Cinema is seen to propagate a "bourgeois world view" (42) and is explained as a spectacle for audiences who are seen as "consumer[s] of ideology," and as "passive and consuming object[s]." They equate Second Cinema with author cinema, filmmaking in which the director is seen as an artist who uses nonstandard cinematographic language, yet is still trapped within the system and operates within the distribution laws of the capitalist system. In contrast, Third Cinema, which the authors advocate in the essay, has to exist in opposition to the political and studio system. To qualify for the term, one or two requirements have to be met: they should be "films that the system cannot assimilate and which are foreign to its needs, or . . . films that directly and explicitly set out to fight the system." This "cinema of liberation" would ideally lead to direct political action or would involve filmmaking by revolutionary groups themselves.

In addition, Solanas and Getino insist that Latin American cinema must cultivate its own identity and ensure that it is not assimilated by the Hollywood film industries. The first rule to follow in the creation of independent Latin American cinematographic languages is that filmmakers must distance themselves from Hollywood models. The authors lament that the distinctiveness of national cinemas has disappeared with the dominance of North American movies (Solanas & Getino, 1997, 41). In response to this, they call for a cinema that recognizes "the great possibility of constructing a liberated personality with each people as the starting point — in a word the decolonization of culture" (37).

This essay, written before the dictatorships that terrorized the southern cone countries in the 1970s and 1980s, was part of a culture that had more hope in the possibilities of socialist revolution. Solanas, like many of his contemporaries, had experiences that led to a shift from a hardline revolutionary position. He lived in Paris, in exile from the Argentine dictatorship, from 1976 until 1984.[3] In line with a generational shift, Solanas has moved away from aligning filmmaking with revolutionary armed struggle and has worked within a commercial system and made films within existing funding and distribution systems. *The Voyage,* for example, was funded by major Spanish, British, Mexican, and French television and film companies.[4]

Despite the fact that, within Solanas's own terms of reference, his films of the 1980s and 1990s can be seen as examples of Second Cinema, many of his political targets remain the same, including a corrupt Latin American political class and U.S. imperialism.[5] Likewise, it is clear from *The Voyage* that, for the director, the answer to the problems posed by the above lies in political protest and organized resistance by the masses. Solanas has remained a central political figure; in 1993, he cofounded the left-wing party El Frente Grande with Chacho Alvarez and Graciela Fernández Grande and was elected to parliament that year. He worked as a member of Parliament until 1997, during which time he continued to oppose Argentine president Carlos Menem and neoliberal economic policies, among other projects (Mahieu, 1999, 88).[6]

In addition, in his filmmaking Solanas is still self-consciously looking for a means of expression in opposition to the commercial Hollywood blockbusters. In his words: "All my cinema is a reaction against Hollywood in which storyline and argument are more important than the person. I try to break from the traditional schemas imposed by television and Hollywood to make my own cinema in my own way" (Nash, 1992, 19).

The director has spoken of his aim in *The Voyage* to create an anti-Hollywood action film,[7] while his coproducer, Envar El Kadri, has talked of how all involved in the project in a range of Latin American countries were "co-workers in the production of a film of high quality, and at the opposite end of a 'Hollywood' style mega-production" (*The Voyage,* video cover sleeve, 1992). This has been a long-standing concern of Solanas's. In 1989, in a book of interviews with Horacio González, he returns to the themes outlined in his essay with Getino. He talks at length of the dominance of a Hollywood-style cinema, which, he claims is most popular in the United States but has been adopted throughout the world (Solanas, 1989, 98), and he attacks the principal ingredients of the international film product (96–102).

A brief examination of Solanas's criticisms of "the Hollywood film" and counterproposals for more "authentic" filmmaking reveals a position that, aside from a shift away from a call to arms, has altered little since the late 1960s. His definitions of the "Hollywood product" are reduced to the action-adventure blockbuster and ignore other types of cinema, as if one model of filmmaking were slavishly followed. He begins by reproaching Hollywood for ignoring the rights of the director (the "author of the image") in the creation of the successful commercial film (96). He attacks the star system in the way that the cinematographic techniques — lighting, narration, scenery, the use of the camera — revolve around the star actor, with a loss in the quality of the images. In his words, the traditional Hollywood movie is characterized by "a language which is at the service of action and information, of dialogue, but not of the creation of images . . . it is nothing other than an illustrated dialogue" (87).[8] He goes on to critique the reliance on the use of suspense to generate interest in the story (97) and the simplification of characters into Manichean archetypes (97). Another area of concern is the overreliance on a realism that aims to show that "this is how life is." For Solanas, the great weakness of this "hyperrealism" is that it limits the spectator's imagination (97). His final point of criticism is the fact that it is a cinema of very strong emotions, which are closer to sport than to art. Clearly, then, he is referring in particular to action/suspense movies, although this is not specified.

What is apparent here is a tendency to provide a monolithic characterization of Hollywood, with little recognition of the wide range of themes, genres, styles and approaches adopted. It is significant that Solanas provides no concrete examples of films that conform to this rather caricatured image of Hollywood. There is also a tendency to ignore auteurist directors working within Hollywood, and although he does state that exceptions to this type of filmmaking can be found in the works of Woody Allen, John Cassavetes, Robert Altman, Francis Ford Coppola and Stanley Kubrick, there is little recognition of a number of new directors who at the time were producing interesting and challenging work.[9] Despite his criticisms, Solanas also shows little concern for gender representations in mainstream film, the subject of much feminist film theory, a lack of concern evident in the representation of women in *The Voyage*.

In opposition to the Hollywood aesthetic, Solanas argues for "open and poetic film making" (97). A poetic film depends on an individual artistic interpretation and transformation of reality (89), using such devices as metaphors, and allegory (88), and creating a film time slower than that of the fast-moving action movie.[10] The characters should act within a world without an enclosed plot structure, where there is no distinction between digression and central action (79–80). The difficulty for the Latin American director, Solanas argues, is to find his or her own images when generations have been brought up with foreign images that have been taken to be universal (88). It is worth noting that this position goes against the trend of films in Argentina today, which, because of a concern with commercial factors, are often "Hollywood-style movie[s] spoken in Spanish" (Falicon, 2000, 328).[11]

Cinematic Approaches Used in The Voyage

The focus of this discussion is an assessment, through a close reading of *The Voyage*, of Solanas's success in creating a form of filmmaking in opposition to his characterization of the dominant Hollywood aesthetic. I argue that the film often achieves this, particularly in the representation of Latin American (geographical) images, the incorporation of digression, the imaginative use of cartoons and music, and the combination of mythical realism, social realism, and a surreal form of satire. Nevertheless, in some respects Solanas fails to address one of the weaknesses he identifies in the Hollywood film: the Manichean division of characters into good and evil. In addition, the film fails to adequately represent the female characters, despite a stated concern for equality of all Latin Americans.

The Voyage does put into practice many of Solanas's views on filmmaking. The journey itself allows for the use of an open plot structure, with no distinction between digression and central action.[12] The diverse landscapes allow the director a range of cinematographic choices for the representation of poetic images, with, for example, some stunning imagery of Ushuaia, Machupichu, and the Amazon River. The journey format presents a series of answers to the question Solanas raises with González, "How do you construct a world of your own images?" (Solanas, 1989, 88). The director and his team turn to Latin America itself to provide the images that are to counter U.S. hegemony. The crew embarks on an ambitious journey of filmmaking to shoot the adventures of Martín (played by Walter Quiroz), the film's protagonist. In the cover text for the video version of *The Voyage*, Horacio González explains the scale of this project:

> The filming of *The Voyage* was a marathon. We travelled over 50,000 kilometers, took over 50 planes, boats, carrying over 800 kilos of equipment. In 16 weeks and 5 countries, we visited cities and places from pre-colonial sites like Machupichu, Maya ruins in Yucatán, and the Serra Pelada gold mine in Brazil.[13]

As Envar El Kadri comments in the cover text for the video version of *The Voyage*, the crews could have shot the entire film in Argentina with its varied geography; however, their epic journey was an integral part of the project.[14]

Through Martín's encounters with the peoples of the continent, the film calls for an integrated identity, and this concept is put into practice at the level of filmmaking. There were film crews from each country to assist in filming, and the nationality of the characters is, to a large degree, reflective of the crews' and includes Argentines, Brazilians, Peruvians, Mexicans, a Chilean, and a Venezuelan.[15] This Pan-American identity, however, is not felt on every level; Martín's mother and father are played by French actors Dominique Sanda and Marc Berman. European companies investing in Latin American cinema often prefer some participation by European actors, as this helps to sell the film to domestic markets.

In the geographical scope of *The Voyage*, Solanas aims to show that "cultural integration in Latin America [is] more than just a dream" (El Kadri, *The Voyage*, cover sleeve, 1992). However, despite the cinematography, which highlights many beautiful facets of Latin American geography, the film is much more than a travelogue. Solanas uses a wide range of approaches in his construction of a filmic world of his own and his collaborators' images.

One of these approaches is to make music an integral component of the film. *The Voyage* is divided into three parts, and Solanas has said that he conceived the film as an opera in three movements, with the first part in Ushuaia characterized by fixed shots and the second and third sections, "Towards Buenos Aires" and "Through Indo-America," characterized by movement to capture the sense of the journey.[16] Solanas, a trained musician, wrote songs with the well-known musicians Egberto Gismonti and Astor Piazzola that act as the motif for the first two sections, and music has an important structural and emotive function within the film. The first song, "Ushuaia," by Martín and Pablo (the real-life musician Fito Páez), expresses the desire to travel and explore, mixed with love and imagined nostalgia for their homeland. The second song, entitled "The Voyage" accompanies the second movement. As Martín is seen cycling out of Ushuaia toward Buenos Aires, a female vocalist (Liliana Herrero) sings of the disintegration of an old identity, as the character is about to embrace new possibilities through the journey. The third song, "Floating in Buenos Aires," is heard as we meet Pablo and his band in the flooded metropolis. Pablo's song describes the citizens' attempts to "float" or survive in a city ruined by corrupt politicians and crooks. The songs speak of movement, imagination, possibilities, and resistance, and in this way highlight the principal themes of the film. In the third section of the film, music is replaced by synthesized human voices, which represent the resistance of the masses and strength in solidarity. These voices are first heard accompanying Tito's drum in the war of noise against the authorities and reproduced at key moments of the film, such as the scene in which the Peruvian peasants resist the debt collection.

A political vision runs through *The Voyage,* and a number of approaches are used to provide that vision. Solanas depends on the use of satire, mythical realism, and social realism for specific political purposes. He divides his characters into good and bad; the common people of Latin America are seen as good, as are those who represent the interests of the people. A series of characters who can lead the people to resist corrupt politicians and the capitalist forces of globalization are given a mythical treatment. In contrast, political figures are seen to be acting against the interests of the masses and are satirized. Solanas coins the term *grotético* to describe the treatment applied to them; they are a mixture of grotesque and pathetic (Yglesias, 1993, 41).[17]

Mythical realism is used to represent a sense of community and resistance to political mismanagement. Solanas creates three highly symbolic characters of mythical status that are rooted in a fictional universe, but who, nevertheless, come to represent political and social realities in Latin America.[18] Solanas has said of them that Alguien Boga (Somebody Sails, played by Franklin Caicedo) symbolizes the permanent exile of the American Indians, Tito el Esperanzador (Tito the Hope Giver, played by Carlos Carella) represents the resistance of the urban masses, and Américo Inconcluso (Americo the Inconclusive, played by Kike Mendive) gives expression to black culture (Castillo, 1993, 43.) The nature of all three in terms of fiction/reality is intentionally ambiguous. They are, at once, cartoon creations of Martín's father, Nicolás, and characters that act as guides to Martín on his travels. This gives them a heroic status, as their mythical condition suggests that they are timeless elements in Latin American liberation struggles.

The other good characters, in addition to Martín, are the common people he meets in his travels. Social realism is used for these encounters with "the people," that is, the peasants in Bolivia and Peru and the miners in Brazil. Here the style is closer to documentary, as Solanas aims to show the lives and hardships of the indigenous and the poor, who are underrepresented in the Latin American media. Satire is reserved for the authorities, in their demands that the national debt be paid by the peasants, with the weight of the produce corresponding to the level of debt. The weight specifications issued over a television attached to a post in the desert and the special debt-collecting trucks add a surreal touch and serve to highlight the gap between the faceless bureaucrats and the people from whom they are stealing.

Solanas, then, does not limit himself to a single approach for any particular time frame. Even before Martín's journey begins, elements of surrealism are introduced to satirize the mismanagement of the "model school" he attends in Ushuaia. Snow is seen entering the classroom and falling directly on the boys, most heavily on Pablo (played by Fito Páez), the least obedient of them; a dog is seen wandering the corridors; teachers' voices are comical, excessively high pitched and nasal, or exaggeratedly slow; and portraits of national historical figures regularly crash to the floor as they fall off the walls. Nondiegetic sound is introduced in the form of screams that accompany the falling portraits, a technique that clearly draws attention to the symbolism: historical figures who fought for the independence of the country are abandoned as the ruling classes sell off the country for a quick profit.

Satire is used in the film to provide negative representations of authority figures. This is the case in the characterization of Garrido (played by Eduardo Rojo), the school's principal, who is the cause of the school's ruin, as he sells off all its assets for personal profits, and in the representation of the president of Argentina (played by Atilio Veronelli) and later in that of the president of Brazil. Politicians, along with the crises they create, are seen through the lens of a ridiculous televisual reality. Thus, Solanas mocks their incompetence with their mediatized attempts to explain the tilting of Ushuaia, the flooding of Buenos Aires, and, in Brazil, the need to wear giant belts as part of the financial adjustment plans.

The Voyage thus draws upon a range of aesthetic styles to critique the ruling classes and to make heroes of those who resist their policies. A rather Manichean approach is used to romanticize the struggles of "the people" and to condemn and dehumanize the political classes. It is worth further analyzing the two categories of characters, as through them Solanas

112

proposes models and antimodels for a Latin American future. It is significant that both heroes and antiheroes are men, whereas the female characters are totally marginalized in this vision of Latin America, ideas that will be developed below.

Satire is reserved principally for a new breed of Latin American leader, seen in Dr. Rana (Dr. Frog), the president of Argentina. Of this character, Solanas has said: "President Rana represents the new politics of South America where we are considered the property of foreign powers. He is the epitome of corruption and betrayal" (Chaudhary, 1992, 8). Although the director sees Rana as a Latin American symbol in general, he can be seen more specifically as a caricature of Carlos Menem, Argentina's president at the time of filming.[19] In 1991, Solanas was shot in the legs during the editing of *The Voyage* as a result of his attacks against the corruption of Menem's regime and the privatization of public services, exactly the focus of his attack against Rana.[20] From 1989 to 1991, the period just before and during the making of *The Voyage*, contrary to his election promises, Menem established himself as an autocratic leader who introduced a package of pro-market reforms (Novaro, 1998, 12). The president turned his back on the traditional Peronism of his Justicialista Party, using his fight against hyper-inflation as an excuse to embrace the technocrats and the new creed of the free market.[21]

In *The Voyage,* parody is used as a weapon to attack politicians and their economic policies. In his travels through Argentina, Martín learns that Patagonia has been sold to the British and American petroleum companies, and politicians are selling off plots of water of the submerged Buenos Aires and making large profits.[22] President Rana, who is responsible for the ethos of shady privatization deals, is like a cartoon character brought to life.[23] He is given the "grotethic" treatment, defined by Solanas as "the fantastic, the illogical and the irrational placed within the everyday" (Yglesias, 1993, 41).[24] Rana is appropriately never seen without his flippers, and his dyed, slicked back hair and white suit project an image of competence and purity. His speech and his mouth are distorted, and it is clear that he has cultivated a mediatized image, made up of sound bites.[25] Rana has created an environment in which he is comfortable: he has flooded Buenos Aires with waters in which human excrement floats, a symbol of corruption and economic mismanagement, and is represented as a slimy amphibian, able to maneuver above and below the water, while encouraging the citizens to keep afloat.[26] The camera provides a close-up of the excrement and shows Martín vomiting, to highlight the horror of this dystopian image of Buenos Aires.

Solanas also uses the *grotético* to satirize globalization and attack neo-colonialism in the scene of the Conference of the Organization of Nations on Their Knees. This is a rather unsubtle parody of the Organization of American States, controlled by the U.S. State Department. Rana gives a speech parodying the acceptance of World Bank and International Monetary Fund adjustment policies, which were adopted by Argentina in the 1990s. In his speech, he uses clichéd political rhetoric to explain why the only viable position is the kneeling position and to reject the vertical position (one of independence and resistance) and the horizontal position (maintaining the status quo). The servants fittingly are dwarfs to ensure that they are not seen to be above the political leader. The satire continues with the representation of the American president (played by Héctor Gance). As another baddie, he is also given a cartoon name, Mr. Wolf, and can be seen as a parody of George Herbert Walker Bush.[27]

The political leaders are thus grotesque cartoon-like characters who are working against the interests of the people they are supposed to serve. Cartoons are used to the opposite effect in the comic strips that Nicolás creates to tell of the injustices of Latin American history. The film is, significantly, dedicated to Hector Oesterheld, an important Argentine comic artist, whose work had a social and political content. He and his four daughters had disappeared during the 1976–1984 dictatorship. Oesterheld had collaborated with Alberto Breccia, the artist whose drawings are used in the film. Solanas claimed that his own experience as a cartoonist from 1956 to 1960 helped him film the drawings (*The Voyage*, video cover sleeve, 1992). It is interesting to note that the cartoons are not animated; rather, voice-overs are used to narrate the stories behind the pictures.[28] In scenes such as the U.S. bombing of Panama, the director uses a range of techniques to capture the horror and injustice of the invasion. Realistic sound effects are used over the drawings of fighter planes and bombs; the editing is extremely rapid, as images of destruction flash onto the screen in quick succession. The camera shows close-ups of disembodied faces, all with large, startled eyes, then pulls back to show viewers the larger scene. The shock and the ensuing chaos are evident, as Breccia and Solanas depict the murders ignored by the world's media.

The cartoons of the U.S. invasion of Panama in 1989 accompany Américo Inconcluso's eyewitness account of the events. He tells Martín the news of the 3,000 dead in six minutes from the aerial bombing.[29] Américo is the voice of popular memory, emphasized by the fact that Martín had heard nothing of the invasion of Panama on the state-controlled media in his travels, as Latin American governments were not willing to antagonize their powerful northern neighbors.[30] In this scene, through the drawings and the character of Américo, it is clear that Solanas uses cartoons to focus attention on the atrocities committed against Latin Americans.

Cartoons are also linked to the creation of the popular Latin American heroes who act as Martín's guides in his voyage. Viewers are first introduced to Américo, Alguien Boga, and Tito in cartoon form to highlight their fictional nature. The characters brought to life act as symbols of facets of Latin American experience. Freed from the constraints of realism, they take on mythical proportions, as a brief analysis of Américo Inconcluso will reveal. As his name suggests, he can be seen to embody the entire continent, with all its uncertainties and unknown futures. He is inconclusive, the film argues, just as Latin American nations are still in the process of formation and have not achieved true independence, because they are at the mercy of corrupt, incompetent rulers and international economic and political bodies led by the United States.

Américo is undoubtedly a good, mythical force; he rescues Martín twice, once early on in his travels as Martín is lost, and again toward the end of the journey, from the jungle after Martín has escaped from gunmen who shot the driver of the truck on which he was riding. Américo's appearance is presented without any explanation, and there is no attempt to account for how he has managed to find Martín's bicycle, which he has at the front of his truck. As Gabriel García Márquez has shown in his own work, the recounting of nonrealistic dramatic events is most effective when the narration treats these events with no surprise, as if they were entirely expected (Mendoza, 1982, 41).[31] Américo is needed, so he appears, obeying a fictional reality; yet, once again, there is a deeper poetic truth in Solanas's playful treatment of fiction.[32] If Américo Inconcluso represents the positive spirit of Latin America, the suggestion is that Martín will be safe in his travels around the continent. Good men, such as Américo, Alguien Boga, and Tito, who fight for their societies, will protect Martín and teach him the value of community, and the importance of resistance.

Américo is a symbol of both oppression and hope, and, as Solanas has said, of black Latin America (*The Voyage*, video cover sleeve, 1992). Born into poverty in Panama, of a Cuban father and a Guatemalan mother, Américo was trapped in conditions of modern-day slavery, working on banana plantations. However, he is now a blind truck driver, traveling the roads of the continent. He never gets lost, as he imagines the road ahead. The allegory here is obvious: the road represents the past, present, and future. Latin Americans are blind to their futures; however, if they learn from their past and keep to the vision inspired by the possibilities of their imaginations, they will create their own paths. This is a key concept of the film and is reflected in the fact that Nicolás's comics are entitled "The Inventor of Paths" ("El Inventor de Caminos"). Américo can also be seen to represent the memory of Latin America, as he remembers every dictatorship and every murder of a hero.[33]

Aside from acting as important symbols, the primary purpose of Américo, Alguien Boga, and Tito is to act as guides to Martín in his search for his father and in his quest to discover Latin America. Like so many Argentine young people, including Che Guevara, Martín explores Latin America to try to find an individual identity within a continental identity.[34] The link with Che is interesting, as there is perhaps an implicit suggestion that Martín's generation needs to develop its own revolutionary models, based on those of Che's generation.

This search for identity is conceived of in exclusively masculine terms. Martín himself is linked not only to Che, but, through his name, to two Argentine male national heroes: José de San Martín, the military leader who with his armies secured Argentine independence and helped secure Chilean independence,[35] and Martín Fierro, the gaucho of José Hernández's narrative poem (1872), who fought to keep a traditional, more egalitarian way of life in the face of modernity. His surname, Nunca, meaning *never* in Spanish, is a reminder to viewers that he is a fiction, a character who has never existed beyond the film.[36] Like his guides, he is a symbol: he represents a generation of men who have to look beyond failed patriarchal models of teachers, political leaders, and even parents to find alternative masculine models, seen in historical heroes and in popular figures, who can teach them the realities of their world and the value of resistance.

Martín discovers a male community in place of the absent father figure he was seeking. Initially, Martín appears to find his father as he is embarking on his journey home, in scenes that would suggest a classic Hollywood-style happy ending. However, the following scene shows a close-up of Martín deep in thought, alone on the bus, which reveals the reunion as a product of his imagination. This leads to his final revelation, which is also a form of liberation: he does not have to look for his father, because his father is always with him. Nicolás Nunca can act as a guide for Martín, as seen by the fact that he is protected by his cartoon creations, inspired by characters he met on the same journey, but he cannot tell Martín how to lead his life. In the same way, the film suggests, Latin Americans have to find their own destinies; they can learn from their forefathers, yet each generation has to confront its own specific problems and face them.[37]

Representations of Women

Destiny in *The Voyage* is reserved for the male characters; the search of a young man for his father, guided by male mythical heroes, is clearly a masculine quest. The women in the film serve only two purposes: Vidala (played by Soledad Alfaro) and Waita (played by Liliana Flores) are objects of desire, and Martín's mother (played by Dominique Sanda) and grandmother (played by Juana Hidalgo) are caregivers and wives.[38] Janaína (played by Angela Correa), Nicolás's former girlfriend, would appear to offer an exception to this, as she is the only woman who has a career (she is a documentary filmmaker). Nevertheless, she makes only a brief appearance, and her only real function is in terms of plot development. This is an important weakness in Solanas's filmmaking and shows a failure to challenge the traditional patriarchal representations of women that have been so prevalent in mainstream cinema. Hollywood films, of which Solanas is so critical, have themselves been rewriting their roles for women, with the figure of the passive, romantic heroine challenged by such blockbusters as *Charlie's Angels* (2001) and *Lara Croft: Tomb Raider* (2001), among others.

Early feminist film critics have argued that in Hollywood films, woman is often "represented as what she represents for a man" (Johnston, 1999, 33).[39] In her essay "Visual Pleasure and Narrative Cinema," on the patriarchal control of the gaze for both characters and spectators within mainstream Hollywood cinema, Laura Mulvey categorizes "woman as image and man as bearer of the look" (Mulvey, 1999, 62). A number of the ideas in this influential essay have been subsequently critiqued, including the neglect of female spectators, gender essentialism in Mulvey's analysis of characterization and spectator behavior, a heterosexual white bias, and the reliance of psychoanalysis (see de Lauretis, 1984; Doane, 1981; Gains, 1988).[40] Nevertheless, Mulvey's central ideas, outlined below, hold true for the representations of women in *The Voyage*, particularly that of Vidala:

> In a world ordered by sexual imbalance, pleasure in looking has been split between active/male and passive/female. The determining male gaze projects its fantasy onto the female figure, which is styled accordingly. In their traditional exhibitionist role women are simultaneously looked at and displayed with their appearance coded for strong visual and erotic impact so that they can be said to connote *to-be-looked-at-ness* (Mulvey, 1999, 63; author's emphasis).

It is interesting that these comments are made about "mainstream Hollywood cinema," whose codes and aesthetics Solanas is so at pains to reject. In his representation of gender, Solanas, then, falls into the rather generalized patriarchal flaws that Mulvey levels at Hollywood up until and including the mid-1970s.

Whereas in Martín, Américo, Tito, and Alguien Boga, the director creates Latin American male heroes, the Latin American woman, seen in Vidala, remains the mysterious, silent object of male desire. She is a character whom, it is suggested, Martín has imagined. This mysterious, silent woman, always seen in a red dress, color coded for desire, is thus given no identity of her own. Although she is never named in the film, we learn from the video sleeve for *The Voyage* that she is Vidala, the messenger of love. She too is a symbol, with her name indicating that she represents life (vida). The soundtrack, which always accompanies her appearance, is the hummed song, "Ushuaia," suggesting that she represents love for the homeland. Yet, unlike the other characters, she does not take on a fully embodied existence; she never speaks and is always about to depart on a bus or a boat. The only physical contact between her and Martín is in his dream, as he makes love to her on idyllic land along the Amazon River, only to wake up alone. Vidala is thus a creation of his fantasy, an object to be looked at and desired. In fact, her idealization depends on the fact that she is a silent nonperson onto whom he can project his fantasies.

The film shows little sensitivity in dealing with the other, "real" romantic figures in Martín's life. His girlfriend, Violeta (played by Christina Becerra), is only ever seen from his perspective. The film focuses on Martín's reaction to Violeta's pregnancy and subsequent abortion; his joy, then pain and anger are represented, while audiences never learn of her emotions regarding this traumatic experience. In fact, she is an entirely undeveloped character. Martín's abandonment of her is justified in the narrative by the fact that she does not consult him before the abortion, and the audience hears nothing more of Violeta.

The representation of Waita, the young Peruvian woman with whom Martín has a sexual encounter, is even more insensitive. It appears as if she is introduced to represent issues of gender, class, and ethnicity, as she is forced to work away from her village in order to eat, is mistreated by the white woman she works for, and is pregnant following her rape by her boss's son. Nevertheless, despite the recent rape, she is shown to be happy to have sex with Martín, whom she has just met. As Martín leaves Peru, the voice-over declares that he is feeling invigorated after this beautiful interlude. Again, the concern is primarily with the male hero and his sexual and emotional needs. Waita has fulfilled these and is dispensed with.

Although *The Voyage* is sensitive to issues of ethnicity and nationality, the journey of discovery is set out as a male project. The film calls for a Latin America where all citizens are equal, while cultural differences are respected. Yet here, the epic search for a national and an individual identity is conceived of in masculine terms, with "woman" as unknowable other. A film that aims to be radical in terms of class politics is conservative in its conceptualization of gender identity. Martín's search for his father and the Latin American fatherland allows him to forge a new identity to represent a new generation of Latin American men. Nevertheless, he is guided by the spirit of the figure of the absent father and sees women as idealized romantic figures, not as cotravellers on the journey of self-discovery. This patriarchal vision of identity embraced in the 1990s by a respected filmmaker in an otherwise often innovative film is of concern to feminists.

Despite of this failure in representing women, Solanas, in large part, suc-ceeds in countering the aesthetics of many Hollywood blockbusters. His focus is on creating a political film filled with Latin American imagery and peopled by Latin American professional and nonprofessional actors.[41] The structure of the journey affords a digressive approach, which Solanas has advocated. Throughout the film, Solanas demonstrates that different subject matters require different styles. He uses his own form of satire to attack political leaders; popular heroes are created using mythical real-ism, and the spirit of survival and resistance of the poor is shown through documentary-style realism.

Music, cartoons, satire, surrealism, and social realism are all harnessed to produce this epic tale of Latin American identity. Nevertheless, there is a lack of subtlety in Solanas's political vision. A cartoon-like sense of good and bad and right and wrong characterizes the representations of the characters, with Américo, Tito, and Alguien the heroes, and Mr. Wolf and Mr. Frog the villains. The former are trying to save Latin America, whereas the latter are seen to be destroying it. The three heroes, to whom, by the end of the film, Martín can be added, represent the interests of "the people" of Latin America. They, the working and peasant classes, are seen in Marxist terms; they are the oppressed and pure of heart, who, despite the dictatorships that have gone before them, are still resisting exploitation by the political classes. The sound of Tito's drum, accompanied by the voices of the downtrodden, is heard calling to battle the drowning Argentines, the debt-ridden Peruvians, and the Brazilian mine workers toiling in slave conditions.

Solanas makes it clear in *The Voyage* that he believes that the old wars are still there to be fought. He remains true to the essence of the dream that sustains his first film, *The Hour of the Furnaces* (*La hora de los hornos,*

119

1968), of an independent Latin America, united in its struggles, based on social equality, and free from the dominance of neocolonialism and cultural imperialism. The ambitious aesthetic and political goals of *The Voyage* highlight the fact that the emancipation of women is overlooked in this master narrative of Latin American liberation.

Creating a Heroine for Our Times: María Luisa Bemberg's *I the Worst of All*

In contrast to *The Voyage,* the emancipation of women is the central concern of María Luisa Bemberg's *I the Worst of All.* Both films comment on what they see as the ills of Latin America; however, they have very different points of focus. As has been seen, Solanas's film locates these ills in neoliberalism and corruption, whereas *I the Worst of All* finds them in discrimination against women and in censorship, although corruption is also attacked. Whereas *The Voyage* promotes equality in class terms, *I the Worst of All* promotes equality in gender terms and makes little mention of class divides. In this film, "the people" of New Spain (Mexico) are not of interest; rather, the focus is on one extraordinary woman, who, the film argues, can serve as a model for women of the future.

I the Worst of All is a filmic biography of the life of the seventeenth-century Mexican nun Sor Juana Inés de la Cruz (1651–1695), considered one of the finest poets, playwrights, and intellectuals of her age. Bemberg's fascination with this historical figure is not isolated. Sor Juana studies have experienced a renaissance among recent researchers, keen to have the contributions of this important woman recognized.[42] In the late twentieth and early twenty-first centuries Sor Juana has been held up by Latin Americanists as an inspirational woman and early feminist.[43] She has come to represent a call for women's entry into Hispanic culture, at a time when Latin American women are just beginning to see a boom in literature and are beginning to make their presence felt in film.[44]

This section focuses on the way in which María Luisa Bemberg reclaims a seventeenth-century woman and makes her into a role model for contemporary audiences. I examine the way in which Sor Juana is re-created and history is interpreted in the film to suit the feminist requirements of a Latin American director in 1990. Before examining the creation of a filmic heroine, a brief introduction to Sor Juana and her cultural importance is necessary in order to place Bemberg's representation within a historical context.

Sor Juana Inés de la Cruz: A Brief Introduction

It is not surprising that Sor Juana has been so attractive to feminist Latin Americanists, nor that María Luisa Bemberg chose to make a film about her. Her appeal lies in the fact that she gained prominence for her works when literary production was almost exclusively masculine. As Octavio Paz tells us, "The literature of New Spain was written by men to be read by men. . . . It is . . . truly extraordinary that the most important writer of New Spain was a woman" (Paz, 1988, 45). In seventeenth-century Mexico, nuns were expected to be self-effacing and dedicated to a life of prayer and meditation. Sor Juana was writing on such "masculine" subjects as philosophy, theology, and romantic love; she was the official poet to the viceroy and vicereine and proudly proclaimed women's rights to take part in the world of the intellect.[45] In addition, it was extremely rare for women in seventeenth-century Spain and its colonies to develop skills beyond basic literacy. To know Latin and to read historical works, all preserves of male scholars, was highly unusual (Lavrin, 1991, 64). Sor Juana was thus an exceptional woman, versed in Latin and classical literature, who had two volumes of her works published in her lifetime and a final volume five years after her death.[46]

There is little contemporary material about Sor Juana's life beyond what she herself wrote,[47] and there has therefore been much speculation as to the motivation for the key events in her life. Sor Juanistas have debated the identity of her father, a man who left her mother when Juana was a child;[48] her reasons for entering the convent when many of her writings do not reveal a spiritual calling; the nature of her relationship with the countess de Paredes, the vicereine (María Luisa Manrique de Lara y Gonzaga), for whom she wrote passionate poetry; what lay behind her fall from grace; and the reasons behind her final confession, in which she renounced her writings and her former identity as a writer.[49]

There is much consensus about a number of these issues. It is generally agreed that Sor Juana entered the convent because it provided a space in which she could dedicate herself to her writings and avoid marriage and the domestic responsibilities that went with it (Paz, 1988; Schons, 1991).[50] Her fall from favor has been carefully chronicled by Dorothy Schons and Octavio Paz, among others, who argue that she was the victim of the virulent misogyny of the archbishop of Mexico, Francisco Aguiar y Seijas; of power struggles between him, the archbishop of Puebla, Manuel Fernández de Santa Cruz, and the viceroy at the time, the Count de Galve; all exacerbated by social unrest.[51]

There is less agreement regarding the sincerity of her abjuration and the nature of her relationship with the countess de Paredes, the vicereine. Was Juana a Christian saint, who realized that she should abandon her writing and offer her life to prayer, or was she a martyr to a misogynistic church that forced her to give up her worldly concerns and her fame? Can the relationship between the two women be categorized as lesbian, or was it a neoplatonic, romantic friendship?[52] These two key issues, Sor Juana's struggles with the Roman Catholic hierarchy that led to her abjuration and the relationship between her and María Luisa Manrique de Lara, frame Bemberg's filmic narrative.

María Luisa Bemberg's Sor Juana Inés de la Cruz

Despite an approximate gap of 300 years, Bemberg clearly felt that a representation of Sor Juana would be relevant to contemporary audiences. In *I the Worst of All,* Bemberg offers her own interpretation of Sor Juana's relationship with the vicereine, her difficulties with the Catholic Church, and her downfall and abjuration. She selectively takes elements of Sor Juana's life to provide an episodic narrative, representing a safe love story in her depiction of an erotic yet chaste relationship between Sor Juana (played by Assumpta Serna) and María Luisa Manrique de Lara (played by Dominique Sanda), and creating a drama through Juana's struggle with a corrupt, misogynistic church that succeeds in breaking her. The timescale of the film is fifteen years before Juana's death and begins in 1680 with the arrival of the archbishop of Mexico (played by Lautaro Murúa) and the viceroy (played by Héctor Alterio) (Scott, 1994, 152). The film thus concentrates on her rise and fall, serving to dramatize her glory and her renunciation of that glory. As will be seen, the film chooses to downplay key historical elements, namely, her religious beliefs and her support of the viceregal colonial system, in order to make Juana into a heroine for our times.

As an artist struggling to have creative control in a male-dominated medium, there are obvious parallels between the careers of María Luisa Bemberg and Sor Juana Inés de la Cruz. Bemberg, who came late to filmmaking, began to write screenplays at forty-eight in the 1970s and became a director at fifty-eight. She wanted control over her own scripts, so she turned to directing (Torrents, 1990, 173).[53] In her career, she made six feature-length films, with *Camila* (1984) the most commercially successful, and she was considered one of the best Latin American directors of her generation.[54]

Bemberg's interest in the feminist movement propelled her to embark on her career, after a life of marriage and bringing up children.[55] She consistently saw filmmaking as an opportunity to promote women's rights and

Sor Juana (Assumpta Serna) and the vicereine (Dominique Sanda) in I the Worst of All.

to represent strong female characters in the male-dominated world of Latin American cinema.[56] She was a founding member of the Unión Feminista Argentina (Argentine Feminist Union) in the 1970s, and set up her own production company, GEA Ciematográfica, with her longtime producer, Lita Stantic.[57] Like Sor Juana, Bemberg was a pioneer in opening the way for women in a male-dominated arena. She took on this role aware that she was attempting to change cultural attitudes, and I the Worst of All clearly fits within her aims of filmmaking. In an interview, she spelled this out:

> The Sor Juana project fits in with what I set out to do when I began to make movies — to change the very *un*interesting image of women that film generally conveyed. When it comes to women, Latin American film is terribly poor and tendentious. Women are generally presented as a function of male ambition and are too often, even today, the object of a distorting, grotesque misogyny. (Pick, 1992–1993, 78).[58]

A seventeenth century woman was thus chosen to serve a contemporary feminist purpose. This is not to criticize Bemberg's approach; rather, it presents an interesting example of how historical figures are reinterpreted according to the needs and values of each new age. As Walter Benjamin argued, history is always used as a commentary on the present. In his words, "History is the subject of a structure whose site is not homogeneous, empty time, but time filled by the presence of the now" (Benjamin, 1973, 252–53). Bemberg aimed to seek out the universal and transhistorical in Sor Juana's story. In her words:

> I was determined to emphasize the universal over the local. The theme of obscurantism is not specifically Mexican; nor are the themes of repression and misogyny limited to the seventeenth century. (Pick, 1992–1993, 80)

Bemberg's film brings an important historical figure to contemporary audiences and uses her to raise key issues for these audiences. The film takes its material from an academic source, the biography by Octavio Paz, the Mexican poet and intellectual. Nevertheless, Bemberg brings a popular touch to her interpretation of Sor Juana in an attempt to make her accessible to a wider audience and to take her beyond the world of the universities. *I the Worst of All* focuses on the misogyny of seventeenth-century ecclesiastical society and Sor Juana's defiance of the Catholic Church, to condemn the transhistorical themes of religious hypocrisy and the repression of women and to make a point about the need to promote women's place in culture. In addition, the cinematography and art direction follow a fascist aesthetic in order to make connections between inquisitorial New Spain and militaristic, dictatorial, and patriarchal societies, so characteristic of Latin America in the 1970s and 1980s.

The historical Juana poses some difficulties when seen through a modern, feminist lens. She was undoubtedly a radical within the context of her society. She was a woman of academic brilliance who asserted her right to study and to engage with the debates of her day, at a time when nuns were loudly proclaiming their unworthiness and finding new ways to mortify their flesh.[59] Nevertheless, she was also a woman of her age, who shared many of the values of her society, values that Bemberg chooses to ignore in her representation. Although she rejected the path of the mystics and the religious fanatics and called into question her vocation as a nun,[60] Catholic orthodoxy shaped Sor Juana's worldview, as it did all intellectuals in seventeenth-century New Spain. She wrote a substantial amount of religious verse; the Christian God was always at the center of her philosophical inquiries, and the Virgin was a major figure in her poetry (Franco, 1989, 51–52). As she herself wrote in "Reply to Sor Philotea," "There is something about treating the Most Blessed Virgin that sets the frostiest heart ablaze" (Trueblood, 1988, 242–43).

Sor Juana was also an important figure in the promotion of colonial rule. She was the semiofficial poet of several viceroys and vicereines, the colonial representatives of the Spanish monarch, and was particularly close to the marquis de la Laguna and the countess de Paredes, writing numerous eulogies to them.[61] She also had important friends in the church, until a series of events isolated her. As Jean Franco perceptively notes, "she was ... a nun living within a system of patronage that she neither resisted nor opposed. It is important to understand that Sor Juana ... was not a lone sniper resisting the state, but was, at times, the very voice of that state" (Franco, 1989, 49).

Bemberg, however, does not focus on Sor Juana's conformity to the contemporary worldview or on her support for the viceregal court. In an attempt to increase her relevance for modern viewers, she concentrates on Sor Juana's rebellion against the Catholic hierarchy and her defense of her right to study, and interprets her relationship with the vicereine as a transgressive love story, preferring to downplay the fact that she was also acting to support a colonial instrument of power. The viceroy and vicereine are only ever seen in the film in terms of their relationship with Sor Juana. Although this is understandable, as this is Sor Juana's film, the impression is gained that their only acts were carried out to protect her from the excesses of the archbishop of Mexico (both frequently promise that no harm will come to her as long as they are in Mexico). This concern for Juana serves to distance them from their roles as representatives of the colonial world order and puts them on the side of good (Sor Juana), as against bad, represented by the archbishop. Sor Juana's loving friendship with the vicereine is thus seen in purely personal terms. This conceptualization is something that Jean Franco warned against due to the submissive position that Sor Juana held within their relationship of patronage. In her words: "it is impossible to separate personal love from love of the body politic, and love of the body politic included the recognition of authority" (Franco, 1989, 50).[62]

Another way in which Bemberg modernizes Sor Juana is to make little of her nun's Catholic beliefs and claim her for a secular audience. Bemberg spoke of the lack of appeal nuns hold for contemporary audiences, and felt that she had to downplay the religious aspect in order to make Sor Juana more interesting. In her words: "I decided that what I had to do was to deconventize the convent, denun the nun" (Bemberg, 1991, 15; my translation). The convent is presented as the scene of intrigues and power struggles, not a place of worship, as Bemberg seeks to demonize the misogynistic archbishop of Mexico, and the establishment he represents. The scene in which this is best demonstrated is in the archbishop's meeting with Sor Ursula (played by Graciela Arújo) and an aide in the convent of San Jerónimo.

Sor Juana (Assumpta Serna) and the archbishop (Lautaro Murúa) in
I the Worst of All.

Here he is seen plotting with Sor Ursula, who represents a repressive order, to secure enough votes to ensure she will be the new abbess. The film relies on lighting and staging to have him represent an evil force. The archbishop's own dark shadow looms over him as he is talking. He is raised above the nuns on a platform, to show his sense of superiority and his self-imposed separation from women, and he further dehumanizes the nuns by insisting that they lower their veils in his presence. His misogyny is such that he refuses to accept Sor Ursula's list that places the nun's in moral categories from her hand, insisting that she give it to his secretary.

It is interesting to note that the representation of the archbishop is historically accurate. His biographer, a contemporary, has written:

[His Honour the Bishop] believed in the importance of guarding his eyes to preserve his chastity; he made sure that women did not visit him except under the most urgent of circumstances, and even then, ... he refused to look at their faces. . . . He considered it a great gift from God that he was nearsighted. (Schons, 1991, 41)[63]

The convent, a female space, has been invaded by oppressive patriarchal forces, which the director equates with fascism. Bemberg spoke of the use of "high angles and grand travelling shots of columns and cupolas, of that huge, hard, imposing proto-fascist baroque architecture whose bad taste only emphasizes the power to which it testifies" (Pick, 1992, 80). She asked her director of photography, Félix Monti, and her art director, Roman Voytek, for blue, cold tones and oppressive and harsh settings for the mise-en-scène to highlight the inquisitorial era (Pick, 1992, 81).[64] In this way, Bemberg makes a generalized historical link between the values of Sor Juana's society and twentieth-century fascism and totalitarianism, so relevant to Argentina's recent history.[65] Sor Juana is often shot behind the bars of the grille that separate her from her guests. This acts as an obvious metaphor for historical and contemporary attempts to keep women barred from cultural and intellectual activity.

In the film, religious devotion is reserved for the fanatical, and the shadow of the Inquisition constantly hangs over Juana. The vicereine is seen frequently warning her to be careful and recounts with horror an auto-da-fé that she witnessed in Spain. Juana is seen to be at risk because of her status as a female "secular" intellectual, who is represented as a woman of little faith. In one exchange with the vicereine, she claims that she cannot hear the voice of God. She is not particularly interested in the day-to-day life of the convent, and only really concerned about her writings and her relationship with María Luisa Manrique. When her confessor, Patre Nuñez de Miranda (played by Alberto Segado) asks her about the lack of God in her poetry, unfitting for a nun, she replies that she wanted to study and that the convent was the only place where this was possible. Conveniently, the film makes little mention of the fact that she wrote a number of *villancicos*, or verses sung on religious occasions.

Sor Juana's cell contrasts with the rest of the convent. It is round, filled with light and books, and she is seen there happily writing, entertaining the vicereine, but never engaged in any religious activity.[66] The director said of the space: "I wanted Juana's cell to be like a round prison, as if it were the equivalent of her own head, like a labyrinth that surrounds her with books, a kind of half-jail, half-refuge" (Pick, 1992, 80–81).

The Mexican nun is seen to symbolize the struggle between freedom and rebellion. She occupies the open space of the intellect within the closed world of patriarchal religious fanaticism. The convent is thus a space where enlightenment and obscurantism do battle. On the side of enlightenment are Juana, her friend Carlos Sigüenza y Góngora (played by Gerardo Romano), Madre Leonor, the first abbess, and the viceroy and vicereine, all fighting for intellectual exploration and a woman's right to study. On the side of obscurantism are the archbishop of Mexico, Padre Miranda, Sor Ursula and the Archbishop of Puebla (played by Franklin Caicedo), who eventually betrays Juana.[67]

The convent is also the setting for an unconventional love story, seen in the relationship between Sor Juana and the vicereine, María Luisa Manrique de Lara.[68] The romantic friendship between the two becomes the site to play out the battle between the two forces and posits a world of feminine secular love as counter to ecclesiastical misogyny. This relationship is the central focus of the film, as it provides the primary emotional energy. It is here that there is the greatest degree of artistic license. This is because very little is known about the countess, and the passionate poems Sor Juana dedicated to her are the only testament to their relationship.[69] Their friendship is represented in the film as ambiguous in nature, charged with an erotic tension, all within the boundaries of Sor Juana's celibacy and María Luisa's official heterosexuality, marked by her marriage and her pregnancy. Despite these obstacles, the countess is the desiring subject, who grows fascinated by Juana and appears to fall in love with her. María Luisa openly flirts with the brilliant nun, shown through Dominique Sanda's burning gaze accompanied by the sexy tones of Cecilia Roth, who provides the voice for the French actress. She comes to represent the physical body, with her pregnancy and her attractiveness, which constantly disturb Juana's attempts to transcend physicality and see their love on an exclusively spiritual plane.

The scene in which Juana discovers that the vicereine is pregnant is an interesting example of the tensions between the physical and the spiritual/intellectual, with each woman placed on separate sides. Juana is visibly disturbed by María Luisa's mothering heterosexual body, as it challenges her attempts to place her body within the abstract. She tells María Luisa "I have a body which in a poem of mine, I call abstract."[70] She claims that her scientific instruments (her astrolabe, telescope, and sundial), her lyre, and her writings are her children. She is uncomfortable when her friend counters this by telling her how beautiful she is when she becomes passionate, and tells her that women without children are incomplete.

This is carried a step further when María Luisa orders the nun to remove her veil, to find the "real" Juana, the woman of flesh and blood within the intellectual genius, a woman who remains elusive. To a degree, María Luisa's gaze is that of the director and the implied audience.[71] She is used as a vehicle to express the desire to know the "true" Juana and falls in love with her, just as the director encourages the audience to do. She represents enlightened, progressive values and soft femininity. Denise Miller has written of the "lighter, golden tones" used for the close-ups of the vicereine (Miller, 2000, 143). These and her bright, ornate clothes contrast with the nuns' dark habits and the dark, shadowy world of the convent. Although there are echoes of traditional representations of sex scenes here, with the dominant partner commanding the submissive partner to undress, the order to remove the veil keeps the action outside the sexual sphere. Juana appears frightened rather than excited, as her attempts to separate physical from spiritual love are directly challenged. María Luisa does not succeed in finding a woman with physical desires, with Bemberg representing her nun as a "pure spirit" dedicated to pursuits of the soul. Her love for María Luisa is thus depicted as spiritual; at one point, Sor Juana tells her confessor that the more she loved the vicereine, the closer she felt to God.[72] The erotic energy is reserved for the vicereine, with her physical desire represented in her longing looks and the kiss she gives Sor Juana on the lips before retreating. Although physically awkward, Juana is seen to have romantic feelings; on María Luisa's departure, she rushes to find a locket her patron has given her and places it lovingly around her neck.

Emilie Bergmann has criticized the scene in which the vicereine commands Juana to remove her veil, arguing that Juana's sexuality is neutralized. In her words, "The shorn head of the unveiled Sor Juana reveals submissiveness rather than a desiring female body" (Bergmann, 1998, 230).[73] The kiss is daring within the context, yet it lacks sexual energy, as it is not reciprocated. Bemberg is true to Paz's interpretation in that the sexuality of the two women is sublimated within their romantic friendship.[74] The countess's words following the embrace, "To remember," indicate that this is not to be taken further, and they can share only a memory of what might have been.[75]

There is a surprising disjunction between the language of the poems Bemberg inserts to illustrate Juana's passion for María Luisa and the reticent way in which she behaves with her. Although, as Bergmann has noted, her most passionate poems are not included, there are extracts that are full of intensity. The following lines hint at an emotional relationship with jealousies, tears, and reconciliations, none of which are represented in the film:

So beloved, put an end to harshness now,
jealous torments will cease if you command,
and doubts no longer trouble your peace of mind
with needless gloom, with insubstantial shams, since,
in that flood of tears, you saw and touched
my broken heart within your very hands. (Trueblood, 1988, 81)[76]

However, these intense words are read peacefully by the vicereine at her home and are later seen by her husband, who indulgently comments that his wife is still breaking hearts. The two women are never seen to quarrel, as is suggested in the poem. The passions contained in the poem sit uneasily within the context and belie Juana's shyness and hesitancy when the two are seen together. All of this reveals Bemberg's vision of the relationship as passionate yet chaste. The nonsexual nature of their relationship vindicates Juana from the charges of the religious authorities, who are shown to condemn Juana for her lascivious imagery in the poems written to the vicereine.

Bemberg deviates from Octavio Paz's biography in that she highlights Juana's poetry written to María Luisa as one of the causes of her downfall. Paz has suggested that her poems to María Luisa did not fall outside the conventions of court eulogies and would not in themselves have caused her problems.[77] Nevertheless, in I the Worst of All, her poems are criticized at a meeting of senior figures of the Catholic Church, instigated by the archbishop, who has been looking for an excuse to attack Sor Juana.[78] She is denied access to her library and forbidden from writing, an order overturned by the viceroy. Her confessor then unsuccessfully tries to sway her from her "amorous disorders." Through her representation of Juana's relationship with María Luisa and her conflict with the church hierarchy over her romantic poems, Bemberg manages to create a sense of Sor Juana's radicalism and passion, while maintaining her purity in sexual terms.

The director follows Paz's interpretation of the relationship between the two women. Reacting to an early German biographer's claims of Juana's masculinity and bisexuality, Paz prefers to see her relationship with María Luisa Manrique de Lara as a loving friendship.[79] He is at great pains to desexualize a woman who wrote many passionate love poems, claiming that "even those inflamed poems cannot be described as Sapphic, except in the sublimated sense of the Renaissance tradition" (Paz, 1988, 506). In the impassioned tone of the poetry dedicated to the countess, Paz sees socially acceptable expressions of devotion by an inferior to her superior (201).[80] For others, Sor Juana has been taken as an early historical lesbian symbol and has been adopted as the patron saint of contemporary gay and lesbian Latino/Latina and Spanish American poets (Bergmann, 1998, 232) Critics such as Emilie Bergmann have begun to seek to address the erotic nature of her love poetry and attack earlier attempts to negate her lesbian identity.[81] In her reading, Bemberg claimed Juana for modern mainstream audiences; a sexual reading of the relationship would have pleased lesbian audiences, but at the time of its release, it may have alienated sections of heterosexual audiences.

Bemberg's representation of Juana's ultimate downfall also follows Paz's historical biography to a degree, although she deviates from his version of events in terms of Juana's own final lack of resistance to ecclesiastical pressures.[82] Her fall from grace is seen to occur when she dares to enter into a theological debate and is betrayed by the archbishop of Puebla, who publishes her refutation of an important Portuguese Jesuit, Antonio de Vieyra.[83] What was radical in this in the seventeenth century was that a woman had dared to challenge the views of a noted theologian, a favorite of Aguiar y Seijas, something that maintains its radicalism today. It is therefore not surprising that this is what Bemberg concentrates on. She does not note that there was a basic conservatism within the contents of the letter itself. In fact, Sor Juana wrote in defense of the church Fathers, Augustine, Thomas Aquinas, and John Chrysostom, regarding Jesus' expressions of love prior to his death, views that had been challenged by Vieyra (Paz, 1988, 391). Like Paz, Bemberg traces her fall from grace to this case, combined with the departure of the viceroy and vicereine, recalled to Spain, and her confessor's withdrawal of his services, which leave her without protectors and isolated.[84]

The film's version of events of both Juana's critique of Vieyra and her later submission to the church hierarchy follows modern ideological requirements. In the first instance, her Catholic orthodoxy is not mentioned, and in the second Juana is seen as totally crushed by the hierarchy. Evidence of Juana's attempts to resist are ignored in order to emphasize her status as a victim of intolerance and misogyny. Paz argues that she must have initially fought against Núñez de Miranda and did not, as Catholic historians have argued, undergo a religious conversion (Paz, 1988, 463).

In the final scenes of the film, which document the last years of Sor Juana's life, the pressures of her circumstances are so great that she surrenders to the will of her confessor and to the church hierarchy. She is seen to renounce all her worldly possessions and concerns, to confess to her sins, to renew her vows, and to take the role of the model nun. Bemberg represents her as a broken woman, who is sincere in her confession, a confession that nullifies her entire life's work. The director deviates from her source book, Octavio Paz's biography, which suggests that fear motivated her actions.[85] In I the Worst of All, Juana expresses fear in her confession to Padre Miranda, but this, she says, is a fear of herself, of not knowing how to live according to the expectations of the church. Paz argues that she must have initially fought against Núñez de Miranda and did not, as Catholic historians have argued, undergo a religious conversion (Paz, 1988, 463). Paz also questions the sincerity of her abjuration, citing evidence that she secretly kept jewels, money, and certain documents, despite her promises to renounce all worldly possessions (467).

There is no suggestion in the film that Juana puts up any resistance to her confessor. The final scenes chronicle her surrender to the church hierarchy. She accepts Padre Miranda's assertion that God wants another Juana, one who is to be a negation of all that she has been. In order to be a model nun, she must abandon all worldly interests, including writing, reading, and her love for María Luisa. She is seen to submit entirely to Padre Miranda's will. In this scene, she is kneeling before him in a large white room, furnished only with long tables covered in white cloth and a large crucifix in the center. Juana too is dressed in a simple white habit, not her usual black and white habit, and is dwarfed by the size of the room and her kneeling position. Padre Miranda, in contrast, is standing over her and is wearing his black cassock. The colors used in this scene have a range of signifiers: the whiteness of the room suggests an ascetic coldness; the white and black clothing of the nun and the priest denote good and evil, with Bemberg reversing the moral codes of the seventeenth-century Catholic Church. Sor Juana's white could also suggest a blank canvas, with the church now able to re-create her in its own image.

From here on her defeat is compounded: she hands over her locket to Padre Miranda, a gift from María Luisa, a sign that she renounces her love, and watches passively as the nuns remove all of her books and other possessions. Finally, she reads out a handwritten confession of her "sins" and a renewal of her vows. Bemberg has used Juana herself as the source and edits her actual words to produce a confession characterized by self-abasement and self-abnegation. Juana speaks of herself as "the most unworthy creature created by Your omnipotence" and declares: "For the crime of having lived in religion without religion like a pagan, condemnation to eternal death would be clemency, for my crimes deserve everlasting Hell."[86]

Bemberg used filmic license effectively to provide an edited version of the renewal of vows. In the editing of historical sources and the way in which she stages Juana's words, the director brought her own interpretation to the nun's emotional state. As she confesses to Sor Ursula and Padre Miranda, seated on a raised stage, and to the few nuns who have not died of the plague, her voice is barely audible, and she appears stooped over the document she is reading. She dramatically brings her hand down on a sharp point in order to draw blood with which to sign her declaration with the words "I the worst of all."[87] The scene cuts to Juana's cell, and the camera pans over her empty bookcases and rests on Juana, huddled in a corner. It is here that the film ends with the victory of Church officials their defeat over the brilliant nun.

The director never questions the sincerity of Juana's actions, and she is never seen to subvert the terms of her penance. Bemberg's interpretation of events are in direct contrast to that of her source historian. Paz argues that Juana did not change her views on women's rights to study, but was motivated by fear, and in her confession used the conventional language of nuns in order to appease her detractors. In his reading, Sor Juana does not negate her life's work with any sincerity. In two key passages he states: "I have no doubt that she defended herself to the last and refused to sign an abdication and nullification of her entire life" (Paz, 1988, 463). And "she cannot, no matter how severe her opinion of her own life and behaviour, have believed she was 'the worst in the world.' She was simply using a common formula of vilification" (465).

The effect of Bemberg's opposing reading of total submission to the Catholic Church and its misogynistic expectations of women emphasizes Juana as a victim of patriarchal forces. Had she been seen to subvert church officials in any way, at the end, they would have appeared less menacing. Sor Juana is also seen to be defeated, as she is alone, once she is unwillingly abandoned by her protectors, and lacks a supportive community.[88] There is an implicit call to contemporary audiences to fight against the dark forces that destroyed this brilliant woman. Viewers, who have been inspired by the life of Juana and have suffered with her downfall and the injustices committed against her, are invited to become the community denied to Juana. Bemberg declared that the aim of her films is to change people's attitudes. In her words: "My goal, which is very ambitious, is to always move spectators, and, if possible, change them so that they will leave the cinema transformed" (Trelles Plazaola, 1991, 113; my translation).

The aim of this film, then, is to call upon audiences to recognize and fight against misogyny and totalitarianism, and thus defend women's rights to have a central position within culture. The director interpreted the late seventeenth century for audiences of the late twentieth century and beyond, as women are still marginalized in culture. This is something Bemberg knew from firsthand experience from her battle to succeed in the male-dominated film world of Argentina.

Much of the film does stand up to historical scrutiny. As has been seen, the archbishop is accurately drawn, Sor Juana's cell is an impressive re-creation, her troubles with the church's hierarchy over her writings have been well documented, and she herself spoke of her lack of vocation and irritation at the communal life of the convent.[89] Nina Scott, a well-known researcher on Sor Juana, was asked by Bemberg to check the script when she was in Argentina. Scott wrote approvingly of the authentic representation of the period, commenting, "Bemberg is a stickler for the historical accuracy of details, an impressive feature of her film" (Scott, 1994, 152). Nevertheless, a modern filmic version of Sor Juana has to be an invention. In the creation of a heroine for contemporary audiences, that invention will need to focus on certain aspects of the character at the expense of others.

Sor Juana was a central figure of a colonial, ecclesiastic society, which had few values a feminist, socially concerned director would claim. Nevertheless, she was a radical figure within the context of her age: the fact that a woman came to represent Mexican culture at a time when women were excluded from that world is remarkable. This was an achievement that was hard fought for and brought her glory and sanction. In I *the Worst of All*, María Luisa Bemberg succeeds in making Sor Juana relevant and appealing to contemporary audiences in a number of ways. She places the poet-nun's struggle with the Catholic Church at the core of the film and humanizes her through her romantic friendship with María Luisa Manrique de Lara, in a representation that downplays the political implications of the viceregal system and will not alienate mainstream audiences with representations of lesbian sexuality. Despite the fact that she is ultimately a victim of the church and of the plague that kills her, the epilogue tells the audience that she was considered one of the greatest poets of the Hispanic golden age.[90] Clearly, the defeat is temporal, and history and Bemberg have restored her to her rightful position.

Conclusion

María Luisa Bemberg re-creates a historical figure to warn against the dangers of totalitarianism and to call for an end to misogyny. The focus in I *the Worst of All* is on a single remarkable woman and her attempts to find intellectual freedom in an inquisitorial age that rejected the notion of female scholars. The film is a powerful homage to Juana's achievements and succeeds in bringing an important historical figure to life for contemporary audiences. Nevertheless, it ignores issues of class, and there are only passing references to the Indians affected by food shortages. The inequalities of the colonial system for the masses living in New Spain are disregarded, as the film's focus is on discrimination against women and on how this affects Sor Juana.

In contrast to I *the Worst of All*, *The Voyage* is concerned with the sufferings of the working and peasant classes; it concentrates on the harm done to the citizens of Latin America by mismanaged neoliberal economic policies, U.S. neocolonial practices, and political corruption. The solution to the problems caused by the above lies in mass resistance led by working-class heroes. Solanas's film is true to the political spirit of Third Cinema, calling for the peoples of Latin America, both young and old, to unite against their leaders and to create a new, socially just order. Nevertheless, this order does not appear to be ready to accept women as equals. None of Solanas's heroic leaders are women, and they, in most cases, are reduced to their traditional roles of loyal wives and objects of masculine desire. In respect to this, *The Voyage*'s strength is *I the Worst of All*'s weakness, and vice versa: Bemberg directs a powerful feminist filmic biography, and Solanas creates an epic struggle for an independent egalitarian Latin America, while her failure to represent inequalities of ethnicity and class is inverted in his failure to represent gender inequalities.

Notes

1. I am grateful to the *Bulletin of Latin American Research* for permission to republish material taken from the article "Heroes, Villains and Women: Representations of Latin America in *The Voyage*" (October 2002).

2. Of this, Solanas has said that his film contains "a range of aesthetic planes; there are somewhat fantastical moments, very magical moments, others which almost take the form of documentary, and very real moments" (Castillo, 1993, 47; my translation).

3. For a brief outline of Solanas's position and work while in Paris, see King (2000, 90–91). Solanas has remained politically active and was a member of the Argentine Parliament from 1993 to 1997.

4. These are Televisión española (TVE, Spain), Channel 4 (UK), Instituto Mexicano de Cine, and, in France, Films A2 and Ministère de la Culture et des Grands Travaux.

5. Agustín Mahieu notes that, although Solanas has moved away from advocating armed struggle and his sense of aesthetics has changed, his ideas have remained the same (Mahieu, 1999, 89). Solanas's first film was the revolutionary *La hora de los hornos* (*The Hour of the Furnaces*, 1968), followed by *Los hijos de Fierro* (1978), *Tangos, el exilio de Gardel* (*Tangos, the Exile of Gardel*, 1986), *Sur* (*The South*, 1987), *El Viaje* (*The Voyage*, 1991), and *La nube* (*The Cloud*, 1998), the story of a group of actors struggling to save their theater, which is to be replaced by a shopping mall.

6. For more on this, see Mahieu (1999).

7. Solanas says this in an Italian interview; see *www.alfea.it/arsenalecinema/center-solanas.html*, 4.

8. My translation.

9. The interviews were published in 1989. At this time, directors such as the Coen brothers, David Lynch, Spike Lee, and Oliver Stone, among others, were making films to which Solanas's criticisms cannot be applied.

10. For more on Solanas's views on the need for national cinemas to respect their own tempo in the face of U.S. media conventions, see Solanas (1989, 90–93).

11. For more on the influence of Hollywood blockbusters on films made in Argentina in the 1990s, see Falicon (2000).

12. For Solanas's comments on the importance of the incorporation of digression into film structures, see Yglesias (1993, 42).

13. From cover sleeve of *The Voyage* (1992). Although the film is entitled *The Voyage* in the English translation, the film in the translated interview is referred to as *The Journey.*

14. El Kadri explains further, "We didn't want 'sets,' we wanted to 'integrate,' we wanted to live the old dream of Latin American co-operation, to know the people and to get away from the imposed clichés that separated us and said we couldn't work together" (video sleeve).

15. Somebody Sails is played by the Chilean actor Franklin Caicedo, who also plays the bishop of Puebla in Bemberg's *I the Worst of All*. Américo Inconcluso is played by Venezuelan Kike Mendive.

16. Interview with Solanas in Italian; see *www.alfea.it/arsenalecinema/center_solanas.htm.*

17. This is not the first time that Solanas has coined an expression to describe an art form that he uses. See, for example, *tanguedia,* a tango comedy/tragedy, which he invents in *Tangos, el exilio de Gardel* (see King, 2000, 94).

18. There are clear parallels here with the literary term *magical realism,* which is used to describe much Latin American fiction, including the writings of Miguel Angel Asturias, Gabriel García Márquez, and Isabel Allende.

19. Tzvi Tal (1998) also makes this point, as does Vivek Chaudhary, who notes that President Rana speaks with the same accent of La Rioja as President Menem and is shown playing tennis, Menem's favorite sport (Chaudhary, 1992, 8). President Menem was in power from 1989 until 1999. He won the Argentine national election of 1995, but the constitution prevented him from standing for a third term. In 2001, he was put under house arrest for six months on charges of smuggling weapons to Croatia and Ecuador, as well as for money laundering linked to Swiss bank accounts. It has been claimed that Menem has $10 million hidden in Swiss accounts, a claim that he has denied. Menem has refused to testify in the investigation, arguing that it is politically motivated, and has stated that he plans to run again for the presidency of Argentina in 2003.

20. Solanas received death threats after denouncing Menem, and was taken to court by the president for slander after he accused Menem of corruption and treason in a national newspaper (Ruby Rich, 1991, 64). The day after he repeated his accusations in court, he was shot by unknown gunmen, who warned him to keep his mouth shut. The attack left Solanas unable to walk for two months, but he remained as defiant as ever in his resistance to Menem.

21. For more on Menem's economic policies and style of government, see Vilas (1998), Azapiazu, Basualdo and Nochteff (1998), and Petras and Vieux, (1994).

22. In an interview, Solanas talked of how he exposed the real-life corruption of Menem's cronies through critical humor. He explained how the vice-governor of Santa Fe, a friend of Menem's stole, an iron bridge, which had fallen in a flood, while another friend of the president's committed fraud with a large number of school aprons (Yglesias, 1993, 41–42). Government officials obviously took these attacks seriously; they attacked the film and accused it of spreading crude propaganda, while refusing any form of financial support. In addition, the film's distributors lost the theaters in which the film was scheduled to be shown (Yglesias, 1993, 42).

23. I owe this observation to Rosa Días, a student in the Latin American studies program, at Portsmouth University.

24. My translation.

25. In the film, the character Rana tells Argentines that they have to keep fishing to partake of the economic miracle, that they should not rock the boat, and reassures them that the depth of the water is within the predicted levels, a clear parody of Menem's reassurance that inflation was under control while national industries were being privatized.

26. Flooding as a metaphor for economic troubles due to neoliberal economic policies was used during the actual floods caused by El Niño. A political joke circulating around Buenos

Aires claimed that "the floods are not the result of the waters rising, but of the fact that the country is sinking" (quoted in Vilas, 1998, 10).

27. In an interview Solanas stated that the film includes attacks on Menem and U.S. President George H. W. Bush (Castillo, 1993, 47).

28. Martín's father supposedly provides the voice-over for most of the cartoon sequences. The voice is actually that of Alberto Selgado, as Marc Berman, the actor who plays Martín's father, is French.

29. In December 1989, the United States invaded Panama to topple General Manuel Noriega and defeat the Panama Defense Forces, in Operation Just Cause. It has been estimated that there were 26,000 U.S troops in the invasion. The U.S. Southern Command forces claimed that their actions resulted in 516 civilian casualties, while Noriega's supporters have argued that between 6,000 and 7,000 civilians lost their lives in the U.S. invasion (Weeks & Gunson, 1991, 4). Conniff suggests that 1,000 Panamanians were killed (Conniff, 1992, 164). On the first night of the invasion, there were 417 explosions, which caused many deaths, and the slums of the capital of Panama City were destroyed (Weeks and Gunson, 1991, 4). These are the events Américo is referring to with the destruction of his neighborhood.

30. It is worth noting that the film's meeting of the Organization of Countries on Their Knees in Panama.

31. Márquez describes the way in which his grandmother, unmoved, would tell him the most amazing stories as if she had just seen them. He claims that this is the method he used for *One Hundred Years of Solitude* (Mendoza, 1982, 41).

32. There are parallels here with the works of Jorge Luis Borges, who is only concerned in his stories with truths that serve his fictions. See, for example, "The Garden of Forking Paths," in which chance is harnessed so that the most unlikely series of events sustain the plot (Borges, 1979).

33. Américo says that he remembers everything, from the murder of Augusto César Sandino to the death of Omar Herrera Torrijos. Torrijos gained control of Panama in a military coup in 1968. He was a dictator, yet he passed some legislation in favor of workers. He died in an unexplained plane crash in 1981. Sandino, a Nicaraguan hero for the left, fought against the ruling Conservatives and U.S. involvement in Nicaraguan affairs. In 1934, he was tricked by the dictator Anastasio Somoza, who, after reaching an agreement with Sandino, executed him.

34. Ernesto (Che) Guevara traveled around Latin America in the early 1950s. In 1951, he traveled through Argentina on his motorbike. In 1952, with his friend Alberto Granados, he spent seven months traveling through Argentina, Chile, Peru, and Colombia. His travels in 1954 took him to Ecuador, Panama, Central America, and Mexico. For more information on Che's travels and his life, see *www.cheguevara.com/*. For his account of the 1952 trip, see Guevara (1989).

35. This point is also made by Strick (1993, 55).

36. Solanas has suggested this is the case when he was asked about Martín's surname. He replied that it is necessary to understand that *The Voyage* is a work of fiction and that cinema is not reality, but can only ever be a poetic representation of reality. For this interview, see www.it/arsenalecinema/center_solanas.htm

37. Of this, Solanas has said that his aim in *The Voyage* was to demystify the role of the father for Martín, to learn about the man, not the ideal. He said that the ending of the film shows that Martín has to rely on himself and learn his own lessons (Castillo, 1993, 45).

38. Martín's mother is dominated by his stepfather; his grandmother, though strong, resists the floods because of her loyalty to her late husband. Martín's sister makes one very brief appearance.

39. See also Smith (1999) and Haskell (1999).

40. All of the essays cited here can be found in Thornham (1999).

41. Even this can be seen as running counter to Hollywood, in the latter's rejection of Latin American actors to play Latin Americans, with studios preferring Spaniards such as Antonio Banderas, Penelope Cruz, and Javier Bardem.

42. There have been many recent works dedicated to the life and works of Sor Juana Inés de la Cruz. Some of the key studies in English are Octavio Paz's *Sor Juana, Her Life and Her World* (1988), Stephanie Merrim's *Feminist Perspectives on Sor Juana Inés de la Cruz* (1991), and Pamela Kirk's *Sor Juana Inés de la Cruz: Religion, Art and Feminism* (1988).

43. Clearly, the use of the term *feminist* is problematic in the seventeenth century. Paz has challenged Dorothy Schons's claim that for Juana is the first American feminist stating, "Neither the word nor the concept existed in the seventeenth century" (Paz, 1988, 486). Jean Franco also challenges the use of the term, arguing that Sor Juana was "pre-feminist insofar as feminism presupposes that women are already participants in the public sphere of debate" (Franco, 1989, xxiii). Both these critiques reveal the dangers of applying contemporary terminology to specific historical periods.

44. For more on women directors in Latin America, see Trelles Plazaola (1991).

45. In her work on the writings of Hispanic nuns, Asunción Lavrin writes, "the struggle for perfection was one of the main purposes of religious life. Physical and spiritual discipline, prayer, meditation, self-effacement, and the constant restraining of human desires were some of the means to achieve perfection within the religious state" (Lavrin, 1991, 145). Jean Franco's book, *Plotting Women: Gender and Representation in Mexico,* includes a chapter on the writings of nuns and the relationship between their writings and confessors and priests. In contrast to the literary production of Sor Juana, confessors controlled the output of their charges, and priests, writing biographies, appropriated their words while claiming authorship (Franco, 1989, 3–15).

46. The first volume was published in 1698, the second in 1692, and the third in 1700. See the chronology of Sor Juana Inés de la Cruz by Victoria Pehl Smith in Merrim (1991, 181–82).

47. For her own defense of her vocation as a student and as a writer against criticism that she should dedicate herself to purely secular matters, see "The Reply to Sor Philotea" in Trueblood (1988, 205–43).

48. For a detailed account of Sor Juana's father's identity and the possible effects on her, see Paz (1988, 63–85).

49. For a review of the critical directions on Sor Juana's life, see Merrim (1991).

50. Schons's article was published published in 1926.

51. For a detailed account of this, see Paz (1988, 438–49).

52. For more on these debates, see Paz (1988).

53. Bemberg started her career as a screen writer for two well-known Argentine directors, Raúl de la Torre and Fernando Ayala (Torrents, 1990, 173).

54. Sadly, María Luisa Bemberg died of cancer on May 7, 1995, at the age of 73.

55. In an interview, Bemberg acknowledged the feminist movement as a creative driving force: "I guess one of the things that brought me to make films was my concern with the women's movement" (Whitaker, 1987, 115). She also claimed that feminism gave her the confidence to believe in herself: "Like so many women, I didn't dare take myself seriously....I kept postponing myself" (ibid.).

56. Bemberg said of women directors: "Making cinema is transgression, an attempt to follow one's fantasies, which is a male sport. To stand up to criticism a woman has to feel pretty strong" (Torrents, 1990, 173).

57. For an analysis of Bemberg's life, times, and filmmaking career, see King (2000, 1–32).

58. Bemberg argues, "the ones who think, the ones who communicate, the ones who dream continue to be the male characters" (Pick, 1992, 78).

59. Of this practice, Paz noted, "If the convents of New Spain did not produce either great mystics or great theologians, they were prodigal in the number of penitents and flagellants"

(Paz, 1988, 122–23). Bemberg represents this in the film when the nuns, desperate in the times of the floods and the plague, walk in procession through the convent, praying and flagellating themselves.

60. In her "Reply to Sor Philotea," Sor Juana admits that the convent provided her the space to continue with her studies (Trueblood, 1988, 212).

61. She also wrote official poems for their predecessors, the marquis and marquise de Mancera.

62. Franco added, "Sor Juana loved the countess as a friend but also as an embodiment of a world order in which she stood for the feminine element" (Franco, 1989, 51). Through her study of Juana's poems, Franco has shown that whereas the vicereine embodied the feminine in the secular world, the Virgin Mary took that role in the religious order.

63. José Lezamis, "De su castidad, mortificación y penitencia," in *Breve relación de la vida y muerte del doctor Francisco de Aguiar y Seixas* (Mexico, 1699). For more fascinating details of the archbishop's extreme misogyny, see Paz (1988, 408–10).

64. Félix Monti has worked as cinematographer on more than twenty films. These include three films by Solanas: *Sur* (*The South*, 1987), *Tangos, el exilio de Gardel* (*Tangos, the Exile of Gardel*, 1986), and *El Viaje* (*The Voyage*, 1991). For other films, see *http://us.imdb.com/Name? Monti,+F%E9lix#Cinematographer*.

65. Some 30,000 Argentines were "disappeared" during the military dictatorship's "dirty war" from 1976 to 1983. For more on this, see *www.derechos.org/nizkor/arg/* and Lewis (2002). Bemberg herself had confrontations with the military regime as she was beginning to make films in the early 1980s. Her film *Señora de nadie* (*Nobody's Wife*, 1982) was initially banned by the censors for its representations of an emancipated woman and a homosexual (Whitaker, 1987, 116).

66. Bemberg is historically accurate, as she relies on Paz's account of Sor Juana's cell (Trelles Plazaola, 1991, 122).

67. Padre Núñez de Miranda, Juana's confessor, is known only as Miranda in the film. Carlos Sigüenza y Góngora was a well-known academic, contemporary, and friend of Juana.

68. Denise Miller notes that the casting of the two lead women reflects the underlying lesbianism in their relationship. She points out that Assumpta Serna (Sor Juana) played a lesbian in *El jardin secreto* (Carlos Suarez, 1991), and Dominque Sanda (María Luisa Manrique de Lara) plays a lesbian in *La voyage en douce* (Michel Deville, 1979) (Miller, 2000, 169). Sanda also has a small role in Solanas's *The Voyage* as Martín's mother. Assumpta Serna is best known for a very different role, that of the female killer in Pedro Almodóvar's *Matador* (1986).

69. Regarding the little that is known about the vicereine, Paz writes, "As for the real person, the Countess de Paredes is not even a shadow for us, merely a name and its echo" (Paz, 1988, 217).

70. The lines she is referring to are the following: "Of one thing I'm sure: that my body / disinclined to this man or that / serves only to house the soul — / you might call it neuter or abstract." They are found in Romance 48, no. 1, in Trueblood's translation (Trueblood, 1988, 31).

71. The fact that they share the same first name is a happy coincidence.

72. This neoplatonic love, characterized by an emphasis on the soul and its separation from the body, is the subject of much of Sor Juana's poetry. A famous example is an extract from her *Romance 19*: "That you're a woman far away / is no hindrance to my love: / for the soul as you well know, / distance and sex don't count" (Trueblood, 1988, 39).

73. Her criticism is extended to the director's failure to include some of the most passionate poems Sor Juana wrote to the countess de Paredes. She writes that Bemberg's "choice of poetic texts recited by the actors and her statements about the film obscure the lesbian reading of that image" (Bergmann, 1998, 230).

74. Of this, Paz has claimed, "The only thing that is sure is that their relationship, though impassioned, was chaste" (Paz, 1988, 217), an assertion that could be questioned when considering the lack of knowledge about this relationship.

75. The kiss is in direct parallel to a scene when a younger Juana lived at court as lady-in-waiting to the marquise de Mancera. The scene shows her receiving a kiss from a suitor and returning it with ardor, "to remember" the experience. Here the kiss is seen as a quasi-scientific experiment and is also lacking in any sexual passion.

76. Poem 164 (poem 22 in the translation by Trueblood, 1988).

77. Juana did face constant pressure to stop her studies by those who felt that studying was incompatible with her role as a nun. Paz writes that clerics and nuns issued "continual rebukes and reprimands," as did her confessor (Paz, 1988, 409). In her "Reply to Sor Philotea," Sor Juana gives examples of typical words addressed to her by nameless critic who claim to protect her: "This study is incompatible with the blessed ignorance to which you are bound. You will lose your way, at such heights your head will be turned by your very perspicacity and sharpness of mind" (Trueblood, 1988, 218).

78. Emilie Bergmann has pointed out that the sonnet censured by the church hierarchy in this scene, was not actually written for the Countess (Bergmann, 1998, 241).

79. Ludwig Pfandl, *Sor Juana Inés de la Cruz, la décima musa de México; Su vida, su poesía, su psique* (1963).

80. See Alan Trueblood's *A Sor Juana Anthology* (1988) for English translations of her poems. The treatment of Juana's sexuality says much about critical discomfort with the subject. Trueblood himself, writing in his introduction about the emphasis on love for women in poems, claims: "The situation has inevitably led in some critical quarters to an assumption of lesbianism or bisexuality. At this distance one can only say that no such assumption is necessary to account for the shadowiness of masculine figures and the warmth of emotion in the poems addressed to other women" (Trueblood, 1988, 12). One could ask why the opposite assumption is not more tenable, given the poetic evidence.

81. See also Urbano and Lopez de Martínez's study of Sor Juana's love poems (1990).

82. Paz questions the sincerity of Juana's submission to church officials and argues that she must have fought against total submission (Paz, 1988, 463).

83. Sor Juana was asked to publish her refutation of a sermon by Antonio de Vieyra, a favorite theologian of the archbishop, Aguiar y Seijas, rival of the archbishop of Puebla, Fernández de Santa Cruz. He then published the refutation under the title "The Athenagoric Letter," which included a prologue by the Archbishop of Puebla, using the pseudonym Sor Philotea, warning Sor Juana to concern herself more with the gospels and less with worldly matters. For more on this, see Paz (1988, chapters 25 and 26).

84. Jean Franco mentions a recently discovered letter by Juana to Nuñez de Miranda, in which she defends her right to study and dismisses him as a confessor (Franco, 1989, 40). This suggests that Juana's struggle with the church hierarchy was more active than in Paz or Bemberg's version.

85. In his words, "Sor Juana's contemporaries and many later critics considered this as a sublime act. It seems to me the gesture of a terrified woman attempting to ward off calamity with the sacrifice of what she most loves" (Paz, 1988, 463).

86. For Paz's account of Sor Juana's confession, see 261–463. Bemberg slightly embellishes extracts from her actual letter of confession, in which she wrote that she has "lived in religion without religion, if not worse than a pagan might live," that her sins are "are great and without equal," and that she deserves "to be condemned to eternal death" in "infinite hells."

87. A year after the renewal of her vows, several months before her death from the plague on April 17, 1695, at the age of forty-four, Sor Juana wrote in the convent's Book of Professions: "I entreat my beloved sisters...to commend me to God, for I have been and am the worst

among them. Of them I ask forgiveness, for the love of God and his Mother. I, worst of all in the world, Juana Inés de la Cruz" (Paz, 1988, 464–50).

88. She is supported only by her friend, the intellectual Carlos de Sigüenza, who is powerless to defend her. Jean Franco has also pointed to her isolation and lack of any female community. She claims that her renunciation of learning "was a defeat for all colonial women. Sor Juana could not found a school. She had no disciples" (Franco, 1989, xv).

89. See "The Reply to Sor Philotea" (Trueblood, 1988, 212).

90. The epilogue begins by telling audiences that Sor Juana died of the plague shortly after her renewal of vows.

5

National Identity and the Family
Pixote by Hector Babenco
and *Central Station* by Walter Salles

Pixote: The Law of the Weakest (*Pixote: a lei do mais fraco,* 1981) by Hector Babenco (b. 1946) and *Central Station,* (*Central do Brasil,* 1998) by Walter Salles (b. 1956) are the two internationally best-known Brazilian films of the 1980s and 1990s, respectively, and among the most successful in critical and commercial terms.[1] Both deal with Brazilian realities in different ways, and can be seen as products of their time in their use of plot, their cinematic approaches, their treatment of politics, and their psychological and historical understanding of the family unit. The films have contrasting approaches in their representation of abandoned children: *Pixote* blurs the boundaries between truth and fiction and relies on social realism, whereas *Central Station* creates a romanticized reality. This chapter attempts to explain the effects of these approaches and explore the images of Brazil that each film projects. It analyzes the ways in which the films understand childhood, the dialectic established between the world of the adult and that of the child, and the symbolic family relationships that are forged. The chapter argues that children are used to represent opposing national visions: corruption, immorality, and hopelessness (*Pixote*) versus spiritual and moral redemption and a sense of national renewal (*Central Station*).

In both films, the narrative is structured around the loss and re-creation of the family unit. *Pixote* plays out a variation of the Freudian oedipal triangle, as socioeconomic realities have produced notions of mother, father, and child that do not fit into the bourgeois models for which Freudian theory was developed. There is a direct relationship between poverty, a culture of violent machismo and the failure of the nuclear family in the film. The harsh realities represented in *Pixote* are only briefly touched on in *Central Station,* with the film preferring to represent a romanticized rural Brazil. The nonnuclear family in both films becomes the structure on which to project conflicting

142

visions of national identity. The flawed family represented in *Pixote* symbolizes a country's failure on a number of levels and the alternative family model proposed in *Central Station* symbolizes the possibilities for national reconstruction. The films' representation of gender relations is inextricably linked to the divergent models of families; thus, each discussion explores the ways in which constructs of masculinity and femininity inform the vision of Brazil. The images of motherhood are central to this vision, and the chapter examines the ways that *Pixote*'s failed maternal models define national failings, while the virginal ideal represented in *Central Station* holds a promise of redemption.

Politics and Film in Brazil in the 1970s and 1980s

A brief social, political, and filmic background for Brazil in the relevant period will provide a framework to better understand the ways in which *Pixote* fictionalizes social realities. *Pixote* was made in 1980, when filmmakers were starting to address the problems in Brazilian society, following the military regime's relaxation of its control of Brazilian society beginning in 1975. There was effectively a military-led government in power in Brazil from 1964 until 1985, with 1968 to 1972 the most brutal period (King, 2000, 111–22; Skidmore & Smith, 1992, 179–84). The government of General Ernesto Geisel introduced limited political reforms beginning in 1974 within a structure of military dictatorship, reforms that had an impact on filmmaking. The state organization Embrafilme expanded in 1975 to take on film production and national and international distribution, and had almost complete control of the film industry in Brazil (Ortiz Ramos, 1987, 411). During this period, Embrafilme was under the control of the respected director Roberto Farias, supported by such important directors as Luís Carlos Barreto and Nelson Pereira dos Santos. This was a time of development for Brazilian cinema. Embrafilme's budget increased substantially, as did the number of films it was responsible for: Embrafilme produced seventeen films in 1970, a figure that rose to twenty-nine in 1976. Spectatorship levels for national films also increased in this period. In 1972, there were an estimated twenty-eight million spectators for national films; by 1975, this figure had risen to fifty-two million. It is worth noting that, despite this success, foreign, principally Hollywood, films still dominated Brazilian movie theaters: 198.5 million viewers saw foreign films, compared with 61.8 million who saw Brazilian films (Ortiz Ramos, 1987, 412).

Embrafilme encouraged films with an emphasis on Brazilian historical and cultural heritage, films that lacked the political radicalism of Cinema Novo.[2] Stam and Xavier (1997) describe the policy:

> By sponsoring serious, mildly subversive literary and historical films, the regime entered into a kind of accord with the better behaved of the opposition filmmakers, permitting some critique, as long as it was confined to respectable literary adaptations or to historical dramas set in the safely remote past. (306)

In addition to the policies of Embrafilme, filmmakers were wary of making radical political statements, in the wake of the violent repressions of the military. Harsh political realities following the coup-within-a-coup had effectively brought revolutionary filmmaking to an end. The military regime of 1968–1972 launched a vicious campaign against revolutionary leftist groups, resulting in their torture, murder, and imprisonment, which left the guerrilla movement defeated by 1973. As part of this campaign, many high-profile leftist filmmakers were forced into exile.[3]

With the defeat of the revolutionary left, the continuing power of the military, widespread police violence in the 1980s, and the demands of the marketplace, filmmaking moved away from a revolutionary agenda, with a redefinition of the overtly political.[4] Nelson Pereira dos Santos, an important Brazilian filmmaker and one of the key figures of Cinema Novo, has argued that, following 1973, "our approach has become less ideological and more anthropological" (Burton, 1986, 134).[5] The critic José Carlos Avellar shares this view of the lack of traditional political radicalism in Brazilian filmmaking of the 1980s; for him, there was a new sense of pessimism because of this lack of political vision. The problems documented in Cinema Novo, including poverty, corruption, and underdevelopment, are still present; however, there is a sense that there are no answers to Brazil's problems. Avellar talks of "the tragic feeling that the problem has no solution. Brazil, love it or leave it. The only escape is to get out" (Avellar, 1997, 36).

Pixote

Co-produced and distributed by Embrafilme, *Pixote* illustrates a number of the above aspects of 1980s filmmaking: it provides an example of the new-found freedom to tackle social problems that could not have been treated during the dictatorship. The film does not seek a political solution to the problems of the street children, and it is characterized by a pessimistic vision.

As with the films of Cinema Novo, Hector Babenco in *Pixote* fixes his direc-
torial eye on the dark corners of Brazil; however, the political critique is
indirect and is filtered through a concentration on personal relationships. No
clear-cut ideological solution to the problems *Pixote* exposes is proposed,
and there is no escape for the protagonists except through the temporary
relief of sex and drugs. *Pixote* focuses on the cruelty of individuals who
abuse the children and on the survival tactics developed by the boys.

Pixote has, in fact, been criticized for its lack of perceived political ideology. Robert Stam, for instance, argued that the film blames individual
institutions, rather than the social system, and lacks political analysis (Stam,
1983, 14).[6] Nevertheless, it can be argued that the representation of social
injustice and the denunciation of institutional violence constitute a type of
political and cultural statement. The lack of resolution and the pessimistic
ending leave the audience with a sense that there are serious social problems that need addressing, even though specific solutions are not offered. A
rejection of party politics is a conscious approach taken by the director, as
a reaction to the failure of political establishments or opposition groups to
offer any practical solutions to the suffering people of Brazil. In his defense
from leftist critics who attacked the film, Babenco made it clear that the
absence of a large-scale political vision is deliberate. He argued, "Left-wing
people want a theorem. They want a formula.... I don't believe in the solution proposed by leftists. I believe only in individual solutions. And I did
Pixote in order to show that. The relationships of one man, two, three, four
or five men, are more important than the whole society" (Csicsery, 1982, 8).[7]

It is understandable that the film places an emphasis on the individual
over the collective in a period that saw dictatorship and successive governments chosen by the military establishment. In a sense, the fact that the
film makes no direct reference to national government is an indictment of
the political system and reflects the historical failure of the state to address
social inequalities. The state is simply bypassed, as it is felt that it has nothing
to offer these children.

Through a focus on a poor, abandoned child, *Pixote* exposes the poverty
of the people of Brazil and highlights the neglect and abuse of the most
vulnerable of Brazil's citizens, its children. The film tells the story of ten-
year-old Pixote (played by Fernando Ramos da Silva), whose father has
died and whose mother has abandoned him; he is living on the streets until
he is put into a reform school/home following a raid of street children after
the murder of a judge. At the home, he makes alliances with the older boys
and acts as a witness to the violence of life for all the boys and to the abuses
committed against them by the authorities. Pixote takes the role of narrative

guide, and his gaze is the dominant one throughout the film. The second part of the film shows him and several other boys, Lilica, Dito, and Chico, on the streets of Sao Paulo and Rio de Janeiro, as they engage in a picaresque life of survival and increasingly serious crime. These boys represent types: Lilica (played by Jorge Juliâo) is the effeminate homosexual; Dito (played by Gilberto Moura) is the macho figure; Chico (played by Edilson Lino) is a younger version of Dito; and Pixote, the youngest, is the street urchin soaking up the influences of the older boys. They escape from the home when Lilica and Pixote fear that their lives are in danger after Pixote has witnessed the murder of their friend, Fumaça (played by Zenildo Oliveira Santos), by the police and Lilica is about to be framed for the murder of his lover, framed and killed, in turn, by the authorities in the home for the murder of Fumaça. Chico and Dito die violent deaths — Dito, at the hands of Pixote, who mistakenly shoots him. Lilica disappears when he is replaced by Sueli (played by Marília Pêra), a "real" woman. At the end of the film, Pixote is left alone and seen walking along the railway track armed with his gun.

Cinematic Approaches

Babenco relies on a realistic approach in an attempt to produce a "true to life" representation of street children in Brazil and to give a social problem a human face, through the close focus on a group of friends, both in the reform school and on the streets of Sao Paulo and Rio de Janeiro. The film is an exposé of the violence, corruption, and ineffectual nature of the authorities. Babenco's initial plan was to make a documentary inside a reform school for abandoned children; however, after ten to twelve weeks of visits, the authorities prevented him from returning to the school, presumably to avoid the bad publicity the film would cause (Csicsery, 1982, 2–3). In a response, Babenco decided "to try to make another reality like the reality they wouldn't permit me to show" (3), and he produced a screenplay with Jorge Duran.[8] The script used 200 interviews with children as source material. Not surprisingly, the film has a documentary quality, as it follows the lives of a group of boys, presenting the action from their perspective.[9]

The naturalism the film achieves is due in large part to the processes used in the direction of the child actors and in their performances. Following the examples of Italian neorealism and Cinema Novo, the director used a combination of professional (adults) and nonprofessional actors (children).[10] The children were carefully selected and very well prepared.[11] Each day they rehearsed and filmed a sequence from the situations in the script, following directions and improvising, without ever reading the screenplay (Csicsery,

1982, 3). The children themselves were from the slums of Sao Paulo, as Babenco did not want actors accustomed to the melodramatic techniques required by Brazilian soap operas. They brought their own language to the situations given to them by the director; as Babenco said, "They gave me the right words, the right sentences" (7). Robert Levine found that 40 percent of the script was changed by Babenco after working with the boys (Levine, 1997, 203).

This process clearly ensures a realistic treatment of the fictional situations as the boys interact with the bourgeois director. Babenco and Duran's screenplay changed following the workshops with the child actors, chosen because of their knowledge of the life the film represents. The result is a realistic portrayal of a specific time period for this sector of Brazilian society, coming partially from the perspective of the boys. Babenco intentionally limited his interference as both cowriter and director in the representation of his characters. In one example, Babenco changed the way in which he filmed a scene, on the advice of Fernando Ramos da Silva. As would be expected, Babenco originally had the young Pixote in another room when Chico and Sueli, the prostitute make love. Fernando insisted that in a nonfictional setting, he would be in the same room watching, and Babenco altered the scene accordingly:

> He [Fernando] corrected me because my understanding and my vision are very bourgeois and moralising. . . . But I learned a lot from the children in the film. What is important is how he feels morality, how he understands morality. What is his relationship to feelings? With responsibility? With love? With real affection? That is important. And that has nothing to do with promiscuity. (Csicsery, 1982, 6)[12]

A child from the *favelas* (slums), living with his or her mother, father, and brothers and sisters in one small house or on the streets clearly has a different sense of sexuality than the bourgeois child, and Babenco argued that he had a responsibility to represent this fact.

Babenco also ensures that *Pixote* is seen to be grounded in Brazilian reality by beginning the film with a series of statistics. The director is seen standing in front of a *favela* in São Paulo.[13] He tells the audience that Brazil has 120 million inhabitants, and that 28 million children in Brazil live below the United Nations' standards for human rights. He adds that there are three million homeless children and explains that those under age eighteen cannot be prosecuted if they break the law.[14] This is an important fact that allows foreign audiences to understand the plot; the children are used by adults to commit crimes, such as drug dealing, because they cannot be prosecuted.

They are, however, detained and sometimes murdered by the police, as the film shows.[15] Babenco then points to Fernando Ramos da Silva, the actor who played Pixote, who is now a few years older; he is seen standing with his mother and some of his nine brothers by their house in the slums. This also serves to give the film a life outside the story, as Fernando's reality continues when Pixote's screen life ends.

The line between fact and fiction is blurred in Fernando's life, following the film, which adds credence to the claims of authenticity that the film makes. Fernando claimed that, following the release of the film, he was persistently harassed by the police (Levine 1997, 208), presumably because they confused the fictional character with the "real" person, they bore grudges against Fernando for the way in which they are represented in *Pixote,* and because he was involved in petty crime following the failure of his acting career.[16] He was arrested twice for minor offenses and tortured. On August 19, 1987, he was shot dead by police.

In his description of the events Robert Levine argues that the police murdered Fernando with no provocation. Audiences watching the video version of the film released after 1987 are told in a postscript that the actor playing the protagonist was violently killed. This inevitably affects the reading of the film, highlighting the links between fiction and reality and adding a shocking and tragic dimension: the final image of the figure of Pixote walking along the railway is one without future, as the character becomes the dead actor in the imagination of audiences.

Using a variety of techniques, such as the appearance of the director to provide the audience with statistics, naturalistic methods of acting, and biographical connections between the child actors and the characters they play, the film creates a link between the real and the fictional. *Pixote* aims to create the impression that the fiction is rooted in the lives of children who originate from the slums of large cities and that the story in the film is not exceptional, but represents a microcosm of a social situation. Indeed, police brutality against petty criminals, both adults and children, has been well documented. The military police who patrolled the streets of Brazilian cities following the defeat of terrorist groups in the late 1960s and 1970s turned their attention to street crime and arrested, tortured, and murdered suspects from the slums with impunity (Pinheiro, 1991; Chevigny, 1991, 207–12). In addition to the police, street children have to contend with death squads, made up of off-duty police officers often working for small business owners who employ them to kill thieves. In 1984, more than over eighty youths were found shot by death squads in the slums of São Paulo, and several members of the military police were found to be involved (Chevigny, 1991, 211).[17]

Despite the factual basis of the representations and the freedom Babenco gave the children to use their own language, this is not a documentary, and the filmmaking process is clearly mediated. The tightly constructed, action-packed fictional plot and the emotional identification between the boys and the audience that is generated mean that *Pixote* can be seen as realistic drama.[18] The film aims to show the dark side of life for abandoned children in Brazil and to earn audience sympathy for them by focusing on their experiences. Randal Johnson explains that "point of view shots, show-ing the world from Pixote's perspective, alternate with an objective camera, revealing the brutality faced by the film's characters" (Johnson, 1987, 45).[19] Pixote's gaze is thus the dominant one throughout the film, and he acts as the witness of events for the audience. An example of this is seen in one of the opening sequences. A young boy is brutally raped by three older boys during the first night that many of the boys spend in the reform school. The scene begins by showing three boys attacking a smaller boy; there is a cut to Pixote, with a close-up of his face illuminated for emphasis. The cam-era then switches back to the rape, and it is now clear that it is being seen through Pixote's eyes. The representation of this scene challenges images of childhood innocence on many levels: older children are the rapists, a younger child is the victim, while the child's point of view adds horror to the attack. In addition, this is a fate that could await Pixote, as a newly arrived younger boy.

The fact that the audience is forced to share this horror with Pixote ensures our sympathy for him. This is a technique used throughout, with audiences shown the cruelty of the authorities through Pixote's eyes. This approach establishes an interesting dialectic between audiences and charac-ters, as middle-class audiences are forced through the eyes of a ten-year-old boy to witness events that are usually hidden from their view. These audi-ences are likely to be from the middle classes, particularly outside Brazil, where the film was very successful on the art house scene.[20] The inten-tion of this is to generate understanding and sympathy for a marginalized group. Frequent close-ups of Pixote's young, bruised face add to the audi-ence's sympathy for the protagonist; he has a disturbing combination of soft childish features and cuts, bruises, and dirt that show the harsh reali-ties of his life. Although the children, once on the streets, reveal themselves to be violent criminals, this can be seen as a response to the violence that surrounds them.

The Family Unit

Relationships, mediated through the reconstructed family unit, provide the focus of concern in *Pixote*. As has been seen, the film is sensitive to issues of class representation; given this, a useful reading of the film can be provided by considering the ways in which it reworks the Freudian oedipal narrative to fit within the social context of street children in Brazil. In *Pixote,* both traditional paternal and maternal figures have been distorted by the violence of the patriarchal model, the total subordination of women, and extreme poverty. As a result, these are children without parents. Corrupt, violent police and reform school staff fail to take the place of absent of fathers, and weak, marginal feminine figures in the school—the teacher, the nurse, and the doctor—and in the streets—Sueli, the prostitute and Debora (played by Elke Maravilha), the drug dealer/club dancer—are unable or unwilling to fill the role of absent mothers. Many of the boys' mothers, forced to work as prostitutes, have abandoned their children. The figure of the mother has thus become a sexualized commodity because of economic and social realities. The confusion that Sigmund Freud argued takes place between mother and whore for the bourgeois male child in the Oedipus complex is in the case of *Pixote,* not a false association to be resolved, but a reality, which clearly affects the boys' relationship with women, as will be seen.[21]

The potential maternal figures, the female "carers" the boys come into brief contact with in the institution, are prevented by the authorities from having meaningful relationships with them. The boys, and Pixote in particular, thus never succeed in disentangling the figure of the mother from the sexual figure of the prostitute, as they are shown no viable alternative models. The boys have an ambivalent relationship with the patriarchal authority figures (the judge, the police officers, the school staff) that have taken the place of their fathers. They clearly hate them and resent them for the violence that they inflict. However, in their dealings with each other, the boys follow the paradigms of power that they have learned from these men, with dominance and submission organized around masculine and feminine gender roles. Failed paternal and maternal models lead the boys to create their own family unit, which takes its most complete form when a small group escape the reform school to make their lives on the streets of São Paulo and Rio. Lilica, the effeminate boy, takes the role of mother, Dito acts out the role of father, and Pixote and Chico take their places as the male children. Lilica is ultimately replaced by Sueli, the biological woman, who takes the role of sexual object for Dito and (failed) surrogate mother for Pixote.

A culture of violent machismo (indirectly linked to the militarism of the era) is blamed for the failures represented in the film. This violence, as well as its relationship to masculine power dynamics, is established from the outset. In the opening scene, the camera provides individual close-ups of a group of boys; their faces are dirty and a number of them have bruises and cuts, presumably caused by beatings given to them by the police during the raid. They are all transfixed, watching something. The audience does not know who these boys are or what they are watching. The boys, however, are united by something. There follows a cut to a small television showing images of two men violently attacking another man, who is on the floor. The next wide-angle shot brings the boys and the images on the television into the same frame, which has the effect of making a connection between their behavior and the culture that surrounds them. This is emphasized by the fact that when the boys are interrupted from their viewing, a fight breaks out between several of them. They are thus marked by the sign of violence; aggression surrounds them, on the television, in the police station, and on the streets.

This violent cult of masculinity is held responsible for the breakdown of biological and symbolic family units. State institutions fail to provide alternative support for these boys without families. The culture within the reform school and the police is rooted in aggressive and exaggerated masculinity and sustained by violence, intimidation and fear, as well as the subordination of femininity. It is significant that in one of the early scenes, Sapato (played by Jardel Filho), the director of the school, and Almir (played by João José Pompeo) the brutal policeman, are shown humiliating Lilica, the effeminate boy, forcing him to dance provocatively by gyrating around Sapato's shoe, which turns from an instrument of parodic seduction to a symbol of violence, as Sapato kicks Lilica away from him.[22] Almir shows his connection with Sapato who then takes over in the humiliation of Lilica, threatening him and then the others with violence if they do not tell him who killed the judge. Lilica, although biologically male, has taken a feminine subject position, and dominance of him heightens the authorities' sense of their power. The plot involving the murder of the judge shows how a law based on masculine power and violence has replaced a civilized rule of law based on the protection of human rights. Street children, living outside the law, have unwittingly murdered the symbol of the law, the judge (who is the victim of a mugging gone wrong); they, in turn, are threatened by the policeman (the supposed upholder of the law), and, in fact, Fumaça, who is suspected of the crime, is later beaten to death on Almir's orders.

The judge (played by Rubens de Faldo), who is brought into the school to investigate the riots, illustrates the ineffectual nature of the legal system, and its failure to understand or protect the boys. It is significant that he adopts a benevolent paternalistic discourse to appeal to them. He has them all gathered outside and, like a vexed headmaster, asks them why is there so much destruction; he says that they should think of the center as a home and tell him everything as they would a father. However, the boys are silent and look down at the ground. He is speaking a foreign language, and is alienated from them by his class and circumstances. These are boys without fathers and the male figures in their lives have abused them. The gentle paternalistic discourse is one that does not exist for these boys. Equally, the judge will never hear the voices of the boys; they are too frightened to tell him the reason for the riots (the murder of their friend), as they know they would also be beaten to death if they talked. The judge's discourse is that of the middle-class family and is directed at the middle-class audiences who have failed to understand these children's reality. His comment that they came to the school to be reintegrated into society is laughable to audiences who have seen the boys struggle to survive amid the violence of the authorities.

The film suggests that a caring maternal model could offer a form of salvation for the boys; however, the power of the patriarchal model defeats any possibility of fulfilling relationships with the feminine figures. The theme of the redeeming maternal figure is established early in the film. Fumaça and Pixote are seen wandering around at night after sharing a joint.[23] Pixote, stoned, is drawn to a statue of the Black Virgin. As he approaches the statue, the camera shoots from above, and he is made to look very small, which suggests a heavenly presence watching him. Pixote emerges from the darkness of the night and is illuminated by the multicolored lights surrounding the image of the Virgin, who is pointing skyward. There follows a long close-up of Pixote, transfixed by the statue, with the focus alternating between Pixote and the Virgin, thus shown in silent dialogue with each other. He is dragged away unwillingly from this state of grace by Fumaça.

This scene establishes a dominant theme of the film: the frustrated search for the mother. Throughout, Pixote is unconsciously seeking a maternal figure, seen in his encounters with the teacher and the psychologist, in in his bonding with Lilica, and his attraction to Debora and Sueli. Pixote's scenes with the women in the school are brief but significant. In a tender scene, a beautiful schoolteacher (played by Arielé Perez) attempts to teach him to read. Pixote shows no interest in the lesson, but when she approaches him and gives him individual attention, he speaks and writes the innocent line "The world is round like an orange" (*"a terra é redonda como uma laranja*"), his voice joining the teacher's. There is a close-up of the two of them joined in this task, as soft, romantic music is heard. This is a brief image of a potential mother-child relationship, which quickly ends. The impossibility of such a relationship in the environment of the reform school is emphasized by the editing: this scene is followed by an abrupt cut to the boys playacting a torture scene, to practice withholding information from the authorities, immediately followed by the rehearsal of a bank holdup. The (masculine) law of violence and crime is perpetuated by the boys and leaves no space for (feminine) care and nurturing, with street education taking the place of a traditional education.

The same point is made even more forcibly with Pixote's brief meeting with the psychologist (played by Isadora de Farias). Pixote is seen playing with a glass globe depicting a snowstorm, the only time he has ever had a toy, and the psychologist encourages him to confide in her. She convinces him that everything he says will be confidential and will go into a report that can help him leave the reform school. Pixote has never before been in a position to trust anyone in authority. In addition, he has no records, and therefore does not officially exist. However, before he can begin to talk to the psychologist, Sapato forces him to leave.[24] Pixote gives the psychologist a long, sad look as she tells him to go, and the same music that was played when Pixote was with the schoolteacher is heard, creating a link between these two scenes of hope and disillusionment. The editing is even more dramatic here, as the following scene shows Pixote and a group of boys taken away by Almir, the policeman, an episode that results in Fumaça's murder.

The feminine order is thus continually weakened by the primacy of the masculine order, a fact that ensures that Pixote's search for the mother figure is destined to fail. This power dynamic is also at the root of the relationships that the boys form among themselves and with others, with their interaction organized around sexuality and power. This is established from the outset, as has been seen, when the older boys show their dominance of the younger through a violent group rape of a young boy. The importance of the family unit is illustrated in the school by the fact that the most powerful couple are Garatão (Claudio Bernardo) and Lilica, who are among the oldest of the boys, both nearing their eighteenth birthday. They come to form an alternative maternal/paternal model for the younger boys in opposition to the dictatorial paternalism of the authorities. It is significant that the riot, led by Lilica, in which all of the boys participate, is sparked by Garatão's murder by the school's staff. Garatão's association with Lilica serves to consolidate his power. His "ownership" of the effeminate boy enhances his masculinity.[25] As is commonly the case in Latin American constructions of sexuality,

Lilica's lovers (Garatão and Dito) do not see themselves and are not seen as homosexual, as they are the active partners.[26] In Brazil, the effeminate, passive homosexual is known as the *viado* (from *veado,* "deer") or *bicha* (the feminine form of "animal") and takes a feminine role.[27] As Richard Parker explains, although the *bicha* or *viado* suffers social stigma, his sexual partner does not: "Precisely because his phallic dominance is preserved through his performance of the active role in sexual intercourse, the *masculinidade* of the *homem* (man) is never called into question, regardless of the biological sex of his partners" (Parker, 1993, 71).[28]

This distinction between the dominant and submissive masculine and feminine man is played out in the relationship between Dito and Lilica. Once the boys have escaped, the two become lovers, which consolidates Dito's position as leader of the group. He is not the most experienced, nor is he the oldest, yet, through "ownership" of Lilica, he comes to adopt an increasingly masculine/machista role (Dito's age is never specified, but he appears to be about sixteen years old). In fact, it is Lilica as the older, most experienced member of the group who has the most contacts with the underworld, is the most streetwise, and would appear to be the natural leader; however, his sexual and gender identity precludes him from this position. Lilica arranges a cocaine deal with Cristal (played by Tony Tornado), his old associate/lover, which Dito wrecks through his naivete. Dito insists on giving Debora the cocaine, mistakenly trusting that she will appear later with the money, despite Lilica's warnings.

The four boys come to form a family group, with Dito and Lilica acting as a form of mother and father to Chico and Pixote. In one scene, just after their escape, Dito and Lilica are seen lying on the grass, while Chico and Pixote are childishly play fighting in the fountain. In this scene, the gender roles between the two lovers are firmly established. Lilica is holding a flower and wearing a feminine halter-neck top. His hair is arranged in a bob, and he is leaning seductively toward his lover. Dito, since his escape, has cultivated a fashionable (in the late 1970s and early 1980s) macho look, with his Afro hairstyle and large shades; he is seen lying on his back, bare chested, revealing a large crucifix, clearly no more than a fashion statement, as he shows no sign of being religious. He mentions how much he would like to go to Copacabana, and Lilica, playing the feminine role, asks if Dito can take them there. Like a good husband and father, Dito promises to take all four of them. The next scene reveals Dito and Lilica having sex, with Dito taking the active role, and the act providing pleasure and consolidating their gendered positions.

This is a fragile family unit based on the need to survive and lacking strong foundations. The "parents" of the group are children themselves, who have not had any successful role models, and thus fail to provide appropriate guidance for Chico and Pixote. Their first failure comes with the attempt to sell cocaine at a nightclub. Lilica and Dito send the two younger boys in, as they are less likely to get into trouble if they are caught. Here, they are repeating the cycle of exploitation that they themselves have been victim of, with adult criminals, such as Cristal, using minors to do their dirty work. This inability to protect the younger two results in Chico's death and Debora's murder. Chico attacks Debora, who has betrayed the group by stealing their cocaine, and she (rather unconvincingly) hits him against the wall, causing him to die. Pixote reacts instinctively and stabs Debora in the stomach, causing her death.

The cause of this terrible accident lies in the fact that these are children playing adult games. Of this scene, Babenco said, "The fight between the woman and the child is the same as children playing in kindergarten. 'Give me my pocketbook.' 'I don't want to give it to you. . . .' Whap" (Csicsery, 1982, 8). However, the drama is generated by the fact that this is not another child, but a woman whom Pixote has seen as a potential mother figure. It could be argued that, on an unconscious level, through a knife attack in the area of her womb, Pixote is taking revenge on the representation of the failed mother. Debora has earlier appealed to Pixote's desire for a maternal figure when she is attempting to win his confidence: she tells Pixote that she has a son of his age and that he can come to her home to play with him. Pixote's face lights up, and he tells the other boys that they should trust her. For Pixote, the fact that Debora has reneged on her promise to take him home is even more serious than her failure to pay the boys for the cocaine.[29]

The unit finally breaks up when the group ally themselves to Sueli, a prostitute. They become involved in a scam that embroils holding up Sueli's clients and stealing from them as they are about to have sex with her. This is, initially, a successful operation, as the men are not in a position to defend themselves or to complain to the police. Lilica, however, is excluded from the group; when Dito becomes Sueli's lover, Lilica sees that he has been replaced and leaves. The feminine man clearly cannot compete with the feminine woman in the construction of Dito's masculinity. This signals the end of the family of boys, and although they form an alternative family unit with Sueli, this is soon destroyed by tensions between Pixote and Dito.

Although Sueli is a mature woman, with many years of experience working on the streets, she is sold to them, which suggests that, even as boys, they have more value in their society than a woman, with prostitutes reduced to objects of exchange. It is significant that as part of the deal with Sueli's previous pimp, Dito buys Pixote a gun for the same price as Sueli (Dito already owns a gun). The purchase of both a woman and a gun gives Dito a sense of his virility; however, it is this machista brand of masculinity that ultimately causes his destruction and that of the pretend family unit. Pixote's gun is, ironically, the instrument of his death. Dito as the flawed father figure is too immature to understand that Pixote is too young to enter the symbolic phallic order of manhood, as represented by the gun.

In a botched holdup of one of Sueli's clients, an American businessman, Pixote mistakenly shoots Dito instead of the client.[30] Dito's sense of power has been enhanced by becoming the lover of a "real" woman, particularly as he steals from her clients and prevents them from having sex with her through the use of his gun. His death at the hands of Pixote reveals the shaky foundations of his power and is a form of unconscious patricide, when looked at within the terms of the film's reworking of the Freudian oedipal narrative. Pixote's mother figure is the prostitute whom his surrogate father now "owns," so Dito, who has already caused Pixote to lose one maternal figure (Lilica), is the rival who stands in the way of Pixote's desire for union with Sueli. Prior to the shooting scene, Pixote and Dito have their first argument over the departure of Lilica, with Pixote defending him from Dito's attacks. Pixote accuses his mother of being a whore, an attack stimulated by the loss of Lilica. Significantly, in response, Dito throws a carton of milk at Pixote after drinking some, with the rejected milk acting as a symbol of the loss of the mother figure. He has the milk through his possession of Sueli and denies it to Pixote. It could be argued that the "accidental" shooting of Dito is motivated, on an unconscious level, by Pixote's desire to gain exclusive ownership over Sueli and to be rid of the dominant paternal figure.

Pixote's tragedy, however, is that, as a result of the shooting, he orphans himself. Sueli, as has been seen, is a flawed maternal figure who does not have the ability or the resources to act as a mother to Pixote.[31] Throughout the film, the traditional virgin/whore dichotomy is played out in the representation of the female characters. The figure of the prostitute traditionally acts as an antithesis to the idealized mother, seen in the image of the Virgin, which earlier so captivates Pixote. He, however, confuses the two figures in his search for a mother because of the lack of availability of other models in his environment. His failure to understand the prostitute's inability to nurture a child is demonstrated on their first meeting; in a graphic and disturbing scene, Sueli explains to Pixote, while sitting on a blood-stained toilet, that she has just aborted the fetus she was carrying inside her. She has

Pixote (Fernando Ramos da Silva) and Sueli (Marília Pêra) in *Pixote*.

done this using knitting needles, and the remains of the fetus are visible in the rubbish bin; Pixote just stares at her, and she threatens to do the same to him with the knitting needles if he does not leave her alone. Pixote is too young to understand and tells the others that he thinks she is unwell, as there is blood in the bathroom.[32] He therefore does not sense her rejection of the maternal role, and for a short time lives out a fantasy that he is her child.

Sueli can be nothing other than a sexual subject. She only knows how to relate to others through her sexuality, and in one scene, when she is trying to bond with Pixote, she asks him if he has ever had a French kiss. He responds in a confused way, kissing her on the mouth as they celebrate their first successful job, and watches fascinated as she and Dito have sex. In the final scene, where he, traumatized by Dito's death, turns to her for solace, there is a further disturbing merging of the maternal and the sexual. He searches for her breast and sucks hard upon her nipple. Initially, she responds to his needs and adopts a maternal language, telling him that "Mummy is here," however, she soon reacts violently against this imposed role, forces him off her, and shouts that she is not his mother and that she hates children. He covers his ears and curls up into a fetal position, initially refusing to accept her rejection. His final departure, in which he prepares to leave and carefully

157

fixes his gun into his trousers, suggests that in response to the rejection of the maternal model, he will take up the phallic, macho position embodied in Dito, a position that has only brought death and destruction.[33] The last scene of the film, in which Pixote is seen walking along a railway track, symbolizing the journey he is on, is thus deeply pessimistic.

Pixote is a film that focuses on problems without proposing any solutions. Through a representation of the hardships faced by the boys, it exposes the total failure of state institutions to care for street children. The realities of life for these children are fictionalized, using an often brutal, realistic approach and naturalistic dialogue and acting techniques. Childhood is never romanticized, and the boys turn to crime and violence as they learn from the examples set by the adults with whom they are in contact. The story rests thematically on a focus on the culture of violent masculinity and the domination of the feminine, which leads to a failure to recognize the needs of children and the creation of flawed family units.

Central Station

In the words of Johnson and Stam (1982):

> Every cinematic tradition has its own intertext. Every film is part of a text larger than itself; each film is a discourse responding to other discourses; each film answers and echoes those that have preceded it. (19)

Central Station, whether consciously or otherwise, offers a response to *Pixote.* It takes the figure of the poor male child and contests the negative images projected in Babenco's film, and instead offers the international market a contrasting, romanticized vision of childhood. Josué, the film's young protagonist, comes to represent innocence, hope, and the possibility of changing one's destiny. The neglect and violence so clearly portrayed in *Pixote* are ignored, and solidarity and love protect the child and allow him to forge a secure identity. In *Central Station,* a positive model of an alternative family is proposed without the figure of the father, who is absent throughout. Josué, whose mother dies early on in the film, looks for help and support from Dora, and she becomes a maternal figure for him. Nevertheless, there is no hint of sexual desire for her, and she gradually becomes associated with the figure of the Christian Virgin. The film bypasses the patriarchal model that so dominates *Pixote* and proposes a maternal-fraternal family unit in which the child, the symbol of Brazil's future, is able to develop.

Pixote and *Central Station* represent childhood in very different ways. There are a number of superficial similarities. Both films feature children of similar ages (Pixote is ten and Josué is nine) who have been left without parents and who try to survive in large, uncaring cities (São Paulo and Rio de Janeiro — *Pixote;* Rio de Janeiro — *Central Station*). Despite the similarities in the ages of Pixote and Josué, there are important differences in the representation of the two. This is seen through their circumstances. Josué has managed to hold on to his childhood innocence because his mother has died; she has not abandoned him. His father may have been an alcoholic, but Josué was protected by his mother, who left her husband when she was still pregnant, and is rescued by Dora, before he turns into a Pixote: a victim of his society who learns to survive by victimizing others. Dora accompanies him on his journey to Bom Jesus do Norte in northeastern Brazil, where he hopes to find his father. In their travels, the two develop a relationship based on caring and learn much about themselves.

Central Station does not deny the reality represented in *Pixote,* as will be seen; however, the film's focus is elsewhere. Whereas *Pixote* reflects the despair following the years of militarism, *Central Station* is a film that represents hope for renewal and a better future. It chooses to represent an optimistic vision of Brazilian society, through the redemption of Dora, initially a hardened, cynical, and materialistic woman, and her gradual adoption of the maternal role. *Pixote*'s realism and pessimism are countered here with a romantic, optimistic vision of reality. Society is equally guilty of neglect of the street child; however, an individual's action, motivated by conscience and concern, is enough to save this child and assure him a future filled with hope. Likewise, the child has a redemptive power as he awakens in the adult compassion and love: in Walter Salles's words, "He is the transforming angel of the story" (James, 1999, 14).

Josué represents innocence and the potential for a better future, in direct contrast to Pixote. Salles has spoken of the symbolic function of his child and adult protagonists: "Dora represents old Brazil: that culture of indifference and cynicism we had in the 70s and 80s, which arose from the idea that we had to be industrialised and any means were acceptable to reach specific ends." Josué, in contrast, "represents the possibility of a certain innocence, of refusing a deterministic future and granting yourself another destiny" (James, 1999, 14). This vision of Brazil, as seen through Dora and Josué, is very different from Babenco's representation of the country. The culture of indifference and cynicism is the same culture that is exposed in *Pixote;* however, the possibility of change and redemption offered to Dora and Josué is refused to both boys and adults in *Pixote. Central Station* ultimately offers a fairytale romance in its reworking of traditional myths, such as the happy return to rural origins, the reuniting of child and family, and the power of the virginal mother figure.

Politics and Film in Brazil in the 1990s

It is worth locating *Central Station* in terms of Brazilian culture and society, in order to account for this shift from realism to romance and from negative to positive representations of childhood and of the future. Certainly, the situation for street children in Brazil did not improve; by the end of the 1990s, it was, in fact, worse, as the statistics demonstrate. Other social indicators are as negative; social inequality was even more pronounced in 1998 than in the early 1980s, with 10 percent of the wealthiest Brazilians taking 47 percent of the national income, and 10 percent earning less than 1 percent of that income (Palast, 1998). Likewise, despite the end of military regimes, there was little faith in the government by the end of the 1990s. Although Fernando Henrique Cardoso's government had initially restored much confidence to the country after the corruption of his predecessor, Collor de Mello, the president lost support toward the end of the decade with his policy of continued privatizations and International Monetary Fund–sponsored austerity programs.

This failure of the political system can explain the rejection of a political solution in *Central Station*. Salles has said that the elite are nowhere to be seen in the film, "because there's nothing to expect from these classes" (Kaufman, 1998, 21) and that individuals have to work to improve their own lives because governments will not help them. However, whereas both *Pixote* and *Central Station* share this refusal to turn to political solutions, understandable following the abuses of military and paramilitary organizations and political corruption in the following civilian governments, *Central Station* presents a way out through personal relationships, which serve to bring hope and salvation, despite the failure of the patriarchal state. Lúcia Nagib has stated that an emphasis on individual destinies, which overcomes social problems, and a shift from political to intimate portraits of characters, are part of a trend in Brazilian cinema (Nagib, 1999, 19).[34] She argues that such films are not political in traditional terms, yet they retain a sense of social solidarity. Filmmakers are now less ambitious than in the times of Cinema Novo, as "none aspire to a revolution or to establish a new art form" (Nagib, 1999, 19; my translation); they are more interested in telling stories and giving voice to characters from the poorer classes. It is interesting that film turns to individuals for values of solidarity and compassion to seek a better society when filmmakers once advocated government-led collectivist systems of revolutionary Marxism.

This shift in approach and positive focus, characteristic of *Central Station*, as well as a number of other recent Brazilian films, can be explained by the changed nature of the film industry itself.[35] It is well known that feel-good stories with sweet, ultimately good children and happy endings have a good success rate at box offices, and there has been a growing awareness of commercial factors in Brazilian cinema, with an increasing reliance on private finance. As Stephanie Dennison notes, "There appears to be a consensus of opinion for the first time among Brazilian filmmakers on the need to make their product more commercially viable" (Dennison, 2000, 143). Although *Pixote* was relatively commercially successful, it could be argued that such harsh images of misery and violence are unlikely to hold much appeal for audiences today. Unlike many films of the 1980s, which focused on the dark side of life in Brazil (Avellar, 1997), there was a stronger sense of the need to entertain the audience in films of the 1990s. Many of the films were likely to have a commercial appeal, with an emphasis on comedies, period dramas, historical farces, children's films, urban dramas, and thrillers (Dennison, 2000, 135; Johnson, 1999, 19). Films also sought to represent popular culture, such as music, football, and religion, while an awareness of an international audience was seen in the use of foreign actors and the "foreigner's perspective" in the film.

This awareness of market forces is understandable when considering the preceding period that saw a crisis of funding, leading to a temporary freeze in filmmaking. Brazilian cinema in 1998 was emerging from one of the worst periods in its history. The year 1990 witnessed the collapse of a national film industry. The corrupt president, Collor de Mello, withdrew all state funding; Embrafilme, the state-funded national film body, was forced to shut down, and the Sarney Law, which provided tax incentives for investment in film and quotas for Brazilian films shown in theaters, was repealed (King, 2000, 270).[36] In 1990, only thirteen films were produced, a figure that dropped to three in 1993. With the fall of Collor and the new regime of Fernando Henrique Cardoso in 1994, the dying film industry was brought back to life. New progressive film laws were introduced. The new version of the Sarney Law, the Audiovisual Law, was passed in 1993. This brought back a quota system and introduced a reduction in tax for companies investing in film. In addition, the law allowed foreign film distributors to invest up to 70 percent of their taxes in Brazilian film. This had the desired effect, with U.S. companies such as Columbia, Warner, and Sony taking up this opportunity (Johnson, 1999, 30; King, 2000, 272; Paxman, 1998, 55).[37]

This availability of funds saw a radical change in the state of Brazilian cinema. By the late 1990s, thirty-five to forty films a year were being made (Mount, 1999, 18). New directors emerged, while well-known directors associated with Cinema Novo continued to make films. Nevertheless, the majority of the funding was from private sources, which led to a heightened awareness of the need to win audiences by ensuring that the films were commercially attractive. In the words of the critic and film editor Inácio Araújo, "Before, producers attempted to make art. Today, the key word is product. What is being asked for . . . are Brazilian films capable of competing with American films" (Palast, 1998). A number of critics have warned against being overcelebratory about the resurgence of Brazilian film in the 1990s. Johnson (1999, 30) points out that most films from that period had a box office draw of less than 300,000 and achieved limited art house release. In most cases, they could not compete commercially against the dominance of U.S. cinema. The fragility of the contemporary Brazilian film markets is also pointed out by Araújo (1999, 90).

A Commercial Success Story

Central Station is a film that has come to represent the boom period of the late 1990s; its main achievement is that it is a film that is successful both as a commercial product and as a work of art, with widespread international art house release. From the start, it set its sights on a world market, with the entry of the screenplay at the Sundance Film Festival (Chaves Tesser, 1999, 144). In Brazil itself, the film was a huge box office hit, beating *Titanic* and *Godzilla* in the top ten list at the time of its release. By March 1999, the film had been seen by 1.3 million spectators (James, 1999, 14). Internationally, by the same time, the film had taken in over $17 million and was distributed by major companies, Miramax in Europe and Sony in the United States (King, 2000, 272). The film was also critically acclaimed and won a number of prestigious awards at international film festivals.[38]

The film has a strong screenplay, based on an original idea by Walter Salles and written by first-time writers João Carneiro and Marcos Bernstein. The strength of the story and the screenplay can be said to be behind the success of the film; it won the Sundance Institute International Award from 2004 screenplays, which, along with the prize money of $310,000, secured a $2.9 million budget, along with French and Swiss producers, notably the five-time Oscar-winning Arthur Cohn (Mount, 1999, 19).[39] The film's success has allowed Salles to make several subsequent films, with international investment, in a short period of time, a luxury denied to most Latin American directors, who are forced to spend years raising money for projects.[40]

What is it about *Central Station* that has attracted so much international attention and won it so many awards? The reasons for the commercial and critical success of *Central Station* are numerous. The story itself has a universal appeal: the death of a mother and the developing maternal/filial relationship between Dora and Josué are guaranteed to move audiences. The theme of the search for the father is at once realistic and mythical and allows the film to be read on various levels. There is the literal desire for a young boy to find his father and the need for the country to seek out its history, to turn to its past for guidance. *Central Station* also gives the audience a sense of insight into Brazil through the characters' journey from Rio to the northeast, without dwelling on the ugliness of the country. Aspects of poverty and violence are glimpsed in the cruelty of Don Pedrâo, his murder of the young thief, and in the organization that buys street children, kills them, and sells their organs. These scenes serve to add emotional impact to the film; however, once Rio is left behind, so too is any sense of evil. The harshness of life for abandoned children, told so graphically in *Pixote*, is thus avoided, as Josué is saved from this fate by Dora. He passes from his mother's care to Dora's and so keeps his innocence. This, along with the fact that street children are rarely seen, allows for a sanitized and romanticized image of children.[41] The film's success also rests on the characterization of Dora and the magnificent acting of Fernanda Montenegro, one of Brazil's most respected theater actresses.[42] Dora initially shares the indifference of the city; her gradual adoption of a maternal role and her shift from a position of coldness and rejection to warmth and love is handled sensitively and is moving while avoiding sentimentality. Through the focus on Dora, the audience is emotionally engaged, as we are shown that individual acts have the power to change lives, clearly a heart-warming, feel-good message.

Perhaps the main selling point of the film is the character of Josué and his portrayal by Vinícius De Oliveira: a beautiful boy, with big eyes and an easy charm. As Josué, an innocent, sweet-natured child, he tries to play at being what he thinks is a man, but is defenseless without a caregiver. It is interesting to examine Salles's comments on the selection of the child actor. The importance of the right choice of child to sell the film can be seen from the fact that 1,500 boys had been given screen tests, and none were felt to be right for the part. Vinícius was not an aspiring actor, but a shoeshine boy who had never seen a film and who approached Salles at an airport looking for business. When Salles, impressed by Vinícius, encouraged him to audition, he insisted that the other shoeshine boys also be tested, a generosity of spirit that moved the director. In his words, "Ultimately, the film is about solidarity and discovering compassion, and he had those qualities

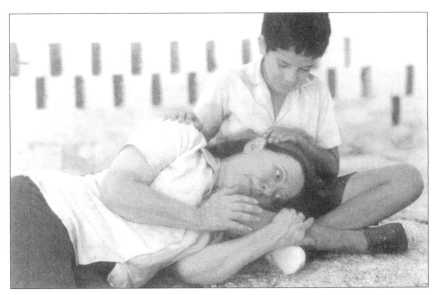

Josué (Vinícius De Oliveira) and Dora (Fernanda Montenegro) in *Central Station*.

ingrained in him" (Flyn, 1998, 10). This is clearly a romantic story, which itself is used to sell the film, as is evident by the fact that it is told in each promotional interview that Salles gave. The follow-up story is also romantic in nature. The production company promised to supply a scholarship to see Vinícius through school and college. In addition, following the film's release, he worked on a local radio show, introducing educational programs made for children who are unable to go to school (James, 1999, 15). Salles explained, "For many Brazilians he's the boy who managed to escape that deterministic future" (ibid.). Even in the biographical lives of the actors who play the children, the contrast between Fernando Ramos da Silva (Pixote) and Vinícius De Oliveira could not be greater; as has been seen, Fernando was murdered by police at the age of nineteen, after a life of petty crime.[43]

Walter Salles's background explains how he is able to make a film that is so attuned to commercial factors, while remaining sensitive to artistic considerations. He started his career making documentaries and advertisements, which he made with the company that he founded in 1986, Video-Filmes (Kaufman, 1998, 19). These two facts are significant, as they reveal a man interested in the representation of social issues and stories of human interest, yet who knows how to sell an idea. *Central Station* incorporates all of these skills. As has been seen, it is a film with a powerful human interest, while a documentary approach is used in the filming of key scenes, such as the letter writers at the station (Central do Brasil), and the pilgrims at Bom Jesus do Norte. The greatest spectacle of the film, the pilgrimage, was not a reenactment, but the actual event. This documentary approach means, for Salles, that such scenes stop "being the representation of the thing and becomes the thing itself" (Kaufman, 1998, 21). The cinematographer, Walter Carvalho, captures both the realism and the power of the atmosphere by using the natural light from the pilgrims' thousands of candles ("Central do Brasil," 1999, 13).

The flexibility of this kind of filmmaking lends a folkloric power to the film and provides a dramatic visual stage for the actors. There is a sense here of cultural tourism, both for the international audience and for the urban Brazilian viewers. Salles has claimed that he wanted to put northeastern Brazil back on the screens, to represent "a physical and human geography that has been absent from Brazilian cinema for a long time" (James, 1999, 14). The film does this in a visually and emotionally appealing way, by focusing on the faith, hopes, and hospitality of the people, not their poverty or misery. Nevertheless, despite the selective use of documentary techniques, Salles has not cultivated a documentary approach in the ways that Babenco has done in *Pixote*. The line between fact and fiction is thus much more obviously delineated in *Central Station*, with the narrative clearly located within the realms of romanticized fiction.

The City

The emotional heart of *Central Station* is found within biological and symbolic family relationships, represented through the death of Josué's mother (played by Soia Lira); the developing bond between Dora and Josué; the search for Jesus, the boy's father; the temporary family unit established with César (played by Othon Bastro), the evangelical truck driver; their acceptance within the spiritual family of pilgrims, and their final encounter with Josué's brothers. As in *Pixote*, the paternal model is flawed, seen in the failure of the state to care for Josué, in the absence of the biological father, and in the greed and brutality of Don Pedrâo (played by Otávio Augusto), a security guard at the train station. Nevertheless, an alternative is found in the development of the maternal and fraternal models, the significance of which will be explored below.

This emotional heart can only begin to take shape as the city is left behind and Dora and Josué travel to the heart of the country. The film is structured in two parts and is organized around urban and rural spaces, with the values the film espouses only present in the small communities of the Sertão and the northeastern town of Bom Jesus do Norte, Pernambuco. The scenes shot in Rio are concentrated on the Central do Brasil, the principal train station in the city, and represent a dehumanized world, where individual identity has been crushed by the multitude. Here, it is suggested, there is little space for family or community. Some 300,000 to 400,000 people pass through the station every day, and the film uses this location to represent the failure of modern Brazil to integrate the range of social classes and to provide social services for the poor. Salles explains that the station provides "a portrait of the urban scenario of Brazil. It's almost a Darwinist place in which only the strong survive" (Kaufman, 1998, 21).

There are many crowd scenes, with long shots of passengers hurrying to get off and on the trains and rushing to get to their destinations. These are interspersed in the opening sequences with the close-ups of customers at Dora's stall. This has the effect of presenting them among the backdrop of the crowd and prevents their character development. Both for the audience and for Dora, these talking heads never acquire the status of individuals worth caring about, with the obvious exception of Josué and Ana, Josué's mother. For a number of these crowd scenes, the camera focuses on the feet of the commuters, a technique that serves to depersonalize them. This effect is also achieved through the use of high angle shots, which ensures that individuals are not distinguished from the mass. A variation on this technique is used following the death of Ana. Josué is left alone and is seen, with a tear-stained face, sitting on a bench, while dissonant music, resembling the sound of trains on tracks, is heard. The camera focuses on him, and because of his size, the passing crowd is seen to be headless, which again serves to highlight the dehumanized nature of the city crowds and Josué's plight. The screenplay highlights this intention, with the crowd described as a "suburban swarm" (Carneiro & Bernstein, 1998, 4).

It is significant that Ana is, in effect, killed by this "suburban swarm." The crowd has its own rhythm, and standing out results in danger. Josué loses his spinning top in the pushing of the mass of people; he goes back to retrieve it, and as his mother stops to look for him, she is run over by a bus. There is no space for play here, as symbolized by the lost toy, and no room for the individual to go against the flow of the crowd. The figure of the mother is thus symbolically murdered by the city, and Dora refuses to take on this role while she is still in Rio. Even when she, tortured by her conscience, rescues Josué from the false adoption agency and accompanies him on his journey to find his father, she intends to leave him to the driver's care, and only continues with him because he gets off the bus.

The film offers a critique of modernity and consumerism, seen in the fact that the city represents a world where material possessions are prized over human life. Don Pedrâo shoots a young man because he steals a Walkman, and nobody protests. In one of the most shocking scenes of the film, Dora symbolically exchanges Josué for a new television. This is apparent when she is seen entering the "adoption" house holding him by the hand; there is then a cut to Dora pulling on a rope, attached to the new television that she has bought, which replaces the boy's hand. She walks home through an underground, suburban complex as she pulls her television, suggesting that her actions have caused her to enter a moral underworld. Once in her apartment, the camera provides a close-up of her television. The screenplay makes it clear that it is to have pride of place in her living room: "On Dora's chest of drawers there is now enthroned a spanking new TV with a 20 inch screen" (Carneiro & Bernstein, 1998, 31). Dora initially prefers to buy into consumer culture and escape through television than to confront the reality of Josué's fate.[44] She admits that she was lying to her best friend Irene (played by Marília Pêra) and that he is not in one of the best children's institutions, saying, "Alright, Irene, I'm lying and you know everything about me. But, just for now, let's watch television." Irene refuses to allow this form of escapism, telling Dora that Josué will be killed for his organs, and says the words that trigger Dora's redemption, "there's a limit to everything!" This forces Dora out of her voyeurism to become engaged with her reality; she acknowledges her responsibility to Josué; without her, he will be murdered, and her conscience refuses to let the television hide this reality. It is significant that when she has reached her destination and is in Bom Jesus do Norte with Josué, she phones Irene to ask her to sell her possessions, and she has forgotten that she owns the television. A concern with others has now replaced her interest in a consumer lifestyle.

Dora comes to represent the cynicism and indifference of the culture predominant in the city. Salles explains:

> In the eighties and nineties, like in many other countries, the only criterion was efficiency. In the name of that, we had unemployment and social violence. Individually, it causes you to ignore others, and there is a loss of identity. Dora in the film is typical of that. (Flyn, 1998, 10)

She has a potentially responsible job, helping the illiterate and semilit-erate to communicate, yet she betrays their trust, by using the letters as entertainment, reading them aloud to Irene. The letters take the place of her faulty television, in providing voyeuristic pleasure in others' misfortunes and seductions, the material of the soap operas of everyday life. Like the television viewer, she passes moral judgment on her customers, choosing not to send the majority of letters, with the additional advantage that she saves on postage. The film suggests that communication, as symbolized in the letters, can break down through this culture of indifference.[45]

Dora initially resists engaging with anyone on a personal level, apart from her old friend Irene. She is particularly annoyed with the return of Ana to rewrite the letter she has sent to her husband, as she is imposing herself on Dora's consciousness. This is compounded by her death and the return of Josué, who wants her to write yet another letter to his father. Her initial rejection of Josué is striking; she refuses to write the letter, as he has no money, and forces him to leave, ignoring him when he later tries to follow her onto the train. She only eventually takes him home when she can make some money from him by selling him to the "adoption" agency. At this stage, Dora can be seen to be actively opposed to family life. She does not send either of Ana's letters, as she has judged that Jesus is an unworthy husband because of his drinking, and appears indifferent to Irene's pleading that the boy deserves to meet his father. She spends much of the time with Josué criticizing his father, despite the fact that he has just lost his mother. This, it is gradually revealed, is not just cruelty or heartlessness, but a reaction to her own family history. When she is on the bus with Josué, she reveals to him, when drunk, that her mother died when she was his age, following her father's drinking and abandonment of them for another woman.[46] In a psychoanalytical reading, it can be seen that Josué's journey to find his father is also Dora's journey to discover/examine her own past and regain a sense of authentic self. At the end of the film, although she is sad to leave Josué, she has learned to accept a maternal role through her relationship with him, and in so doing has reconnected emotionally with the family unit. Her final words, expressed significantly in a letter to Josué, are an acknowledgment of the importance of family. She says that she is afraid that her surrogate son will forget her, and that she misses her dead father.

The romance of the film depends on conservative representations of gender. The initially negative representation of Dora is linked to her rejection of traditional feminine qualities (mothering, wearing feminine clothes and makeup), as well as her declared dislike of men in general.[47] The screenplay describes her clothes, when she is first seen, as "almost masculine" and explains "that Dora has no interest in making herself attractive" (Carneiro & Bernstein, 1998, 2). Dora's self-improvement is linked to her adoption of the maternal role, and a more feminine identity. Her final redemption is symbolized by the fact that before she leaves Josué in his brothers' house, she is seen putting on the new, flowery mauve dress that he has bought for her and carefully applying lipstick. Likewise, Josué's attempts to construct his own masculinity throughout the film are based on traditional patriarchal values, which are not problematized. He is surprised that Dora and Irene can live without a man to protect them, claims that his mother managed without his father, as she had him to look after her, and confuses masculine and Christian codes, when he attempts to impress César with fabricated accounts of the women he has had sex with in Rio. He idealizes his father, particularly his ability to make things as a carpenter, and refuses to accept Dora's warnings about him. The more traditionally feminine Dora looks, the happier he is to be with her. He tells her that she looks much better with lipstick, and, as has been seen, it is he who buys her the dress.

The Journey to the Northeast

The conservatism in the representation of gender relations is also evident in the vision of the ideal future of the country. The film suggests that the best way to deal with the problems of the city is to simply leave it behind and return to a romanticized rural life. Inequalities and the problems of the millions of street children who are never rescued are thus largely ignored. In *Central Station*, the characters are seen as deeply connected to the land they inhabit, with the individual formed by his or her environment. Solidarity between the characters can only be fostered once the dehumanizing site of the city, symbolized by the station, is left behind. Salles has said that he has turned to the Sertão and to poor rural communities precisely because they have been abandoned by official politics and, as a result, maintain a sense of integrity. In the director's words, "If innocence and solidarity still exist anywhere it is here" (James, 1999, 15). There is clearly a romanticizing of the Sertão, with its poverty ignored. Salles's Sertão is a romantic landscape used to suggest an uncorrupted Brazil, where more humane values can be found.

The film clearly fictionalizes rural and urban spaces, demonizing and romanticizing them, and creates characters that come to represent these spaces. Whereas the unredeemed Dora shares the values of the city, Josué embodies the supposed innocence of the northeast, the region of his conception. In order for Dora to develop, she has to travel though Brazil and leave behind the values of the city, associated with the mismanagement of the country. Likewise, if Josué stays in Rio, he will be killed, resulting in the symbolic death of innocence. It is significant that following his rescue, Dora is forced to leave, as she has put her own life in danger through this act of kindness.[48] This point emphasizes the link between people and places; a new, more caring Dora cannot survive in Rio.

The shift from the urban to rural setting is reflected in the cinematographic techniques used. In the city, colors are dull, sounds merge into each other, and, as Salles points out, everything Dora sees is out of focus, except when she wants money (Kaufman, 1998, 20). The colors that begin to appear on the journey reflect her clearer view of the world. Walter Carvalho, the cinematographer, has discussed the two approaches he took when filming in the city and on the journey. In the area of the station, he used closed lenses to create a sense of claustrophobia and imprisonment. Once they are on the open road, the focus is on movement, and "the gradually opened lenses start little by little to reveal the space" (Carvalho, 1999, 12). In the majority of cases, natural light is used, both in the station and outdoors, as Carvalho prefers not to interfere with lighting where possible (13). There is a striking contrast between the dull colors of the station concourse and the blue skies seen when Josué and Dora are on the bus, and this reflects the hope the journey brings them. This message is enhanced by the romantic, harmonious soundtrack that accompanies them on their travels.[49]

The hope in *Central Station* lies in the possibility of forging positive symbolic and biological family relationships. This, in the context of the film, is only possible in a rural setting, where strong communities still exist. The strongest symbolic relationship is the maternal/filial bond that develops between Dora and Josué, which is allowed to flourish in the rural landscape. Although it may appear that his need for her is greater, by the end of the film it has become clear that he has filled an equally strong emotional need, and that while she saves him from a life on the streets or murder by the adoption scam group, he also saves her from her emotional emptiness.

It has been argued that before Dora can take on a maternal role, she has to shed her city identity. This is symbolized by the fact that she loses all the money she has left on the bus for Josué when he leaves his backpack behind. The money that she had was tainted, as it came from the deception of her clients; she is now forced to rely on strangers and her wits to ensure that the two of them reach their destination, and consequently has to forge relationships with others. She does admittedly steal food, as does Josué; however, this is in a different moral category from deceiving her clients, as it is needed for their survival. The fact that she actually sends the letters (to Jesus, the saints, and personal contacts) that she writes for people at the pilgrimage and that the money she earns through this is legitimate signals her moral redemption. This scene is in direct contrast to that in which customers dictate letters in Rio. The letters themselves are of a less selfish nature, such as those that thank Jesus for favors granted, and the customers are happier, with one beaming man declaring himself the happiest man in the world. Dora clearly cares about these people, and makes empathetic noises and comments as they are speaking.

This moral salvation seen in the midst of a pilgrimage would seem to necessitate a religious reading of the film; yet *Central Station* takes an interesting and ambivalent approach to religion and the concept of the religious family. To an extent, Christianity is the focus of criticism. This can be seen in the representation of César, the truck driver who offers them a lift. The three of them soon come to form a brief, alternative family unit, with Dora and César taking the role of mother and father for Josué. César takes the boy on his lap and lets him drive, and he and Dora begin to have intimate chats, while Josué is at one point mistaken for their son. Paradoxically, through his evangelical, sexless brand of Christianity and his relationship with the "holy" family, César is unable to sustain relationships, and create a family of his own. He is frightened away by Josué's talk of loose women in Rio and Dora's seduction. After being tempted to drink a beer, he abandons them while Dora is in the toilets putting on some makeup. Salles confirms the intention to provide a negative representation of the evangelist in an interview: "I'm really critical of these evangelist guys you see on television. They benefit from the lack of knowledge of the common people. And they diminish the possibilities of one's life. So the truck driver is not supposed to drink or smoke. And he is definitely not supposed to have sexual relationships. This sort of thinking is spreading all over Brazil, like an incredible disease" (O'Sullivan, 1999, 9).

This critique of religion appears to continue in the representation of Josué's father, seen in the fact that he is called Jesus. The name is prevalent in the film (as it is in Brazil); Jesus (father) is thought to be living in Bom Jesus do Norte (literally, Good Jesus of the North), while a pilgrimage sees devotees traveling to the town in search of the Christian Jesus. Josué's father is never actually seen in the film; his is both a symbolic and a real absence. Jesus has left the family home; he has drunk away his lottery winnings, left for Rio to try to find Ana, and has not returned. His letter to Ana, which Dora reads, suggests he has gone to the gold mines to find work. He certainly is not the savior that his son was looking for and shows no interest in the boy. He has never met Josué, as Ana was pregnant when she left him, and Jesus does not even mention him in his letter to Ana. It is obvious that Dora makes up the part of the letter that refers to Josué to protect his feelings.

Nevertheless, religion is not uniformly criticized in the film. There has been a tendency in Brazilian film following the early days of Cinema Novo to take a less critical line toward popular culture. Religion is no longer seen in Marxist terms as the opium of people, and a cause of the misery of the masses, as in the early films of Glauber Rocha, but is seen as a rich an interesting form of cultural expression (King, 2000, 119; Nagib, 1999, 25).[50] Dos Santos's influential manifesto stressed the need to affirm, not reject, popular culture (Burton, 1988, 133 — 141), and most filmmakers from the 1970s have accepted this principle. It is interesting that *Central Station* at once criticizes Christianity, yet celebrates the faith of the pilgrims. This can be explained by the cultural trend that refuses to condemn the beliefs of the popular classes, and also by Salles's background as a documentary filmmaker. He explains:

> As a sometime documentarist I forgot I was an atheist and tried instead to be faithful to what I was seeing and to integrate these elements into the film. The Virgin Mary of the Candlelight pilgrimage brings the possibility of a ray of light in the darkness which in a way is emblematic of cinema itself. (James, 1999, 14)

Salles's understanding and representation of these beliefs do not mean that he shares them; they can, he argues, be explained in terms of the need of people who have received no state help and have nowhere else to turn. In his words, "These communities have been abandoned for so long they don't expect anything from earthly powers" (James, 1999, 14). The film, therefore, takes a complex approach to religion. The scriptwriters and the director give a negative representation of the religion of the truck driver and subtly suggest that both the Christian and biological Jesus cannot bring redemption for Josué, while the popular beliefs of the pilgrims are respected and are used for their dramatic power.

The pilgrims rescue Dora and Josué, after César has abandoned them, and they are welcomed into this religious community, with Josué joining in the songs to the Virgin Mary of the Candlelight on the truck. The plot cleverly plays with the fact that they are also seeking Jesus in Bom Jesus do Norte. The pilgrimage provides a spiritual framework for Josué to symbolically bury his mother. As they all rest in the Sertão, Dora takes Josué and his mother's handkerchief and places it on a crucifix on a rock, among the flowers and candles the pilgrims have left. The pilgrimage also creates a dramatic backdrop for Dora's final transformation. Josué has run off after she, tired and hungry, has exploded in anger at him. In her search for him, she stumbles into the miracle room, a womblike cave full of candlelight and photographs to the Virgin and Jesus and praying women. She cries the boy's name amid the loud praying voices. The camera shows events from her perspective, and as she begins to feel faint, the field of vision is blurred; when she grows dizzy, the images in the room start to spin round. As the scene climaxes, shots of a spinning Catherine wheel outside alternate with images of Dora in the miracle room. As she faints, the Catherine wheel explodes, leaving an image of the Virgin and baby Jesus in its center. The mother and son imagery is clearly echoed in the fact that Dora has completed her spiritual awakening and can now accept the maternal role. She awakes to find her head in Josué's lap in the main square, with him stroking her hair, and she, visibly moved, hesitantly pats his knee.

Central Station is an allegorical film, with Brazil itself represented in the cinematic landscape and in the characters. Josué represents the possibilities of the country; the return to the northeast represents the search for community, which, it is suggested, only exists in a more traditional society. As Salles explains, "The journey of the boy trying to redefine his future and find his roots is emblematic of a country trying to tackle these same problems" (James, 1999, 14). The emigrational waves to the cities and a national focus on modernization have not brought prosperity to the poor, and the alienation of the poorer classes is represented in the death of Ana and the abandonment and attempt to murder Josué. The film therefore looks for "an innocence lost in the same place those people left, like a nation yearning for its roots" (Salles quoted in Cowan, 1998, 72). This place is no paradise, as is clear from the artificial development, with identical houses, created in Bom Jesus do Norte.[51] Josué's brothers are squatting in one of these houses, as their father left them without money.[52] Yet, despite these difficulties, the brothers themselves have retained a sense of innocence and are working to improve their lives. Here again individuals are left to struggle for self-improvement and survival because of government mismanagement.

As has been seen, the allegorical nature of the film is found not only in the landscape but also in family relationships. The failure of Jesus, the biological father, seems to suggest that the future of the country does not lie in the example of the previous generation, or in Christianity. In contrast, Jesus' two sons, the biblically named Moisés (played by Caio Junqueira) and Isaías (Matheus Nachtergaele), Josué's half brothers, welcome him into their home, before they even know his true relationship to them, and the film ends with the suggestion that he has found his home and a loving family. The name Moisés is particularly significant here, as the biblical Moses leads the Children of Israel to their redemption in the promised homeland. The northeast can be seen as Josué's homeland, and it is here that Dora finds redemption. Josué's happy ending is shown in one of the final scenes, which shows the three of them sharing a large bed, with Josué spread out between his brothers (the other bed has been given to Dora). The fact that he finds his future with his brothers, not his father, is significant, and symbolizes the need for a break with the values of the previous generation and for the current generations to work together. The professions of the two older boys are also significant; Moisés is a builder and Isaías a carpenter, jobs that can be seen to symbolize the rebuilding of the country. This was also the profession of their father, but he, through personal failings, could not succeed in his work. Solidarity is thus seen in fraternal, not patriarchal, relationships.

Dora's redemption can also be seen in allegorical, gendered terms. She accepts her "natural" feminine role as a caring maternal figure and can thus contribute to the (masculine) future of her country. She also learns the value of communication and finds her role as the facilitator of relationships between people, another traditional feminine role. Through its characters, *Central Station* proposes a romantic vision of Brazil, based on a return to a traditional, rural way of life, with a caring symbolic family unit at its center. Despite the rejection of patriarchy, many traditional gender roles are not challenged; the men in this vision will work together to build the country, whereas the ideal woman, whom Dora becomes, is still rooted in the mythology of the virginal mother.

Conclusion

The family unit is the focal point for contrasting allegorical national representations in *Central Station* and *Pixote*. This is predicated on the orphaned child at the center of both films and the relationships that he forges with others. Pixote and Josué serve to represent the present and future of Brazil. Pixote's fate provides an essentially pessimistic vision of the country, as he is let down by flawed maternal and paternal models. The film rewrites the oedipal drama for the street child and focuses on the desires of a boy who will never have a mother or father. Pixote's doomed search for maternal figures represents the failure of the motherland (Brazil) to sustain her children (the poor and disenfranchised), and the continued dominance of violent patriarchal values.

In contrast, *Central Station* presents the family as the liberating force of the country. Through the relationship that Josué forms with Dora (the maternal figure) and his brothers, his future is seen to be positive. Dora is a positive antithesis of Sueli, the prostitute and failed mother. As has been seen, connections are made between Dora and the Virgin, and her embracing of the maternal role not only saves Josué, but also brings her redemption. A nation that has been let down by the state, represented by the absence of the father and the killing of the mother, is transformed by love and solidarity, found in the symbolic and biological family unit. Josué, in contrast to Pixote, his filmic predecessor, is represented as a good, unspoiled character who, away from the contaminating elements of the city, will help to build the country's future, seen in the suggestion that he will take up carpentry, the family trade.

Despite Babenco's insistence that his is not a political film, *Pixote* can be seen to be a more radical film than *Central Station,* in its representation of social reality and in its conceptualization of gender relations. *Pixote* relies on a broadly reflectionalist model, in that, within the conventions of realistic drama, it aims to represent life as it is for Brazil's street children. Although it does not present any answers to the problems of the street children, it exposes the many injustices that they face and shows a face of the country unseen in tourist images of carnivals and beaches. The film also offers a critique of the gender systems that sustain social relations within this class in Brazil and offers a realistic representation of the expression of sexualities, exploring the relationship between gender, sexuality, and power. *Central Station* differs from *Pixote* in that it uses a transformative mode; that is, the filmmaker and collaborators use the medium to suggest an idealized, romanticized reality.[53] Thus, the child is rescued before he turns into a Pixote, with the film eager to create a romanticized, audience-friendly, rural Brazil, and not focus on the country's dark side. The film takes a conservative view of gender relations, and through Dora's journey, it is suggested that in women's rediscovery of their traditional femininity and mothering instincts lies the key to personal and national redemption.

Notes

1. *Pixote* won the Silver Leopard at the Locarno Festival, the Critics Prize at the San Sebastian Film Festival, and the U.S. Film Critics Association prize for best foreign film of the year (1981). It was also nominated for a Golden Globe as best foreign film; the film missed an Oscar nomination because of release dates. See page 178, note 45, for details on *Central Station*. *City of God* (*Cidade de Deus*, 2002) directed by Fernando Meirelles and Kátia Lund, follows in the tradition of *Pixote*. *City of God* is a powerful exploration of gang violence in one of Rio de Janeiro's *favelas* and children's place in that violence. At the time of this writing, the film is being shown in the United States and in Europe. It is expected to break international box office records for a Brazilian film.

2. Filmmakers of Cinema Novo included Carlos Diegues, Glauber Rocha, Nelson Pereira dos Santos, and Joaquim Pedro de Andrade. This was not a monolithic aesthetic movement with a single approach; what united the directors was a belief in independent, socially conscious cinema that could play an important part in the social transformation of Brazilian society (see Johnson, 1998; Johnson & Stam, 1982). In his manifesto for revolutionary filmmaking, Glauber Rocha argues that "the most noble cultural manifestation of hunger is violence," as this encompasses love, "not a love of complacency or contemplation but rather of action and transformation" (Johnson & Stam, 1982, 70). The violence of the hungry is revolutionary, as "it is the initial moment when the colonizer becomes aware of the colonized. Only when

confronted with violence does the colonizer understand, through horror, the strength of the culture he exploits" (70).

3. Key directors were forced into exile, and strict censorship meant that films had to rely on allegory to treat any political themes (Johnson & Stam, 1982, 38). Carlos Diegues went to Paris for two years, from 1969 to 1971; Walter Lima Jr. was imprisoned in 1970 for forty-five days without trial (56); and Ana Carolina, a writer and director known for her political documentaries, was imprisoned in the early 1970s for ten months without trial. Ruy Guerra and Glauber Rocha were also forced into exile in this period (King, 2000, 115; Stone, 1997, 52–56).

4. In the words of the prominent Brazilian filmmaker Carlos Diegues, "What's political is the fact that cinema has changed our way of looking at the world, not the power relationships portrayed in the film" (Burton, 1988, 174).

5. This shift in approach clearly fits into B. Ruby Rich's model of Latin American cinema's movement from the "revolutionary" to the "revelatory" (Ruby Rich, 1997, 282; see introduction, p. 5).

6. In addition, Stam claimed that the creation of one-dimensional stereotypes as the "baddies" of the piece means that middle-class audiences are not directly addressed in the film. In other words, they/we are absolved of any guilt for the class system responsible for the situation of the street children. Many on the right have also criticized the film for "suggesting that society's ills breed crime and depravity" (Levine, 1997, 206).

7. Babenco also stated, "I don't believe in political messages or flags.... The most important thing in my films are the interrelations between these people, these children" (Stam, 1983, 7).

8. Babenco bought the rights to José Louzeira's novel *Infância das mortes* but used little of the novel in the film (Csicsery, 1982, 3).

9. For more on this, see Johnson (1987), who analyzes the cinematic and rhetorical devices used to give Babenco's *Pixote* and *Lúcio Flávio* (1977) a documentary tone.

10. Johnson and Stam (1982) commented on the influence of Italian neorealism on Cinema Novo films made in the 1950s, in terms of location shooting, "non-professional actors, popular themes and a simple, straightforward cinematographic language" (32). The influence of neorealism in *Pixote* is evident, particularly in its representation of poverty, its subject matter, and its use of nonprofessional actors. The film has also been compared with Luis Buñuel's *Los olvidados* (*The Young and the Damned*, 1950) and François Truffaut's *Les quatre cents coups* (*The 400 Blows*, 1959); see Hawken and Litewski (1983, 70).

11. There was a thorough casting process, in which 7 main child actors were selected from 800. The actors then participated in workshops for a period of seven months in preparation for the film (Csicsery, 1982, 4).

12. In its screening in Britain, this scene from *Pixote* was cut, a decision taken under the Child Protection Act, which forbids showing minors in the same frame as adults having sex (Hawken & Chaim Litewski, 1983, 70).

13. Luis Buñuel uses a similar technique in *Los olvidados*, his film about the lives of street children in Mexico. A narrator tells the audience that "the film is entirely based on real-life events, and all the characters are authentic."

14. The figures have greatly increased since 1980, and it is now estimated that Brazil has ten million street children. See *www.foundation.novartis.com/social_development/brazilian_street _children.htm*, accessed January 22, 2003. I have used the term *child* for any character under 18, as according to Brazilian law, they are still considered minors until this age.

15. Interestingly, this introduction was given only in the version of the film destined for foreign release, because it was felt that a Brazilian audience would be familiar with these facts (Johnson, 1987, 44)

16. After a brief appearance in a soap opera on Globo television, Fernando was fired for being unable to work within the shows's structure, and to learn his lines (Levine, 1997, 211). All the child actors in the film returned to their former lives of poverty, except for Jorge Juliâo (Lilica), who had a brief acting career.

17. Jubilee Action reports the following on its Web site: "Backed by citizen groups and commercial establishments, death squads have become more and more violent in their goal to 'clean-up' the streets and 'guarantee public safety.' It is estimated by childcare agencies that up to 5 or 6 children a day are assassinated on Rio's streets, even conservative figures put the number at 2 killings every day." *www.jubileeaction.demon.co.uk/jubileeaction/reports/braz il.html*; accessed November 30, 2001.

18. This categorization is given by Johnson (1987, 36).

19. The cinematographer is Rodolfo Sánches.

20. See note 1. Hawken and Litewski (1983) wrote that the film initially had a limited success in Brazil among bourgeois audiences, until it began to win prizes abroad, and as a result gained a wider release, and larger audiences.

21. In the Oedipus complex, Freud, controversially, argued that the male child on discovering his mother's sexuality, associates her with a whore, then begins to desire her and to see his father as a rival (Freud, 1977, 237–38). In the case of the "successful," bourgeois male child, the Oedipus complex is a phase, and this confusion is resolved; see "The Dissolution of the Oedipus Complex," (Freud, 1977, 315–22).

22. It is worth noting that *sapato* means "shoe" in Portuguese; perhaps his name hints at his domination over the boys.

23. Fumaça, a nickname, means "smoke" in Portuguese, a name given to him because of his love for marijuana.

24. This is the second time Pixote is denied an official existence; at the beginning of the film, a bureaucrat insists that his father is missing, not dead, as Pixote claims.

25. It is interesting that the representation of sexuality and, in particular, homosexuality was the reason that *Pixote* was rejected for the Havana Film Festival: "They [festival authorities] said that the film has too much immorality and that homosexuality is a capitalist sickness" (Csicsery, 1982, 10).

26. Babenco has said of Lilica: "[He] takes the place of the woman in the family — in this kind of family. I have empathy with the character and I like him, but he's mostly there because he exists" (Csicsery, 1982, 9).

27. When the boys are by the sea, after their escape, Lilica asks what can a *bicha* expect from life, to which Pixote replies, "Nothing, Lilica."

28. For more on homosexuality in Latin America, see Murray (1995). Part 3 of this book, with chapters by a selection of authors, is dedicated to homosexuality in Brazil.

29. In their strategy for survival, the boys immediately discount the tragic events in this scene, as seen in the swift cut to Pixote, Lilica, and Dito, who are taking refuge in a childhood space. The three are shown happily playing pinball at a fairground, as if Chico had never existed.

30. Pixote calls out Dito's name, telling him to shoot. This causes confusion, with Dito reprimanding Pixote for using his name. Sueli tells Pixote to shoot, as the American client is coming for Dito. This is prefigured in the first part of the film, when the boys role-play the holdup of a bank. Pixote's role is to act as a lookout. Dito angrily stops playing when Pixote calls out his name. Clearly, Pixote's preparation for a life of crime is insufficient.

31. Babenco has made it clear in an interview that Sueli is a victim of circumstances, and not to be blamed for this rejection. In his words, "She doesn't have the structure to accept him. Can you imagine an ending where Sueli tells Pixote to stay with her?" (Csicsery, 1982, 10).

32. They also misunderstand the situation when Pixote refers to blood, and assume she is menstruating. This reveals a failure to consider this woman's needs and their use of her

as a commodity to bring them money, and act as a sex object, in Dito's case. Her previous pimp/lover has left her, presumably because of the pregnancy.

33. The power of the gun and the status it gives the boys are part of the culture of the street in Brazil. This scene was improvised by Fernando Ramos da Silva, who played Pixote, and was not in the original screenplay (Csicsery, 1982, 4).

34. Nagib cites as examples *Central Station,* Tata Amaral's *Um céu de estrelas (A Starry Sky,* 1997), Sérgio Rezende's *Guerra de Canudos (Battle of Canudos,* 1997), and *Baile perfumado (Perfumed Ball,* 1997) by Lírio Ferreira and Paulo Caldas.

35. See Nagib (1999) and Dennison (2000) for other examples of successful Brazilian films of the 1990s.

36. Collor de Mello was impeached in September 1992 on corruption charges, and was voted out of the Senate three months later.

37. Warner Bros. invested in *Orfeu* (Carlos Diegues, 1999), a $7 million remake of *Black Orpheus;* Miramax, in the Oscar-nominated *Four Days in September* (Bruno Barreto, 1998). Columbia has invested in a number of films, although not all were as successful as Sérgio Rezende's *Battle of Canudos* (1997) (Paxman, 1998, 55).

38. The awards include a Golden Bear at the Berlin Film Festival (1999), a Silver Condor for best foreign film at the Argentinean Film Critics Association (2000), a Golden Globe for best foreign language film (1999), the BAFTA Film Award for best film not in the English language (1999), and a number of awards for Walter Salles at the 1998 Havana Film Festival. The film was also nominated for an Oscar for best foreign language film (1999).

39. The French production companies included Canal + and MACT Productions. The Brazilian companies were Riofilme and Salles's company, Video-Filmes.

40. These are *O primeiro dia (Midnight,* 1998), directed with Daniela Thomas, and *Abril despedaçado (Behind the Sun,* 2000). At the time of this writing, Salles is directing *Diarios de motocicleta (The Motorcycle Diaries),* starring Gael García Bernal. Salles's growing reputation is reflected in the fact that he was one of the judges at the 2002 Cannes International Film Festival.

41. The murdered radio thief is described in the screenplay as 18 years old and cannot therefore be seen as a child. Some street children are glimpsed in the station; however, they simply provide a backdrop and are there to suggest what fate would await Josué without Dora.

42. Fernanda Montenegro received an Oscar nomination for best actress in a leading role (1999).

43. The directors seem to have chosen both their lead characters based on moral qualities. In contrast to Walter Salles, Hector Babenco cast Fernando Ramos da Silva as Pixote because of his lack of moral awareness and self-promotion. In his words, "He didn't believe in anything. His life was [a] daily fight with reality. . . . The reality of Fernando's life is the same as Pixote's" (Csicsery, 1982, 6).

44. In an interview, Salles has criticized television for its failure to represent Brazilians: "What we saw was a colonised version of ourselves" (O'Sullivan, 1999, 10). He makes it clear that he believes that cinema can counter this: "The public are returning to see their own reflection in the movie theatres which shows how television has failed to supply this reflection" (James, 1999, 14).

45. The idea for *Central Station* came from a documentary that Salles had made, *Socorro Nobre (Life Somewhere Else,* 1995), which is the story of the relationship based on letters between a semiliterate female prisoner, Socorro Nobre, and a visual artist, Frans Krajcberg. Of this film Salles has said, "I never forgot the difference those letters made to these people's lives. And it was the exact opposite to the lack of communication I was seeing in Brazil at the time" (Flyn, 1998, 10). In fact, the first letter writer to approach Dora in the station concourse is Socorro Nobre, which highlights the thematic link between the two films.

46. At one point, she tells Josué that she once came across her father on the streets as an adult, and that when she stopped him, he did not recognize her, but attempted to flirt with her.

47. While they are on the bus, she begins to verbally abuse a man because he looks as if he is a father. The revelation of this personal history and her subsequent failure to have a romantic relationship ensure that her rejection by the evangelical, teetotaling truckdriver is particularly poignant.

48. Don Pedrâo, a man whom the audience already knows as a killer, is seen ominously questioning Irene at her apartment, following Dora's rescue of Josué.

49. The soundtrack was composed by Jacques Morelenbaum and Antonio Pinot and played by a string orchestra (Chaves Tesser, 1999, 144).

50. Along with *Central Station*, Nagib gives the example of *Crede-mi* (1997) by Bia Lessa and Dany Roland (Nagib, 1999, 24).

51. This development is, for Salles, an example of "urban areas in the middle of nowhere, with no economic activities that can make them work" (Kaufman, 1998, 21).

52. This hints at sympathies with the Brazilian Landless Workers Movement (Movimento dos Trabalhadores Rurais Sem Terra), a large-scale popular organization that illegally occupies land as a way of providing an income for the landless and attacking the large-scale inequality in the distribution of land; see www.mstbrazil.org.

53. I am grateful to Sue Harper for the idea of the reflectionalist/transformative model.

6

Making Connections

On starting this book, I was aware of a number of discrete themes in the films selected that I would pursue in the analyses of them. These include the nature of the individual's relationship to changes in revolutionary society (*Memories of Underdevelopment* and *Strawberry and Chocolate*); modernization, class divides, and changes in gender roles (*Like Water for Chocolate* and *Amores perros*); the aftermath of dictatorship (*Amnesia* and *The Frontier*); the effects of neoliberalism, corruption, and globalization (*The Voyage*); discrimination against women and censorship (*I the Worst of All*); and society's neglect of its children (*Pixote* and *Central Station*).[1]

These topics were examined in the relevant chapters; nevertheless, during the writing process, thematic parallels began to emerge that were not immediately apparent. These allow connections to be established between some of the films and suggest that they are responding, each in its own way, to elements of shared realities. Thus, two interconnected themes appear in a number of films studied: these are the failure of the state to assume its responsibilities and the absence or failure of the father. The most obvious example of this was seen in *Pixote*, where semi-orphaned young street children suffer abuse at the hands of flawed surrogate paternal figures, the police, and the "reform" school authorities, acting within a corrupt and violent patriarchal system. The father figure in a number of cases comes to act as a metaphor for the state. In *Central Station,* the father that Josué is searching for is never found, suggesting the absence of any paternalistic state solution to Brazil's problems. In *Amores perros,* the characters are united by their lack of a father, or by inabilities to assume their responsibilities as fathers, and it was argued that, here too, parallels are drawn between an ineffective state machinery and a failure to provide a paternal model. In fact, it is worth mentioning that there are no positive father figures in any of the films studied here. This is inevitably a conscious or unconscious commentary on the failed masculine models of a previous generation.

Mothers do not figure so prominently in these films, with the exception of *Like Water for Chocolate,* which, as was seen, features the demonized, masculinized Mama Elena. There is also less consistency in the types of maternal representations seen. They range from the traditional models of suffering, passive women (*Amores perros, The Voyage*), to women forced to earn their livings as prostitutes (*Pixote*), to the grieving Maite in *The Frontier,* who comes to represent the Chilean mothers of the disappeared, to Dora in *Central Station,* who gradually finds her redemption in her adoption of the maternal role. Despite this range of representations, there are no "liberated" mothers (positive maternal figures, who are independent, working women) featured in any of the films studied.

Creating New Worlds

This perceived failure of parental models, and of previous generations, leads many of the films to suggest that hope for a better future lies in a new generation. *Memories of Underdevelopment* illustrates this by paradoxically focusing on an antimodel. It suggests that the new revolutionary people of Cuba will form a better country by rejecting Sergio's elitist individualism and by forging a national collective identity. Several of the more recent films feature young men who, it is suggested, are to make a positive contribution to their respective country's future. In *The Voyage,* Martín comes to understand that, with the help of popular leaders, he has to look for the answers to his own problems and those of his society if he is to play a meaningful part in the fight for justice. David in *Strawberry and Chocolate* is groomed by Diego as a future cultural leader who will be able to follow a revolutionary path while accepting a heterogeneous Cuba. Josué in *Central Station* will learn his path from his brothers, not his father, and it is suggested that he will become a carpenter, a man who can help to rebuild his country. In the case of the Chilean films examined, both Ramírez and Ramiro confront their country's past and emerge as new men ready to play a role in the transitional period. These films, then, have a sense of hope. In an inverse reworking of the biblical myth of the Promised Land, they are concerned with a search for the causes of destruction, in order to propose the creation of better worlds.

Although this is a pattern that emerges, I do not want to suggest that all the films studied can be analyzed in terms of thematic unity. *Pixote,* in contrast to the above-mentioned texts, features boys and young men who either die or await a future of violence and likely death. It is a deterministic, pessimistic film that sees future generations destroyed by the neglect and mistakes of their elders. The flawed models presented by the authorities result in the boys being unable to break the cycle of violence as they reproduce their behavior patterns. *Amores perros,* though not as pessimistic as *Pixote,* cannot be said to represent a new generation who will lead their country to a better future. Octavio, the youngest of the male protagonists, goes on a personal journey and learns from his mistakes. Nevertheless, Mexico City is represented as a violent, corrupt (and vibrant) space that has corrupted all the characters, and the open ending creates uncertainty as to whether he will be able to fully escape the violence of the city.

Despite the difference in terms of optimistic national visions, these two films can also be said to create new cinematic worlds. *Pixote* achieves this in the way that it projects naturalistic images of Brazilian street children, unseen in previous Brazilian films. *Amores perros* brings a new, exciting style to Mexican cinema that incorporates elements of youth culture, sophisticated plot development, and original editing techniques, to represent a range of realities in modern Mexico City.

Although the above texts represent new filmic possibilities, it has been argued throughout that they are predominantly male projections of national realities, with national identities linked to masculine identities. Only two films, *Like Water for Chocolate* and *I the Worst of All,* have exclusively female protagonists. Both are concerned with redefining women's identities, and both turn to the past to suggest role models for contemporary and future women. This, however, is where the similarities end. It was argued that *Like Water for Chocolate,* in its creation of a traditional, romantic heroine, seeks to promote women's return to a feminine domestic space. In contrast, it was seen that Sor Juana is represented as a proto-feminist, who challenges rather than reinforces traditional gender divides and is reinterpreted for contemporary audiences. The fact that the only women in this corpus of films who can be seen as radical in feminist terms are the seventeenth-century figures of Sor Juana Inés de la Cruz and the vicereine suggests that there is plenty of scope for more liberating, exciting images of women in the twenty-first century.

The Boom in Latin American Films

The popularity of Latin American cinema has grown recently, thanks to a number of strong films that have done extremely well at the box office and won recognition at international film festivals. This "boom" in the past applied to the work of novelists like Gabriel García Márquez, Mario Vargas Llosa, Carlos Fuentes, Julio Cortázar, who achieved unparalleled international commercial success beginning in the 1960s. A similar phenomenon can be seen in the appreciation of the work a new generation of auteurs/directors including Alfonso Cuarón, Guillermo del Toro, Walter Salles, and Alejandro González Iñárritu. The films that have generated a buzz include *Central Station, Amores perros, Y Tu Mama También,* Salles's *Abril despedaçado (Behind the Sun,* 2001), *Perfume de violetas: nadie te oye* (*Violet Perfume: No One Is Listening,* 2001), directed by Marisa Sistach, *Cidade de Deus (City of God,* 2002), directed by Fernando Meirelles and Kátia Lund, and *Nueve reinas (Nine Queens,* 2000) and *El hijo de la novia,* (*Son of the Bride,* 2001), by the Argentine directors Fabián Bielinsky and Juan José Campanella, respectively. They have shown global distributors and producers that investment in Latin American cinema can reap large financial rewards, and which, it is hoped, will lead to more funding for individual projects. This trend is reinforced by the Oscar nominations announced in February 2003. Brothers Alfonso and Carlos Cuarón were nominated for best screenplay written directly for the screen for *Y tu mamá también,* while *El crimen del padre Amaro (The Crime of Father Amaro,* 2002), directed by Carlos Carrera, received a nomination for best foreign-language film.

Films from Mexico, Brazil, and Argentina have been at the forefront of this movement. Their success may help forge a marketing trend that will allow filmmakers from other Latin American countries to gain the funding that they need to break through into international markets. It should be mentioned that in the case of Argentina, however, the crash of the banking system beginning in December 2001, foreseen and dramatized particularly effectively in *Nine Queens,* has led to near paralysis in Argentine filmmaking (Hopewell & de Pablos, 2001).

The success of these films has highlighted a recent trend in the funding of Latin American films: the increased reliance on private finance for production and distribution. In many cases, it is no longer possible to talk in terms of national film industries in the traditional sense. That is, a number of directors no longer need to depend on state-sponsored film institutes. New and existing Latin American, European, and North American production companies have turned filmmaking into a commercial enterprise.[2] This means that cinema production is no longer so closely linked to state policy, a link that, as has been seen, can lead to disastrous results.[3] This also means that directors can worry less about censorship and self-censorship, something that, as has also been seen, has been a problem in the specific cases of Mexico and Cuba, and also in Brazil, Chile, and Argentina in the periods of military rule. In addition, films that secure funding from international companies are promoted using resources at their disposal. In the words of the well-known Mexican director, Guillermo del Toro: "When you let in private investors, you're suddenly dealing with people who'll make an effort to recoup their capital, so they'll promote your film in a way that would never have happened in the past" (Brooks, 2002).

The success of individual films has enhanced the careers of their directors, a number of whom have been offered work in Hollywood based on the success of Spanish language films made in their own countries. Mexican directors figure among those who have made the transition to Hollywood, as seen in the examples of Alfonso Cuarón and Guillermo del Toro. Cuáron made *A Little Princess* (1995) and *Great Expectations* (1998) after his successful Mexican film *Sólo con tu pareja* (*Love in the Time of Hysteria,* 1991). He returned to Mexico to make *Y tu mamá también,* and has now been signed up to direct the third and fourth Harry Potter films, *Harry Potter and the Prisoner of Azkaban* (2004) and *Harry Potter and the Goblet of Fire* (2005). Del Toro has had a similar trajectory; following *Cronos* (1993), he directed the Hollywood films *Mimic* (1997) and *Blade II* (2002), in between making a personal project, *El espinazo del diablo* (*The Devil's Backbone,* 2001), a film set in Spain during the civil war.[4]

Despite all these apparent advantages, there are disadvantages in what could be seen as the privatization of filmmaking. The success of the above directors in Hollywood is an inevitable loss for their national cinemas, even if, as in the case of Cuarón and del Toro, they continue to make Spanish-language films. Also, the fact that primary considerations have become commercial means that producers are less likely to support experimental filmmaking or politically radical projects. Films that are felt to be of less interest in international terms and that do not have important backers lack an effective distribution network and are given an extremely limited release.[5] The success of individual films can mask the overall picture. Production companies will take risks only on a limited number of films, and without effective state support, there cannot be genuinely vibrant film cultures in Latin America. As Néstor García Canclini has argued, the state should not abandon its cultural responsibilities and should try to "prevent the subordination of public interests to market forces" (García Canclini, 1997, 252). He argues:

> We must revise the state's function in and responsibility for education and culture. . . . [We must] reconsider the state as a locus of public interest, as arbiter or guarantor of the collective need for information, recreation, and innovation, and not to subordinate these needs under commercial viability. (ibid., 251)

In order, then, to support the development of national film industries on a larger scale, a combined approach would appear to be necessary. In other words, state-funded film institutes need to take on a role of cultivating national cinema production and be prepared to invest in films by new directors with interesting ideas. Private funding will continue for projects with a more commercial transnational appeal. The hope is that this will result in an even more dynamic Latin American cinema, prepared to further experiment with form and with a broader range of representations that will include more characters from the poor and indigenous communities of Latin America and better developed female characters. In an age that talks of global and local markets, there should be a place for films with transnational appeal as well as films aimed at national audiences.

Notes

1. See the introduction for more on the themes addressed in this book.

2. One example of an exciting new Latin American production company is The Tequila Gang, formed by Guillermo del Toro, Laura Esquivel, Bertha Navarro, Rosa Bosch, and Alejandra Moreno Toscano, with the aim of supporting Hispanic films. The company has coproduced del Toro's *El espinazo del diablo* (*The Devil's Backbone*, 2001) and *La fiebre del loco* (*Loco Fever*, 2001) by the Chilean director Andrés Wood, among others. See *www.cineaste.com/current/deltoro.html* for more details.

3. For an explanation of this in the case of Mexico and Brazil, see chapters 2 and 5.

4. For an interview with Guillermo del Toro, see *www.cineaste.com/current/deltoro.html*. Another young Latin American director who has gained international status is Walter Salles, who, at the time of this writing, is making *Diarios de motocicleta* (*The Motorcycle Diaries*), a coproduction with FilmFour, Senator Films, and Southfork Pictures, based on the diaries of a young Che Guevara and starring Gael García Bernal (*Amores perros* and *Y tu mamá también*).

5. For a discussion of this problem in the Mexican context, see Rashkin (2001, 14–15).

Filmography

Tomás Gutiérrez Alea[1]

Guantanamera (1994)

Fresa y chocolate (*Strawberry and Chocolate*, 1993) (with Juan Carlos Tabío)

Contigo en la distancia (*Far Apart*, 1991)

Cartas del parque (*Letters from the Park*, 1988)

Hasta cierto punto (*Up to a Certain Point*, 1984)

Los sobrevivientes (*The Survivors*, 1979)

De cierta manera (*One Way or Another*, 1977)

La última cena (*The Last Supper*, 1976)

Pelea cubana contra los demonios (*Cuban Fight against Demons*, 1971)

Memorias del subdesarrollo (*Memories of Underdevelopment*, 1968)

La muerte de un burócrata (*Death of a Bureaucrat*, 1966)

Las doce sillas (*The Twelve Chairs*, 1962)

Alfonso Arau

Zapata (2002)

Picking up the Pieces (2000)

Walk in the Clouds (1995)

Como agua para chocolate (*Like Water for Chocolate*, 1991)

Mojado Power (1979)

Tacos de oro (1975)

Calzonzín inspector (*Inspector Calzonzin*, 1973)

El aguila descalza (*The Barefoot Eagle*, 1969)

María Luisa Bemberg

De eso no se habla (*We Don't Want to Talk about It,* 1993)

Yo la peor de todas (*I the Worst of All,* 1990)

Miss Mary (1986)

Camila (1984)

Señora de nadie (*Nobody's Wife,* 1982)

Triángulo de cuatro (*Triangle of Four,* 1974)

Crónica de una señora (*Chronicle of a Lady,* 1970)

Hector Babenco

Corazón iluminado (*Foolish Heart,* 1998)

At Play in the Fields of the Lord (1991)

Ironweed (1987)

Kiss of the Spider Woman (1985)

Pixote: A lei do mais fraco (*Pixote: The Law of the Weakest,* 1981)

O passageiro da agonia Lucio Flavio (*Lucio Flavio,* 1977)

Rei da noite (*King of the Night,* 1975)

Alejandro González Iñárritu

Amores perros (*Love's a Bitch,* 2000)

Gonzálo Justiniano

Tuve un sueño contigo (1999)

Amnesia (1994)

Caluga o menta (*Candy or Mint,* 1990)

Sussi (1987)

Hijos de la guerra fría (1986)

Ricardo Larraín

El entusiasmo (*Enthusiasm*, 1998)

La frontera (*The Frontier*, 1991)

Walter Salles

Abril despedaçado (*Behind the Sun*, 2001)

Central do Brasil (*Central Station*, 1998)

Terra estrangeira (*Foreign Land*, 1995)

A grande arte (*Exposure*, 1991)

Fernando Solanas

La nube (*The Cloud*, 1998)

El viaje (*The Voyage*, 1991)

Sur (*The South*, 1987)

Tangos, el exilio de Gardel (*Tangos, the Exile of Gardel*, 1986)

Los hijos de Fierro (1972)

La hora de los hornos (*The Hour of the Furnaces*, 1968) (with Octavío Getino)

Notes

1. Only films that have been released internationally have been given an English title; only feature films are included.

Bibliography

General Sources

Benjamin, W. 1973. *Illuminations*, London: Fontana Press.

Borges, J. L. 1979. *Labyrinths*. Middlesex and New York: Penguin Books.

Borges, J. L. 1992. *Ficciones*. Madrid: Alianza Editorial.

Bromley, R. 1989. Natural boundaries: The social function of popular fiction. In *The Study of Popular Fiction: A Source Book*, edited by B. Ashley, 147–55. London: Pinter Publishers.

de Lauretis, T. 1999. Oedipus interruptus. In *Feminist Film Theory: A Reader*, edited by S. Thornham. Edinburgh: Edinburgh University Press.

Doane, M. A. 1999. Film and the masquerade: Theorising the female spectator. In *Feminist Film Theory: A Reader*, edited by S. Thornham. Edinburgh: Edinburgh University Press.

Freud, S. 1977. *On Sexuality: Three Essays on the Theory of Sexuality*. London and New York: Penguin Books.

Gaines, J. 1999. White privilege and looking relations: Race and gender in feminist film theory. In *Feminist Film Theory: A Reader*, edited by S. Thornham. Edinburgh: Edinburgh University Press.

Gledhill, C., ed. 1987. *Home Is Where the Heart Is: Studies in Melodrama and the Woman's Film*. London: British Film Institute.

Haskell, M. 1999. The woman's film. In *Feminist Film Theory: A Reader*, edited by S. Thornham. Edinburgh: Edinburgh University Press.

Higson, A. 2000. The limiting imagination of national cinema., In *Cinema and Nation*, edited by M. Hjort, and S. Mackenzie, 63–74. London and New York: Routledge.

Hjort, M. 2000. Themes of nation. In *Cinema and Nation*. edited by M. Hjort and S. Mackenzie, 103–17. London and New York: Routledge.

Hoare, Q., and G. Nowell Smith, eds. 1971. *Selections from the Prison Notebooks of Antonio Gramsci*. London: Lawrence and Wishhart.

Hoskins, C., S. Mcfadyen, and A. Finn. 1999. *Global Television and Film: An Introduction to the Economics of the Business*. Oxford: Oxford University Press.

Kaplan, A. E. 1987. Mothering, feminism and representation: The maternal in melodrama and the women's film 1910–40. In *Home is Where the Heart Is: Studies in Melodrama and the Woman's Film*, edited by C. Gledhill, 113–37. London: British Film Institute.

Labanyi, J. 1999. Fetishism and the problem of sexual difference in Buñuels's *Tristana* (1970). In *Spanish Cinema: The Auteurist Tradition*, edited by P. W. Evans. Oxford: Oxford University Press.

Lamarque, P. and S. Haugom Olsen. 1994. *Truth, Fiction and Literature: A Philosophical Perspective*. Oxford: Clarendon Press.

Mulvey, L. 1999. Visual pleasure and narrative cinema. In *Passionate Detachments: An Introduction to Feminist Film Theory*, edited by S. Thornham, 58–69. London and New York: Arnold.

Nicholson, L., ed. 1990. *Feminism/Postmodernism*. London: Routledge.

Radway, J. 1984. *Reading the Romance: Women, Patriarchy, and Popular Literature*. Chapel Hill: University of North Carolina Press.

Scott, J. 1990. Deconstructing equality-versus-difference. In *Conflicts in Feminism*, edited by M. Hirsh and E. Fox Keller. New York and London: Routledge.

Smith, S. 1999. The image of women in film: Some suggestions for future research. In *Feminist Film Theory: A Reader*, edited by S. Thornham. Edinburgh: Edinburgh University Press.

Solanas, F. 1989. *La Mirada: Reflexiones sobre cine y cultura*. Buenos Aires: Puntosur.

Stone, J. 1997. *Eye on the World: Conversations with International Filmmakers*. Los Angeles: Silman-James Press.

Thornham, S., ed. 1997. *Passionate Detachments: An Introduction to Feminist Film Theory*. London and New York: Arnold.

Thornham, S., ed. 1999. *Feminist Film Theory: A Reader*, Edinburgh: Edinburgh University Press.

Turim, M. 1989. *Flashbacks in Film: Memory and History*. London and New York: Routledge.

Weeks, J., and P. Gunson. 1991. *Panama: Made in the USA*. London: Latin America Bureau.

Latin American and Latin American Film

Brooks, X. 2002. First Steps in Latin. *The Guardian*, July 19. Available at *www.guardian.co.uk/friday_review/story/0,3605,757334,00.html*; accessed July 19, 2002.

Burton, J. 1983. *The New Latin American Cinema: An Annotated Bibliography of Sources in English, Spanish and Portuguese, 1960–1980*. New York: Smyrna Press.

Burton, J. 1997. Film artisans and film industries in LA, 1956–80: Theoretical and critical implications of variations in modes of filmic production and consumption. In *New Latin American Cinema: Vol. 1, Theory, Practices and Transcontinental Practices*, edited by M. T. Martin, 157–84. Detroit: Wayne State University Press.

Burton, J. 1986. *Cinema and Social Change in Latin America: Conversations with Film Makers*. Austin: University of Texas Press.

Castillo, D. 1992. *Talking Back: A Latin American Feminist Criticism*, New York: Cornell University Press.

Chanan, M. 1983. *Twenty-five Years of the New Latin American Cinema*. London: BFI.

Chevigny, P. 1991. Police deadly force as social control: Jamaica, Brazil and Argentina. In *Vigilantism and the State in Modern Latin America: Essays on Extralegal Violence*, edited by M. K. Huggins, 189–212. New York: Praeger.

Conniff, M. L. 1992. *Panama and the United States: The Forced Alliance*. Atlanta: University of Georgia Press.

Franco, J. 1989. *Plotting Women: Gender and Representation in Mexico*. London and New York: Verso.

García Canclini, N. 1997. Will there be a Latin American cinema in the year 2000? Visual culture in a postnational era. In *Framing Latin American Cinema: Contemporary Critical Perspectives*, edited by A. M. Stock, 246–258. Minneapolis: University of Minnesota Press.

García Espinosa, J. 1997. For an imperfect cinema. In *New Latin American Cinema: Vol. 1, Theory, Practices and Transcontinental Practices*, edited by M. T. Martin, 71–82. Detroit: Wayne University Press.

Getino, O. 1997. Some notes on the concept of a "Third Cinema." *New Latin American Cinema: Vol. 1, Theory, Practices and Transcontinental Practices*, edited by M. T. Martin, 99–107. Detroit: Wayne University Press.

Guevara, C. 1989. *The Motorcycle Diaries: A Journey around South America*, translated by Ann Wright. London: Verso.

Gunson, P., and J. Weeks. 1991. *Panama Made in The U.S.A.* London: LAB Books.

Gutiérrez Alea, T. 1997. The viewer's dialectic. In *New Latin American Cinema*: Vol. 1, *Theory, Practices and Transcontinental Practices*, edited by M. T. Martin, 108–31. Detroit: Wayne University Press.

King, J. 2000. *Magic Reels: A History of Cinema in Latin America*. London and New York: Verso.

Martin, M. T., ed. 1997a. *New Latin American Cinema*: Vol. 1, *Theory, Practices and Transcontinental Practices*. Detroit: Wayne State University Press.

Martin, M. T., ed. 1997b. *New Latin American Cinema*: Vol. 2, *Studies of National Cinemas*. Detroit: Wayne State University Press.

Mendoza, P. A. 1982. *El olor de la Guayaba*. Bogotá: Oveja Negra.

Mora, G. 1989. Crítica feminista: Apuntes sobre definiciones y problemas. In *Cultural and Historical Grounding for Hispanic and Luso-Brazilian Feminist Literary Criticism*, edited by H. Vidal, 2–10. Minneapolis, Minnesota: Institute for the Study of Ideologies and Literature.

Muñoz, B. 1982. *Sons of the Wind: The Search for Identity in Spanish American Indian Literature*. New Brunswick, NJ: Rutgers University Press.

Murray, S. O. 1995. *Latin American Male Homosexualities*. Albuquerque: University of New Mexico Press.

Petras, J. and S. Vieux. 1994. The transition to authoritarian electoral regimes in Latin America. *Latin American Perspectives* 21, no. 4:5–20.

Pinheiro, P. S. 1991. Police and political crisis: The case of the military police. In *Vigilantism and the State in Modern Latin America: Essays on Extralegal Violence*, edited by M. K. Huggins, 167–87. New York: Praeger.

Rix, R., and R. Rodríguez-Saona, eds. 1997. *Changing Reels: Latin American Cinema against the Odds*. Leeds: Trinity and All Saints University College.

Rowe, W. 1997. Magical realism. In *Encyclopedia of Latin American Literature*, edited by V. Smith, 506–7. Chicago: Fitzroy Dearborn.

Ruby Rich, B. 1997. An/other view of Latin American cinema. In *New Latin American Cinema*: Vol. 1, *Theory, Practices and Transcontinental Practices*, edited by M. T. Martin, 273–97. Detroit: Wayne State University Press.

Skidmore, T. E., and P. H. Smith. 1992. *Modern Latin America*. 3d ed. New York and Oxford: Oxford University Press.

Solanas, F., and O. Getino. 1997. Towards a Third Cinema: Notes and experiences for the development of a cinema of liberation in the Third World. In In *New Latin American Cinema*: Vol. 1, *Theory, Practices and Transcontinental Practices*, edited by M. T. Martin, 33–58. Detroit: Wayne University Press.

Stock, A. M., ed. 1997. *Framing Latin American Cinema: Contemporary Critical Perspectives*. Minneapolis: University of Minnesota Press.

Trelles Plazaola, L. 1991. *Cine y mujer en América Latina: directoras de largometrajes de ficción*. San Juan: Editorial de la Universidad de Puerto Rico.

Cuba and Cuban Film

Bonachea, R. E., and N. P. Valdés, eds. 1969. *Ché: A selection of The Works of Ernesto Guevara*. Cambridge, MA, and London: The MIT Press.

Burton, J. 1977. Individual fulfilment and collective achievement: An interview with Tomás Gutiérrez Alea. *Cineaste* 8:8–21.

Chanan, M. 1985. *The Cuban Image: Cinema and Cultural Politics in Cuba*. London: BFI.

Chanan, M. 1997. Cuban cinema in the 1990s. In *Changing Reels: Latin American Cinema against the Odds,* edited by R. Rix and R. Rodríguez-Saona, 1–15. Leeds: Trinity and All Saints University College.

Davies, C. 1996. Recent Cuban fiction films: Identification, interpretation, disorder. *Bulletin of Latin American Research* 15, no. 2:77–192.

Dolgoff, S. 1976. *The Cuban Revolution.* Quebec: Black Rose Books.

Evora, J. A. 1996. *Tomás Gutiérrez Alea.* Madrid: Ediciones Cátedra.

Gutiérrez Alea, T. 1975. Respuesta a Cine Cubano. In *Cine y Revolución en Cuba,* edited by J. Alvarez, A. Guevara, T. Gutiérrez Alea, and H. Solás, 99–107. Barcelona: Editorial Fontamara.

Ibarra, M. 1995. Guantanamera, es un retrato fiel de Cuba. *Cambio* 16:79.

Johnson, H. 1965. *The Bay of Pigs: The Invasion of Cuba by Brigade 2506.* London: Hutchinson of London.

Lockwood, L. 1990. *Castro's Cuba, Cuba's Fidel.* San Francisco and Oxford: Westview Press.

Lumsden, I. 1996. *Machos, Maricones and Gays: Cuba and Homosexuality.* Philadelphia: Temple University Press.

Stone, J. 1997. Interview with Tomás Gutiérrez Alea. In *Eye on the World: Conversations with International Filmmakers,* edited by J. Stone, 123–26. Los Angeles: Silman-James Press.

Memories of Underdevelopment

Burton, J. 1977. Memories of underdevelopment in the land of overdevelopment. *Cineaste* 8:16–21, 58–59.

Burton, J. 1984. Modernist form in land in anguish and memories of underdevelopment. *Post Script: Essays in Film and the Humanities* 3/2 (Winter): 65–84.

Desnoes, E. 1971. *Memories of Underdevelopment.* Middlesex: André Deutsch Penguin.

Fernández, H., D. I. Grossvogel, and E. R. Monegal. 1974. 3/on 2: Desnoes, Gutiérrez Alea. *Diacritics* (Winter): 51–64.

López, A. M. 1995. *Memorias* of a home: Mapping the revolution (and the making of exiles?). *Revista Canadiense de Estudios Hispánicos* 10, no. 1:4–17.

Miller, P. 1999. *Memories of Underdevelopment,* thirty years later: An interview with Sergio Corrieri. *Cineaste* 25, no. 1:20–23.

Myerson, M. 1973. *Memories of Underdevelopment: The Revolutionary films of Cuba.* New York: Grossman.

Strawberry and Chocolate

Bejel, E. 1997. *Strawberry and Chocolate:* Coming out of the Cuban closet? *South Atlantic Quarterly* 96, no. 1:65–82.

Paz, S. 1994. Interview with Teresa Toledo. *Sight and Sound* 4 December, 33–34.

Paz, S. 1995. *Strawberry and Chocolate.* London: Bloomsbury.

Quiroga, J. 1997. Homosexualities in the tropic of revolution. In *Sex and Sexuality in Latin America,.* edited by D. Balderston and D. J. Guy, 133–51. New York and London: New York University Press.

Santí, E. M. 1998. *Fresa y chocolate:* The rhetoric of Cuban reconciliation. *Modern Language Notes* 113, no. 2: 407–25.

Smith, P. J. 1994. The Language of *Strawberry. Sight and Sound* 4 December, 30–33.

Smith, P. J. 1996. *Fresa y chocolate (Strawberry and Chocolate):* Cinema as guided tour. In *Vision Machines, Cinema Literature and Sexuality in Spain and Cuba, 1983–93.* edited by P. J. Smith, 81–100. London: Verso.

West, D. 1995. Ice cream and tolerance: Interviews with Tomás Gutiérrez Alea, and Juan Carlos Tabío. *Cineaste* 21, nos. 1–2:16–22.

Wilkinson, S. 1999. Homosexuality and the repression of intellectuals in *Fresa y chocolate* and *Máscaras*. *Bulletin of Latin American Research* 18, no. 1:17–33.

Mexico and Mexican Film

Chun, K. 2002. What is a Ghost?: An interview with Guillermo del Toro. *Cineaste* 27, no. 2. (Available at *www.cineaste.com/current/deltoro.html*; accessed July 2002.

De La Rosa, M. E. 1994. *Mujeres mexicanas de éxito.* Mexico City: Planeta.

Hellman, J. 1978. *Mexico in Crisis.* New York: Holmes and Meir.

Maciel, D. 1999. Cinema and the state in contemporary Mexico, 1970–1999. In *Mexico's Cinema: A Century of Film and Filmmakers,* edited by J. Hershfield, and D. Maciel. Wilmington, DE: SR Books.

Ramírez Berg, C. 1989. The image of women in recent Mexican cinema. *Journal of Latin American Popular Culture* 8:157–79.

Rashkin, E. 2001. *Women Filmmakers in Mexico: The Country in Which We Dream.* Austin: University of Texas Press.

Riquer Fernández, F. 1992. La identidad femenina en la frontera entre la conciencia y la interacción social. In *La voluntad de ser: mujeres en los noventa,* edited by J. M. Tarrés, 51–64. Mexico City: El Colegio de México.

Russell, P. L. 1994. *Mexico Under Salinas:* Austin: Mexico Resource Centre.

Segre, E. 1997. "La desnacionalización de la pantalla": Mexican cinema in the 1990s. In *Changing Reels: Latin American Cinema against the Odds,* edited by R. Rix and R. Rodríguez-Saona, 33–57. Leeds: Trinity and All Saints University College.

Tarrés, M. L. 1992. *La voluntad de ser: Mujeres en los noventa.* Mexico City: El Colegio de México.

Torrents, N. 1993. Mexican cinema comes alive. In *Mediating Two Worlds: Cinematic Encounters in the Americas,* edited by J. King, A. López, and M. Alvarado, 222–29. London: BFI Publishing.

Like Water for Chocolate

Billen, S. 1993 How to cook up a storm. *The (London) Times,* September 30, 35.

Business data for *Como agua para chocolate.* Nd. (Available at *www.usimdb.com;* accessed March 2002.)

Castrillón, M. L. 1993. *Como agua para chocolate,* de Alfonso Arau: La imagen del realismo mágico. *Kinetoscopio* (May–June): 53–57.

Donahue, D. 1993. *Like Water for Chocolate. USA Today*/International Edition, October 19, 9A.

Espinosa, P. 1995. Niega Arau que la PGR exista demanda en su contra. *La Jornada,* September 17, 26.

Esquivel, L. 1989. *Como agua para chocolate.* Mexico City: Planeta Mexicana.

Esquivel, L. 1995. *La ley del amor.* Barcelona: Plaza y Janés.

Feay, S. 1993. Tita on the edge. *Time Out,* October 6, 72.

Finnegan, N. 1999. Boiling point: *Like Water for Chocolate* and the boundaries of Mexican identity. *Bulletin of Latin American Research* 8, no. 3:311–26.

Galvin, Brendan. 1993/1994. Mexican magic. *Film Ireland* (December–January): 24–26.

González Stephan, B. 1991. "Para comerte major": cultura calibanesca y formas literarias alternativas. *Casa de las Américas* 185:81–93.

Ibsen, K. 1995. On recipes, reading and revolution: Postboom parody in *Como agua para chocolate. Hispanic Review* 63:133–46.

Kraniauskas, J. 1993. *Como agua para chocolate. Sight and Sound* 3, no. 10: 42–43.

Lillo, G. and M. Sarafati-Arnaud. 1994. *Como agua para chocolate:* determinaciones de la lectura en el contexto posmoderno. *Revista Canadiense de Estudios Hispánicos* 18:479–90.

Loewenstein, C. 1994. Revolución interior al exterior: An interview with Laura Esquivel. *Southwest Review* 79, no. 4:592–607.

Pérez Turrent, T. 1994. Entre agua y chocolate. *Dicine* 55:8–11.

Shaw, D., and B. Rollet. 1994. *Como agua para chocolate:* Some of the reasons for its success. *Travesía: Journal of Latin American Cultural Studies* 3, nos. 1–2: 82–92.

Stone, J. 1997. Alfonso Arau. In *Eye on the World: Conversations with International Filmmakers,* edited by J. Stone, 463–65. Los Angeles: Silman-James Press.

Amores perros

Barton, R. 2001. *Amores perros* (Life's a Bitch). *Film Ireland* (June/July): 38–39.

Chumo, P. N. 2000. Script review *Amores perros. Creative Screenwriting* 8, no. 2: 10–12.

Fernstein, H. 2002. Mexican Rave. *The Guardian,* April 10, 14–15.

Franco Reyes, S. 2001. La cinta de González Iñárritu recaudó un millón de dólares en 163 salas. *El Universal,* April 23, 1.

Hernández Cerda, E. 2001. *Amores perros* ganó como el video mexicano más vendido. *El Universal,* October 8, 9.

Koehler, R. 2002. How auds learned to love subtitles. *Variety,* January 13. (Available at *www.variety.com/index.asp?layout=upsell_article&articleID=VR1117858466&cs=1;* accessed June 1, 2002.)

Lawrenson, E. 2001. Pup fiction. *Sight and Sound* 11, no. 5:: 28–29.

Limited release B.O. winners. 2001. *Variety,* July 26. (Available at *www.variety.com/av_result .asp?articleid=VR1117850355&query=vr1117850355&display=vr1117850355;* accessed June 1, 2002.)

Niogret, H. 2000. Entretien Alejandro González Iñárritu: aller au fonds des choses. *Positif* no. 477 (November): 24–28.

Oppenheimer, J. 2001. A dog's life. *American Photographer,* April 30, 21–27.

Patterson, J. 2001. Aztec cameras. *The Guardian,* May 18. (Available at *www.guardian.co.uk/ Archive/Article/0,4273,4188495,00.html.*)

Pérez Soler, B. 2001a. *Amores perros. Fade* 6, no. 3:19.

Pérez Soler, B. 2001b. Pup fiction. *Sight and Sound* 11, no. 5:: 29.

Tegel, S. 2001a. "Perros" fetches profit for Estudio. *Variety,* March 2. (Available at *www.variety .com/index.asp?layout=story&articleid=VR1117795720&categoryid;* accessed May 22, 2002.)

Tegel, S. 2001b. New bucks bump Mex B.O. *Variety,* March 2. (Available at *www.variety .com/index.asp?layout=story&articleid=VR 1117795696&categoryid=;* accessed May 22, 2002.)

Tegel, S. 2001c. Mexican filmmakers cheer amendment. *Variety,* April 2. (Available at *www .variety.com/index.asp?layout=story&articleid=VR 1117796194&categoryid=;* accessed May 22, 2002.)

Chile and Chilean Film

Collier, S., and W. F. Sater. 1996. *A History of Chile, 1808–1994.* Cambridge: Cambridge University Press.

Derechos Chile. Available at *www.derechoschile.com/english/about.htm;* accessed December 2001.)

Dorfman, A. 1995. *La muerte y la doncella.* Madrid: Ollero y Ramos.

Dorfman, A., with T. Kushner. 1997. *Widows.* London: Nick Hern Books.

Jocelyn-Holt Letelier, A. 1998. *El Chile perplejo: Del avanzar sin transar al transar sin parar.* Santiago: Planeta/Ariel.

King, J. 1997. Chilean cinema in revolution and exile. In *New Latin American Cinema:* Vol. 2 *Studies of National Cinemas,* edited by M. T. Martin, 397–419. Detroit: Wayne University Press.

Pick, Z. M. 1997. Chilean cinema in exile. In *New Latin American Cinema:* Vol. 2 *Studies of National Cinemas,* edited by M. T. Martin, 423–40. Detroit: Wayne University Press.

Richard, N. 1997. *Residuos y metáforas: ensayos de crítica cultural sobre el Chile de la Transición.* Santiago: Cuarto Propio.

Skármeta, A. 1997. Europe: An indispensable link in the production and circulation of Latin American Cinema. In *New Latin American Cinema:* Vol. 2 *Studies of National Cinemas,* edited by M. T. Martin, 263–69. Detroit: Wayne University Press.

The Frontier

Castrillón, M. L. 1993. Límite a un estado del alma. *Kinetoscopio* (May–June): 25–29.

Mouesca, J. 1997. *La Frontera.* In *Cine chileno: veinte años, 1970–1990,* Santiago: Ministerio de Educación.

Rodríguez, A. 1993. Ricardo Larraín y su opera prima: traspasando *The Frontier. Kinetoscopio* (May–June): 30–33.

Smith, P. J. 1995. *La Frontera. Sight and Sound,* 5, no. 5: 46.

The Frontier. www.filmo.cl.pages/LARRAIN.HTM. (Accessed October 8, 2001.)

Amnesia

García, J., and A. Ricagno. 1995. Entrevista a Gonzalo Justiniano: sin amnesia. *Amante Cine* 43, September 26, 26.

Perriam, C. 1996. *La Frontera.* Paper presented at Conference. Change and Identity: An "Anglo" — "Latin" Encounter, August, Newcastle University, Newcastle, England.

Awards for *Amnesia. http://us.imdb.com/Tawards?0109105.* (Accessed October 9, 2001.)

Argentina and Argentine Film

Azapiazu, D., E. Basualdo, and H. Nochteff. 1998. Menem's great swindle: Convertibility, inequality and the neoliberal shock. *NACLA Report on the Americas* 31, no. 6:16–19.

Falicon, T. L. 2000. Argentina's blockbuster movies and the politics of culture under neoliberalism 1989–98. *Media, Culture and Society* 22, no. 3:327–42.

Gonzales, H. 1992. Interview with Fernando Solanas. Video sleeve.

Hopewell, J., and E. de Pablos. 2001. Argentine Helmers slam gov't over pic production. *Variety,* 31 January. (Available at *www.variety.com.*)

Lewis, P. H. 2002. *Guerillas and Generals: The "Dirty War" in Argentina*. Westport, CT: Greenwood.

Mahieu, J. A. 1999. Fernando Solanas: del cine político a las metáforas de un país. *Cuadernos hispánicos* 592:83–89.

Novaro, M. 1998. Shifting alliances: Party politics in Argentina. *NACLA Report on the Americas* 31, no. 6:11–15.

Vilas, C. M. 1998. Under fire: Menenism and the politics of opposition in Argentina. *NACLA Report on the Americas* 31, no. 6:10–11.

Yglesias, J. 1993. Fernando Solanas, cuatro respuestas para Jorge Yglesias. *Cine Cubano* 138:41–42.

The Voyage

Castillo, L. 1993. Con Solanas proa hacia un viaje real . . . e imaginario. *Cine Cubano* 138:43–47.

Chaudhary, V. 1992. Film-maker woos Argentines with vision of another country. *The Guardian*, 11 May, 8.

Nash, E. 1992. Stepping into the firing line. *The Independent*, 22 May, 19.

Ruby Rich, B. 1991. Tangles Argentina. *The Village Voice*, 30 July, 64.

Strick, P. 1993. El Viaje (*The Voyage*). *Sight and Sound* 3, no. 9:55.

Tal, T. 1998. Del cine-guerrilla a lo "grotético" — La representación cinematográfica del latino-americanismo en dos films de Fernando Solanas: *La hora de los hornos* y *El viaje*. in *Cultura Visual en America Latina* 9, no. 1. (Available *www.tau.ac.il/eial/IX_l/tzvital.html*.)

I the Worst of All

Bemberg, M. L. 1991. Somos la mitad del mundo. *Cine Cubano* 132:11–17.

Bergmann, E. 1998. Abjection and ambiguity: Lesbian desire in Bemberg's *Yo la peor de todas*. In *Hispanisms and Homosexualities*. edited by S. Molloy and R. Mckee, 229–47. Durham. NC and London: Duke University Press.

King, J. 2000b. María Luisa Bemberg and Argentine Culture. In *An Argentine Passion: María Luisa Bemberg and Her Films*, edited by in J. King, S. Whitaker, and R. Bosch, 1–32. London, New York: Verso.

Kirk, P. 1988. *Sor Juana Inés de la Cruz: Religion, Art and Feminism*. New York: Continuum.

Lavrin, A. 1991. Unlike Sor Juana: The model nun in the religious literature of colonial Mexico. In *Feminist Perspectives on Sor Juana Inés de la Cruz*, edited by S. Merrim, 61–85. Detroit: Wayne University Press.

Merrim, S. 1991. Towards a feminist reading of Sor Juana Inés de la Cruz: Past, present, and future directions in Sor Juana criticism. In *Feminist Perspectives on Sor Juana Inés de la Cruz*, edited by S. Merrim, 11–37. Detroit: Wayne University Press.

Merrim, S., ed. 1991. *Feminist Perspectives on Sor Juana Inés de la Cruz*. Detroit: Wayne State University Press.

Miller, D. 2000. María Luisa Bemberg's interpretation of Octavio Paz's Sor Juana. In *An Argentine Passion: María Luisa Bemberg and Her Films*, edited by J. King, S. Whitaker and R. Bosch, 137–73. New York: Verso.

Paz, O. 1988. *Sor Juana and Her World*. Translated by Margaret Sayers Peden. Boston: Faber and Faber.

Pick, Z. 1992–1993. An interview with María Luisa Bemberg. *Journal of Film and Video* 94, nos. 3–4:76–82.

Schons, D. 1991. Some obscure points in the life of Sor Juana Inés de la Cruz. In *Perspectives on Sor Juana Inés de la Cruz,* edited by S. Merrim, 38–60. Detroit: Wayne University Press.

Scott, N. 1994. 'or Juana and her world. *Latin American Research Review* 29, no. 1:143–54.

Torrents, N. 1990. One woman's cinema: Interview with María Luisa Bemberg. In *Knives and Angels: Women Writers in Latin America.* edited by S. Bassnett, 171–75. London and New Jersey: Zed Books,

Trueblood, A. S. 1988. *A Sor Juana Anthology: Introduction and Translation.* Cambridge, MA, and London: Harvard University Press.

Vernaglione, P. 1990. Conversazione con María Luisa Bemberg. *Filmcritica* 41 (September–October): 480–81.

Urbano, V., and A. López de Martínez, eds. 1990. *Sor Juana Inés de la Cruz: amor, poesía, soledumbre.* Potomac, MD: Scripta Humanistica.

Whitaker, S. 1987. Pride and prejudice: María Luisa Bemberg. *The Garden of Forking Paths: Argentinian Cinema.* edited by J. King and N. Torrents, 115–28. London: British Film Institute Publications.

Argentina, Derechos Humanos. *www.derechos.org/nizkor/arg/.* (Accessed June 2002.)

Félix Montior. *http://us.imdb.com/Name?Monti,+F%E9lix#Cinematographer.* (Accessed June 2002.)

Brazil and Brazilian Cinema

Araújo, I. 1999. A new beginning. In *Cinema Novo and Beyond.* edited by J. L. Vieira, 87–92. West Haven, CT: Herlin Press.

Avellar, J. C. 1997. Backwards blindness: Brazilian cinema of the 1980s. In *Framing Latin American Cinema: Contemporary Critical Perspectives,* edited by Ann Marie Stock, 26–56. Minneapolis: University of Minnesota Press.

Dennison, S. 2000. A Meeting of two worlds: Recent trends in Brazilian cinema. *Journal of Iberian and Latin American Studies* 6, no. 2:131–44.

James, N. 1999. Heartbreak and miracles. *Sight and Sound* 9, no. 3:12–15.

Johnson, R. 1999. New beginnings, old beginnings. In *Cinema Novo and Beyond,* edited by J. L. Vieira, 19–32. West Haven, CT: Herlin Press.

Johnson, R., and R. Stam. 1982. *Brazilian Cinema.* London and Toronto: Associated University Presses.

Nagib, L. 1999. Tendências do cinema Brasileiro actual. *Studies in Latin American Popular Culture* 18:19–32.

Ortiz Ramos, J. M. 1987. O cinema Brasileiro contemporâneo (1970–1987). In *História do Cinema Brasileiro.* edited by F. Ramos, 401–54. São Paulo: Art Editora.

Palast, G. 1998. Lights out across Rio? World Bank is to blame. *The Guardian,* December 6. (Available at *www.guardian.co.uk/Archive/Article/0,4273,3846389,00,html;* accessed December 30, 2001.)

Parker, R. 1993. "Within four walls": Brazilian sexual culture and HIV/AIDS. In *Sexuality, Politics and AIDS in Brazil,* edited by H. Daniel and R. Parker, 65–84. London and Washington, D.C.: The Falmer Press.

Paxman, A. 1998. Jungle fever: Hollywood meets vine as film biz rolls. *Variety,* 21–27 December, 55–61.

Pereira dos Santos, N. 1986. Towards a popular cinema. In *Cinema and Social Change In Latin America: Conversations with Filmmakers,* edited by J. Burton, 133–41. Austin: University of Texas Press.

Stam, R., and I. Xavier. 1997. Transformation of national allegory: Brazilian cinema from dictatorship to redemocratization." In *New Latin American Cinema*, Vol. 2: *Studies of National Cinemas*, edited by M. T. Martin, 295–322. Detroit: Wayne University Press.

Central Station

Central do Brasil: An award-winning Brazilian road movie. *In Camera* (July):12–13.

Carneiro, J. E. and M. Bernstein. 1999. *Central Station.* Translated by John Gledson. London: Bloomsbury.

Chaves Tesser, C. 1999. Central do brasil. *Chasqui* 28:142–44.

Cowan, N. 1998. Special Delivery. *Filmmaker* 6, no. 2:72.

Crespi, A. 1999. Nel coure del Brasile. *Cineforum* no. 380:18–19.

Flyn, B. 1998. Shoe-shine star. *The Guardian,* August 24, 10.

James, N. 1999. Heartbreak and miracles. *Sight and Sound* 9, no. 3:12–15.

Kaufman, A. 1998. Sentimental journey as national allegory: An interview with Walter Salles. *Cineaste* 24, no. 1:19–21.

Mount, C. 1999. Native art (interview with Walter Salles). *Creation* (March): 18–19.

O'Sullivan, C. 1999. Still Walter runs deep. *The Observer,* March 7, 9–10.

Pixote

Csicsery, G. 1982. Individual solutions: An interview with Hector Babenco. *Film Quarterly* 36, no. 1: 2–15.

Hawken, J., and C. Litewski. 1983. Exploitation for export: Preview a prize-winning Brazilian film. *Screen* 24, no. 2:66–70.

Johnson, R. 1987. The romance-Reportagem and the cinema: Babenco's *Lúcio Flávio* and *Pixote. Luso Brazilian Review* 24, no. 2: 35–48.

Levine, R. M. 1997. *Pixote:* Fiction and reality in Brazilian life. *Based on a True Story Latin American History at the Movies,* edited by D. F. Stevens, 201–24. Wilmington, DE: SR Books.

Stam, R. 1983. *Pixote. Cineaste* 12, no. 3:14–15.

Stone, J. 1997. Hector Babenco. In *Eye on the World: Conversations with International Filmmakers,* edited by J. Stone, 41–46. Los Angeles: Silman-James Press.

Index of Film Titles

Index of Names